ONLINE PROFESSIONAL DEVELOPMENT FOR TEACHERS

Online Professional Development for Teachers

Emerging Models and Methods

Edited by
Chris Dede

HARVARD EDUCATION PRESS

CAMBRIDGE, MASSACHUSETTS

Library of Congress Control Number 2005937617

Paperback ISBN 1-891792-73-3
Library Edition ISBN 1-891792-74-1

13-Digit Paperback ISBN 978-1-891792-73-1
13-Digit Library Edition ISBN 978-1-891792-74-8

Published by Harvard Education Press,
an imprint of the Harvard Education Publishing Group

Harvard Education Press
8 Story Street
Cambridge, MA 02138

Cover Design: Alyssa Morris

The typefaces used in this book are ITC Stone Serif for text and ITC Stone Sans for display.

Printed in Canada

Contents

Preface

This conference volume stems from the third in a series of invitational conferences at the Harvard Graduate School of Education (HGSE), each with the goal of finding a synthesis between research and practice to create what we call *usable knowledge*. An analogy in medicine is Louis Pasteur's studies of inoculation as a way to prevent deadly diseases such as smallpox. Pasteur began with a major concern of society—infectious diseases—and conducted research that not only made great strides in solving this problem, but also advanced basic theoretical knowledge about infection and the immune system. HGSE is committed to conducting research about important educational issues through studies that provide both theoretical insights and proven methods. With this in mind, the Usable Knowledge Conferences at HGSE aim to disseminate what we know about ways to design, manage, and support education research that will enable educators to ensure that all students meet or exceed standards in core subjects and skills.

In March 2003, we hosted the first such conference, "Scaling Up Success: Lessons Learned from Technology-Based Educational Improvement." For this invitational research conference, participants heard from leading scholars working on challenges of transfer, generalization, and adaptation of successful educational interventions. The result of this conference was a volume of the same name, describing different models for adapting an innovation successful in some local settings to effective usage in a wide range of contexts. We held our second Usable Knowledge Conference in October 2004. Focusing on the topic of "Mind, Brain, and Education," conference participants heard from researchers proactively building linkages between cognitive neuroscience and educational practice. It is our hope that these conferences and their proceedings have helped inform and will continue to help inform both practitioners and the public about effective educational practices.

Online teacher professional development, the topic of our third Usable Knowledge Conference and this book, is a very important type of educational practice, as making teaching more effective is the heart of educational improvement. As you will see in perusing this volume, conference present-ers and participants developed important types of usable knowledge: synthe-sizing current findings from exemplary projects, building collective insights from these results, and proposing key themes and related methodologies for studying the evolution of effective online teacher professional development models. Everyone present at this conference, whether in research or practice, held an important piece of the online teacher professional development puz-zle; working conferences such as this one provide an opportunity to put the puzzle together.

Ten chapters in this book each describe an exemplary online teacher pro-fessional development model with a substantial record of success. Some models focus on targeting teachers at specific points in the pipeline, as does the eMentoring for Student Success project, which provides science-specific mentoring and professional development for early-career science teachers via an online community. Other models, such as the Quest Atlantis Project and HGSE's WIDE World, help teachers not just to learn new skills and methods, but also to truly change and advance their teaching practice. Some mod-els seek to utilize and disseminate rich sources of education information, as does Seminars on Science at the American Museum of Natural History. And still others engender an organizational capacity-building approach, as does the EdTech Leaders Online program. Faced with many choices, organizations using or planning to initiate online teacher professional development can become confused and overwhelmed. These groups will directly benefit from the ideas in this conference volume.

We are grateful to Katharine E. and Albert W. Merck for their generous funding of these conferences, as well as many other HGSE activities. My thanks also go out to the National Science Foundation for being our partner in this effort. And I would be very much remiss if I did not thank Chris Dede, our conference organizer, and all the HGSE faculty members and students who made this initiative possible. To advance this usable knowledge initia-tive, we invite you to join us not only by sharing the ideas in this volume with others, but also by sharing your work with the education community.

Kathleen McCartney
Acting Dean
Harvard Graduate School of Education

The Evolution of Online Teacher Professional Development

Chris Dede

In an era of school reform, many consider the education and professional development of teachers as the keystone to educational improvement.[1] Sparked by a need to meet the student achievement goals mandated by the Elementary and Secondary Education Act reauthorization and the No Child Left Behind legislation, a plethora of professional development programs have arisen, and many administrators have expanded the time they devote to enhancing teachers' knowledge and skills. But this increase comes at a price in resources and energy. School districts spend the equivalent of 200 dollars per pupil on professional development, and these learning experiences add both time and effort demands to teachers' already busy schedules.[2] While we as a profession need to build teachers' capacity for improvement, we also need to be sure that time, effort, and scarce resources are expended only on quality programs that teach with and about best practices.

Unfortunately, many teacher professional development programs are not of high quality, offering "fragmented, intellectually superficial" seminars.[3] In addition, face-to-face "pull-out" programs are unable to provide ongoing daily guidance for teachers as they attempt to implement novel curricula or pedagogies.[4] This problem of just-in-time support is exacerbated when teachers attempt to implement new strategies in environments made hostile by reluctant peers or administrators who see those innovations as undercutting the current school culture. Further, conventional approaches to professional development typically fail to provide day-to-day professional mentoring for entry-level teachers. This lack of support is a major factor underlying the

1

nearly 50 percent attrition rate among new teachers within their first five years in the classroom. As a result of all these factors, teachers often become frustrated with professional development, at times because it is ineffectual and at times because it requires sacrifices disproportionate to the professional enhancement it provides.

The need for professional development that is tailored to teachers' busy schedules, that draws on valuable resources not available locally, and that provides work-embedded support has stimulated the creation of online teacher professional development programs. Generally, these programs are available to teachers at their convenience and provide just-in-time assistance. In addition, they often give schools access to experts and archival resources that fiscal and logistical constraints would otherwise limit. A range of objectives for educational improvement underlie these online teacher professional development ventures, such as introducing new curricula, altering teachers' beliefs and instructional and assessment practices, changing school organization and culture, and enhancing relationships between school and community.

Currently, many initiatives in online teacher professional development are serving large numbers of educators. However, while such programs are propagating rapidly and consuming substantial resources both fiscally and logistically, little is known about best practices for the design and implementation of these alternative models for professional enhancement. Evidence of effectiveness is generally lacking, anecdotal, or based on participant surveys completed immediately after learning experiences, rather than later when a better sense of long-range impact is attainable. Therefore, while online programs help with teachers' time constraints, they may do little to dispel educators' distrust of professional development programs that are often inadequate, whether face-to-face or online. This volume examines alternative models for using interactive media to build teachers' capacity to enhance student learning and analyzes those models' current strengths and limits to develop insights for policy, practice, and research.

ALTERNATIVE MODELS OF ONLINE TEACHER PROFESSIONAL DEVELOPMENT

Online teacher professional development programs are diverse in their models, expressing a spectrum of purposes, learner objectives, content areas, pedagogies, delivery methods, and assessment and evaluation methods. A range of goals for educational improvement underlie these ventures, among them introducing new curricula, altering teachers' instructional and assessment practices, changing school organization and culture, and enhancing relationships between district and community. Online teacher professional development programs also diverge in the type and balance of content and skills taught, which can include subject-matter knowledge for teaching, comprehension of student thinking, instructional practices, assessment strategies, classroom management, epistemic perspective (such as multiculturalism or universal design for learning), or the leadership of educational improvement.

Likewise, a range of pedagogical methods for individual and collaborative teacher learning underlie the various online teacher professional development models, including reading and discussing the research literature, trying out new approaches in the classroom and reflecting on what happens, sharing best practices with other teachers who have similar professional roles, viewing annotated video cases of practice, interacting with subject-matter experts, exploring libraries of resources, or having a mentoring relationship with an expert teacher. For these various pedagogical approaches, the roles played by instructors, facilitators, subject-matter experts, or mentors vary, as do the assumptions, theories, or research findings about adult learning that provide the rationale for a particular pedagogical approach.

Further, online teacher professional development programs can deliver their instruction completely through media or use a blended or hybrid approach that includes some face-to-face interaction. A variety of technologies are available as delivery media, from downloaded texts to annotated video cases, and these interactive media enable participant interaction either synchronously or asynchronously. In addition, these technologies have novel capabilities to collect rich, real-time assessment data on participants' learning that can formatively guide instruction while also providing summative information on learning outcomes. All of these dimensions create a complex design-space that enables a broad spectrum of alternative models for online teacher professional development.

DETERMINING THE VALUE OF ONLINE TEACHER PROFESSIONAL DEVELOPMENT

Measuring the educational effectiveness of an online teacher professional development program is a major challenge, in part because effectiveness includes complex dimensions of scalability, sustainability, and cost-benefit. How should designers define success for their particular model, and what evidence should they collect to determine whether a particular implementation has attained its objectives? Assessing *impact* (the degree of transformation in practice) and *reach* (the number of teachers and organizations influenced) is important but complicated. In educational settings where multiple school-change and professional development initiatives are underway simultaneously, and students move from teacher to teacher, determining the unique contribution of a particular professional development program to a teacher's effectiveness is very hard. Gauging the effect of professional development investments on student achievement or understanding is even more difficult, as is comparing the utility of these expenditures to alternative investments such as reducing class size or increasing the technology infrastructure for student learning.

Faced with this array of issues, many organizations currently using or planning to initiate online teacher professional development programs are confused. Designers of both conventional and online teacher professional development, as well as teacher educators, developers of distance education, policymakers, and scholars, can benefit from research findings that contrast current characteristics of alternative models of exemplary online teacher professional development, build collective insights to guide design and implementation, and propose key themes and related methodologies for studying the evolution of effective models. Alas, as discussed in the first chapter of this volume, most of what is published about teacher professional development—whether face-to-face or online—does not present these types of findings in the context of well-designed empirical research studies. This book is designed to address this scholarly shortfall.

THE GENESIS OF THIS VOLUME

I discussed plans for a conference on this topic with Michael Haney and Robert Sherwood, two program officers in the Division of Elementary, Secondary, and Informal Education at the National Science Foundation. Both were enthusiastic about studying current exemplary models of online teacher professional development to develop cross-case analyses and to chart an agenda for future research. Through a grant, they provided cofunding for the conference and the development of the research agenda. (However, any opinions, findings, and conclusions or recommendations expressed in this volume are those of the authors and do not necessarily reflect the views of the National Science Foundation.)

I selected ten exemplary online teacher professional development programs whose representatives would present models at the conference. This selection was based on a variety of factors: quality and maturity of the program; relevance to math, science, engineering, or technology education; and inclusion of a spectrum of models based on different types of content, pedagogies, and audiences. The designers of each model prepared a conference paper read in advance by participants, based on a template I provided to ensure that the models included comparable information to facilitate cross-case comparisons. Edited versions of those conference papers comprise chapters 2 through 11 of this volume. Collectively, these cases present a valuable diagnostic picture about the current state of high-end online teacher professional development.

A team of four advanced HGSE doctoral students (Lisa Breit, Diane Jass Ketelhut, Erin McCloskey, and Pamela Whitehouse) worked with me as an intellectual steering committee to shape the design and implementation of the conference, including whom to invite. The hundred participants who accepted our invitation to this research conference included scholars developing and studying teacher professional development (both face-to-face and online), practitioners who had experience with various forms of teacher professional development, experts in several aspects of distance learning, national and state policymakers, vendors, funders, and HGSE faculty and students. Gathering together enabled representatives of these various sectors to share their insights and to make essential connections between theory and practice, the lack of which can often undercut the scaling up of promising innovations.

During the conference, representatives of each online teacher professional development program gave a brief summary of that model, including remarks by a designer and by a teacher or an evaluator who presented an on-the-ground perspective. The majority of each session was devoted to attendees' discussing the strengths and limits of that model and generating ideas for further design, implementation, and research.

Beyond conference sessions presenting the ten models, other sessions focused on identifying similarities and differences among these models and their underlying theories, as well as on delineating implications of a comparative analysis for educational practice and policy. Conference participants also discussed research methods and an agenda for further studies needed. Insights from those discussions are presented in chapter 12 of this volume. I and the team of doctoral students also prepared an overview of current research in online teacher professional development. A condensed version of this study is presented in chapter 1. Additional details about the conference are available at http://gseweb.harvard.edu/~uk/otpd/index.htm.

OVERVIEW OF THE TEN MODELS

Here are brief summaries of the ten online teacher professional development programs. They appear in this text in the same order in which they were presented at the conference.

The EdTech Leaders Online (ETLO) program at Education Development Center, Inc. (discussed in chapter 2) focuses on enabling clients to develop their organization's capacity to provide effective online professional development to K–12 teachers and administrators. ETLO courses are conducted entirely online, with teams from a district participating alongside teams from other districts around the country. During an initial course, participants select one of the 30 ETLO workshops to implement during their practicum, become familiar with its contents, and plan all the details of offering it locally. In this model, the participants who have been trained via this learning experience then implement and facilitate online workshops provided by ETLO while receiving ongoing support both from ETLO staff and from an online forum. ETLO staff focus on the quality of the implementation of clients' programs and the quality of the online workshops they offer, how each client's online professional development program is integrated into overall professional development plans, how it will be sustained, and how it helps the client meet teacher-quality goals.

The WIDE World teacher professional development program (chapter 3) offers online courses designed to foster teachers' application of research-based strategies in planning curriculum and fostering and assessing students' learning. (WIDE stands for Wide-scale Interactive Development for Educators.) These strategies include the Teaching for Understanding framework, applications of Gardner's theory of multiple intelligences, and the synthesis of these models in differentiating instruction for diverse learners and integrating new technologies to improve student performance. WIDE World's primary format comprises online readings, asynchronous discussions, and interactive tools. A central component of the WIDE World model is tailored support from an expert online coach for every participant.

PBS TeacherLine and Concord Consortium's Seeing Math Secondary project (chapter 4) are five-year grants supported by the U.S. Department of Education through the Ready to Teach funding program. Both these models, which draw on one another for design insights, provide high-quality professional development for K–12 teachers with the goals of improving teacher performance and increasing student achievement. While both projects focus on mathematics teaching, PBS TeacherLine has also coordinated the development of online courses in the areas of reading, science, curriculum and instruction, and the integration of technology to enhance student learning. All courses were developed with input from K–12 education leaders and research experts, and the courses target areas in which a high percentage of teachers lack content knowledge or teaching skills. The courses provide opportunities for teachers to assess the current capabilities and potential misconceptions of their students, with the objectives of supporting teachers as they make decisions that improve their teaching strategies and prompting teachers to develop activities or instructional units that they will try in their classrooms.

The eMentoring for Student Success project (chapter 5)—funded by the National Science Foundation and cosponsored by the National Science Teachers Association; the New Teacher Center at the University of California, Santa Cruz; and the Science/Math Resource Center and Burns Telecom Center at Montana State University—is designed to increase student achievement in science by providing early-career middle- and high school science teachers with science-specific mentoring and professional development through an online learning community. Emphasizing inquiry into science content and into the ways students think and learn about science, this model facilitates discussion and collaboration among novice science teachers, experienced science teachers, and research scientists. Each new teacher receives support from a mentor who has taught the same content at the same grade level. Mentors receive extensive training in online interactions, content and pedagogical coaching skills, and best practices in science education to ensure that they can apply effective coaching skills in an asynchronous online learning environment. New teachers are paired with a mentor from the same state, so that conversations about standards, assessment, and curricula take account of local contexts.

TERC and Lesley University have collaborated to develop a fully online Masters in Science Education program for K–8 teachers (chapter 6). Participants build their science content knowledge and teaching skills through a combination of on- and offline learning, as well as discussions with course colleagues that take place in online study groups of five to seven, which are engineered in such a way that they foster the development of a collective understanding. Modules are cofacilitated by a scientist and a science educator: the scientist guides participants in their acquisition of science content, skills, and habits of mind, while the science educator coaches participants as they learn about and try new teaching and assessment strategies in their classrooms. Students receive kits that allow them to conduct science investigations at home and report on and discuss them in study groups. In order to prepare for teaching online, new faculty participate in a four-week online seminar designed specifically for the program.

The American Museum of Natural History's scientific staff and extensive resources were leveraged to create Seminars on Science (chapter 7), a set of online courses in the life, earth, and physical sciences. Seminars on Science provides teachers with an opportunity to deepen their content knowledge, to interact with working scientists and master science educators, and to gain valuable resources for their classrooms. Courses are six weeks long, organized into weekly modules with content from diverse media, required assignments, and participation in asynchronous discussion forums. The weekly modules are typically framed around one essential question such as "What is energy?" "How has the atmosphere evolved?" or "What threatens the diversity of fish?" as well as desired outcomes. Participants read essays, view images and videos that present experiences such as laboratory tour, experience interactive simulations, and explore related websites. Discussion forums provide a space for expert-novice interactions among research scientists, expert science teachers, and learners.

Sasha Barab and his colleagues at Indiana University have developed an embedded framework for supporting professional development, Learning through Enacting Innovation (chapter 8), that highlights three core conceptual biases and tensions (drawing on formal and informal experiences, using traditional and innovative curricula, and supporting individual and collaborative reflection). This framework supports teachers in implementing the Quest Atlantis Project as part of their classroom offerings. Quest Atlantis uses immersive technologies, draws upon the genre of computer and video games in informing its design, requires deep levels of student inquiry, and often challenges or modifies teachers' usual roles as facilitators of learning. Teachers discuss their Quest Atlantis experiences with other teachers or with the research/design team through face-to-face dialogue in school hallways or the teacher lounge, through text-based interactions over e-mail or on project bulletin boards, or by individually and collaboratively examining videos of teacher practice and examples of student work. This embedded professional development model uses an electronic knowledge network, the Inquiry Learning Forum, to support a web-based community of in-service and pre-service mathematics and science teachers sharing, improving, and creating inquiry-based pedagogical practices.

Also from Indiana University, Learning to Teach with Technology Studio (LTTS) (chapter 9) is a teacher professional development system that consists of 60 online problem-centered courses and a custom learning management system (LMS). LTTS was built to address four design commitments derived from the theory and research on professional development, which lead to twelve design principles that instantiate the LTTS course model and LMS support environment. Because learners can begin an LTTS course at any time and move at their own pace, a teacher comes to the LTTS website when she or he has the time and the need for professional development, rather than be constrained by a fixed syllabus schedule or the need to meet the schedules of other students. Rather than a class of students, she or he will work one on one with a mentor who will provide feedback on work as well as encouragement and guidance when needed. In this model, each teacher begins by reading a curriculum problem and an approach to addressing that problem; she or he then undertakes five to seven tasks serving as proximal objectives for the overall goal of building a lesson plan consistent with the problem statement and principles for inquiry-based instruction.

The WGBH Educational Foundation has developed a set of online professional development courses for K–12 teachers as part of its Teachers' Domain (TD) digital library initiative (chapter 10). To enhance adult learning, a centerpiece of this model is to embed rich media drawn from WGBH productions into these courses, as teachers who learn using such media are more likely to transfer this experience to their classroom practice. Video segments, typically three to five minutes in length, are often reedited and renarrated to match K–12 curricular needs; other materials in TD come from partner organizations, and others are newly produced for the service. Each media artifact is supported by a resource page, which presents a background essay that provides the teacher (or upper-level student) with context for understanding the content of the resource, discussion questions, and correlation to state and national standards. Lesson plans use many of the resources, modeling best practices and use of rich media in the classroom.

The Milwaukee Public Schools' Professional Support Portal (chapter 11) promotes teachers' flexible thinking and collaborations while ensuring opportunities for access to information, experts, and colleagues. The portal program builds on the district's existing successes in professional development by creating a virtual umbrella under which current strengths and new, externally guided insights can merge. This model is based on the design concept that schools are communities of learners in which strategies support distributed learning not only among students and educators within a particular building, but also among stakeholders in the greater community and beyond. The portal permits each user to personalize the presentation and organization of information that appears on the screen; in addition, the portal offers a smorgasbord of tools and applications, all accessible through a single login and overarching interface, enabling the user to move among them without interruption. Finally, the portal incorporates space where multiple users can post shared documents, leave comments for each another on an asynchronous bulletin board, or have synchronous chats—all activities that support online collaboration.

These ten models span the design-space for online teacher professional development along a number of dimensions:

- *Sponsor:* Some models come from nonprofit organizations (such as research and development centers or professional organizations), others from educational institutions (universities and school districts), and one each from a public television station and a museum.
- *Audience:* Some models involve individual teachers choosing to participate, others provide services to schools as organizational units, and one is internally sponsored by a school district.
- *Content:* The knowledge and skills inculcated by these models include disciplinary knowledge related to curriculum, content-specific pedagogy, skills in technology use and integration, and just-in-time advice on classroom challenges.
- *Pedagogy:* These models utilize combinations of pedagogies based on learning theories such as guided social constructivism, coaching, mentoring or apprenticeship, and communities of practice.
- *Media:* These models span a variety of interactive media, synchronous and asynchronous, and frequently blend online and face-to-face learning.
- *Assessment, evaluation, and research:* Depending on their maturity, these models apply a range of methodologies to understand what participants are learning, whether the program is effective, and how and why the model succeeds in what it does well.

As noted earlier, chapter 12 delineates insights that emerged from conference discussions of these models. In particular, four core dimensions are highlighted, each with intrinsic tensions:

1. *Design for incremental learning versus design for transformation:* reaching today's students, but preparing them for a future quite different from the present.
2. *Tensions among stakeholders' agendas:* partisan concerns of regulators, funders, designers and vendors, school administrators, and scholars.
3. *Customization versus generalizability:* "boutique" versus generic programs, and individual needs versus external mandates.
4. *Research versus program evaluation:* determining not simply *whether* and *where* a model works, but also *why*.

Chapter 12 sketches how the ten models attempt to resolve tensions along these dimensions, as well as the implications for funders, policymakers and regulators, and administrators and school leaders.

Online teacher professional development has great potential to assist in educational improvement, but realizing that vision will involve a combination of creative design and rigorous research. As discussed in chapter 12, design-based research is a scholarly strategy in which researchers perturb typical learning settings by introducing evocative, theory-influenced designs, then study effects on practice and policy, in addition to articulating implications for theory and methodology.[5] Design-based research is the primary method I use in my scholarly studies, and experience has convinced me that this combination of freewheeling and constrained thinking is central to developing new ways to build educators' professional capacity—but it is not easy to attain. I hope this book convinces you to join all those who contributed to this volume in the important enterprise of aiding online teacher professional development's evolution, through innovative design and instruction, meticulous research and evaluation, and informed policy and investment.

An Overview of Current Findings from Empirical Research on Online Teacher Professional Development

Pamela L. Whitehouse, Lisa A. Breit, Erin M. McCloskey, Diane Jass Ketelhut, and Chris Dede

The need for professional development that can be customized to fit teachers' busy schedules, that draws on powerful resources often not available locally, and that can provide real-time, ongoing, work-embedded support has prompted the creation of online teacher professional development programs. However, while such programs are propagating rapidly and consuming substantial resources both fiscally and logistically, little is known about best practices for the design and implementation of these online teacher professional development models. In this chapter, we present highlights from a synthesis of what is known and not known in terms of recent empirical research about online teacher professional development (oTPD).[1] We have limited the scope of our study to synthesizing research that is based on substantial empirical evidence and has been published in a scholarly journal or similar venue within the past five years. We offer this analysis as a step toward illuminating best practices and evolving a research agenda based on findings and insights from current online teacher professional development models.

VISUAL DEPICTIONS OF THE STATE OF RESEARCH IN ONLINE TEACHER PROFESSIONAL DEVELOPMENT

This study attempts to organize the field of oTPD into major categories and to "place" the accumulated empirical research evidence (the known) into each category. Categories relatively unpopulated with research findings provide a measure of what is not known. This mapping of known and unknown facets of oTPD can aid in developing a research agenda for the field. Advance organizers, as defined by Ausubel, create a conceptual framework that helps participants organize a topic at the largest grain size before delving into details and specific examples.[2] By using an advance organizer, participants keep the forest in view even while observing and learning from individual trees. Since the purpose of this book is to learn from specific research and to map a larger plan for future research, it is crucial that we do not lose sight of the forest while learning from specific examples.

We propose a graphic display to organize the field of online teacher professional development. Use of this visual organizer identifies the density gra-

FIGURE 1 "Flow" Perspective on Online Teacher Professional Development

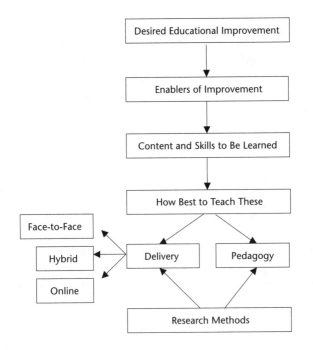

dient of findings and improves discussion about those findings by giving us a common language. However, imposing an organization on the field does not come without problems. The act of creating the organizer can explicitly or implicitly impose a bias or perspective to the data. In addition, in designing such an organizer we risk inadvertently missing a category, thereby diminishing the utility of its portrayal. Therefore, the task we set ourselves was to design a graphical display of what is known and unknown about online teacher professional development and have it be general enough not to limit thinking while specific enough to show relationships—and to do so as objectively as possible.

We considered several formats for our organizer, reviewing ones already in use in the literature. Unfortunately for our purposes, these were either based in a specific theory or presented specific relationships between categories. We developed our own organizer, and its categories are based on specific areas (or "buckets") of research interests rather than theoretical relationships. Figure 1 shows the model we developed for synthesizing the research on oTPD.

This organizer still implies specific relationships that the research findings may or may not validate; on balance, we feel that its advantages outweigh its disadvantages. At the very end of this chapter, we present further thoughts about a "next generation" organizer.

SELECTING RESEARCH LITERATURE TO REVIEW

As we searched through hundreds of articles, papers, and book chapters published in the last decade, we focused on exploring the contours of recent research about online models for teacher professional development (although a few studies are included from the general teacher professional development literature as well). What were the topics and outcomes on which these scholars focused their attention? What empirical methods did they use, and what obstacles and challenges did they encounter? What patterns of findings are beginning to emerge?

Studies of oTPD varied in orientation. Some of the literature we reviewed dealt with professional development with a particular content focus (such as math, science, technology skills, or reading), a specific program approach (such as Understanding by Design), or a particular orientation toward teacher learning (such as mentoring, community of practice, or cognitive apprenticeship). We encountered a fair amount of work that was anecdotal, describing professional development programs or "lessons learned" without providing full details of the participants, setting, research questions, methods of data collection, or strategies for analysis. Also, a great deal of the literature was theoretical, conceptual, or polemical—all categories outside the scope of this report.

We did not limit our review of the literature to a particular theoretical approach, pedagogy, technology, academic discipline, or method of professional development. Rather, we attempted to identify a group of empirical studies that contained findings based on rigorous methods of data collection and analysis; often, these included a mixture of qualitative and quantitative approaches. In searching, we cast a wide net, reviewing nearly 400 articles about online, face-to-face, and hybrid teacher professional development programs.[3] Below we review in detail 40 research studies that met our criteria for high-quality empirical research. While the group of studies in this review is by no means exhaustive, we believe that collectively they represent the types of empirical research that have been conducted on oTPD to date.

The research focus and stated purpose of these 40 studies addressed five main areas of concern:

- *Design of professional development:* The purpose of the study is to use empirical data to contribute to innovations in or improvements to the design of professional development content, instruction, delivery, or administration, focusing on factors such as program model, policy influences, contextual factors, or best practices.
- *Effectiveness of professional development:* The purpose of the study is to measure outcomes of professional development, such as participation levels, participant satisfaction, program quality in relation to a standard, or other intended effects or outcomes.
- *Technology to support professional development:* The purpose of the study is to test or improve the design of a technology learning environment, tool, or online delivery system, or to gauge the effect of using a particular technology to support aspects of teachers' learning.
- *Online communication and professional development:* The purpose of the study is to understand how instructors, moderators, or facilitators can support teachers' learning through effective discourse in an online environment, or to describe the characteristics of teachers' online discourse (effects of gender, age, years of teaching experience, types of interactions, substantive versus superficial discourse, power dynamics, and so on).
- *Research methods:* The study discusses important issues and appropriate research methods for studying teacher professional development.

Most of the studies we reviewed address more than one area of concern. For example, a study that looks at design of an online discussion environment to support teacher professional development may also examine the particular qualities of discourse in that environment, as well as the role of discussion facilitators.

PURPOSES OF PROFESSIONAL DEVELOPMENT

The empirical studies we reviewed addressed one or more of the five areas of research described above. The professional development programs and settings from which their data were drawn also addressed a variety of school needs and reflect a wide range of theories about what teachers need to know, how teachers learn, the best conditions for learning, and how technology might support learning. In the following sections we sketch out the wide range of theories applied to oTPD design and pedagogy.

Fostering Teachers' Abilities to Use Inquiry-Based, Constructivist Pedagogies with Students

One group of teacher professional development (TPD) programs focused on changes in teachers' thinking and practice in their instruction of students toward what could broadly be described as a more constructivist approach. Derry, Seymour, Steinkuehler, Lee, and Siegel, through a TPD program called the Knowledge Building Community Model, studied how discourse in an online environment could help preservice teachers and their in-service mentors shift from didactic methods of instruction to problem-based learning (PBL).[4] Hawkes and Good as well as Hawkes and Romiszowski looked at how computer-mediated collaborative dialogue compared with face-to-face dialogue to foster critical reflection among teachers learning to design curriculum for problem-based learning.[5] Barnett, Keating, Harwood, and Saam studied teachers' Web-based discussions focused on "inquiry-based pedagogies."[6]

As another means of defining the objectives of professional development, Porter, Garet, Desimone, Yoon, and Birman examined longitudinal data from the National Evaluation of the Eisenhower Professional Development Program in order to identify best practices that "enhance teaching and, ultimately, improve student learning."[7] Specifically, they looked at teacher professional development effectiveness and quality, as well as teachers' perceptions of how Eisenhower-sponsored professional development contributed to changes in their classroom practices. Models of professional development varied among schools participating in the Eisenhower program, and this study does not provide details of their individual offerings. However, the working definitions of "effective instruction" and "good teaching practice" used in the study indicate that the Eisenhower-intended educational improvements included both increased alignment with national standards for math (NCTM) and science (NRC) and the cultivation of teaching strategies to promote inquiry, higher-order thinking, and active, project-centered instruction.

As another example of delineating the objectives of professional development, Clarke and Hollingsworth examined data from three Australian TPD programs (the ARTISM Study, the EMIC Study, and the Negotiation of Meaning Project) to illustrate their model of teachers' professional growth.[8] While the desired educational outcomes of these three TPD programs were not described in detail in Clarke and Hollingsworth's paper, one can infer what kinds of instructional changes might have been intended from their report of how teachers in these programs changed practice (emphasis on student participation, use of extended investigation projects tied to real-world contexts, increase in student self-assessment, attention to different learning styles, and generation of problem-solving strategies).

Fishman, Marx, Best, and Tal, in one of the only studies to examine teacher and student outcomes directly linked to teacher professional development goals, used data from the implementation of a LeTUS (Learning Technologies in Urban Schools) program in Detroit to develop an analytic framework linking teacher professional development to teachers' and students' learning.[9] The aim of LeTUS is for middle-school science teachers to learn to develop and implement project-based science curricula that help students meet district standards. Similarly, Neale, Smith, and Johnson explored how effectively teachers learned and implemented "conceptual change" teaching strategies for elementary school science—an approach involving greater use of inquiry in the classroom.[10] Like the Fishman et al. study, Neale, Smith, and Johnson's study attempts to measure the effect of professional development on teachers' practice and students' learning.

Fostering Teachers' Abilities to Create Communities of Practice among Students

Another group of professional development programs represented in these studies focused on fostering teachers' abilities to create communities of practice among students in their classrooms, often aided by an online communications component. In general, encouraging the articulation and exchange of practice knowledge, creating opportunities for collaboration around common objectives, developing a common language, and supporting a culture of professional learning are among the desired educational improvements that communities of practice are intended to support.[11] For example, Barab, Barnett, and Squire studied a practice community model for preservice teachers at Indiana University.[12] The premise of this online TPD program is that teachers learn through social and professional apprenticeship. They must first experience the reflection, collaboration, and negotiation of meaning of a learning community directly in order to create such learning communities in their own classrooms.

Even if desired educational improvements are not explicitly stated in the research on teacher professional development oriented toward communities of practice, an implied intention appears to be that articulating and sharing practice knowledge, reflecting on one's practice, collaborating, and engaging in dialogue are desirable aims in and of themselves and are likely to lead to changes in the instruction of students. Sherer, Shea, and Kristensen described how an online "Faculty Learning Community Portal" helped sustain interaction and learning among higher-education faculty.[13] Koku and Wellman conducted a similar study of university faculty using TeachNet to strengthen interdisciplinary exchange.[14] Both studies were designed to observe and describe how faculty interactions evolved in their respective online forums, but neither described the student learning or instructional improvements these portals were developed to cultivate.

The goals of online and face-to-face mathematics workshops for preservice teachers in Taiwan, studied by Yang and Liu, were more explicit: to improve teacher-interns' repertoires of mathematics knowledge and curricula through "cognitive apprenticeship."[15] Schaverien reports on the use of a research-based, Web-delivered "context" called the Generative Virtual Classroom (GVC), which was designed to help preservice teachers and others develop their ability "to recognize, describe, analyze and theorize learning."[16] One aim of the GVC is to accelerate the process by which undergraduate teacher-interns learn how to teach science with technology. Similarly, Wearmouth, Smith, and Soler described a TPD program to reduce isolation and provide access to expertise for special education teachers.[17] Another aim of this program was to develop a knowledge-building community of teacher researchers. Nemirovsky and Galvis go further in articulating the aims of a TPD program that uses online video cases as the basis for "grounded," specific discussion of instructional practice and content knowledge.[18] The aim of this program is to help teachers jointly invoke a shared language, focus on evidence, and avoid generalizations—and possibly to foster these types of thinking skills in students through using similar forms of discussion in classroom instruction.

Fostering the Intellectual Development of Teachers in Order to Increase Student Learning

Many of the programs examined in this research were intended to foster the intellectual development of teachers: their knowledge of content in their academic disciplines and of pedagogical strategies related to that content. Renninger and Shumar studied how teachers engaged in rich discourse using the extensive content resources and communication tools available in the Math Forum.[19] As described by Porter et al., the Eisenhower-sponsored TPD programs—the Inquiry Learning Forum, the RUSMP Summer Campus, and LeTUS—were developed in part to support the improvement of teachers' math and/or science knowledge.[20] Dutro, Fiske, Koch, Roop, and Wixson studied a Michigan program to improve teachers' knowledge of curriculum standards in language arts.[21]

In several of these studies, teachers' learning to integrate new technology in instruction was the desired educational improvement. Leach, Patel, Peters, Power, Ahmed, and Makalima's study of Project DEEP looked at how teachers learned to use handheld computers to improve the teaching of literacy, numeracy, and science in primary schools in Egypt and South Africa.[22] Harris and Grandgenett studied how learning to use Internet tools and resources in instruction influenced teachers' pedagogy overall.[23] Mouza as well as Curtis and Lawson also studied teachers' learning to integrate new technology in instruction.[24]

FINDINGS ABOUT MEASURING EFFECTIVENESS

Overall, while all of the research we reviewed drew empirical data from actual teacher professional development situations, it is notable that only a few studies were concerned with measuring how effectively the desired educational improvements at the heart of these interventions or programs were realized. Few studies attempted to measure observable changes in teachers' knowledge or skill as a result of TPD, and fewer addressed the ultimate effect of TPD on student learning. Rather, the studies tend to look more closely at various aspects of the design, delivery, and use of oTPD—effects such as discourse patterns, contextual influences, and the formation of practice communities with conditions that support interaction, collaboration, participation, and teacher self-efficacy within these communities.

One study that attempted to document change in both teachers' approaches and evidence of student learning was published by WestEd.[25] Using case studies, the WestEd researchers examined best practices of eight diverse schools that were recipients of the National Awards Program for Model Professional Development. At all eight sites, students made significant academic gains, regardless of socioeconomic factors, and teachers were able to describe consistently the pervasive changes in school culture, infrastructure, and their own knowledge and skills that contributed to these gains.

Even so, for the majority of this group of studies, it appears that the purpose and desired outcomes of current research on oTPD are not often closely wedded to the aims and desired outcomes of the specific TPD program being studied. It is sometimes difficult, therefore, to discern how usable knowledge generated by these studies connects clearly and directly back to the concerns and perspectives of school leaders, teachers, and ultimately their students (as opposed to the work of university researchers and TPD designers).

FINDINGS ABOUT ENABLERS OF IMPROVEMENT

Table 1 shows specifically what aspects of teacher knowledge, skill, or practice the TPD interventions in the studies in our review were trying to change in order to enable educational improvement. The table headings indicate the emphasis of each intervention, as follows:

- *Subject knowledge:* Focused efforts on improving teachers' knowledge depth in their academic discipline, such as math, special education, science, or language arts.
- *Pedagogical knowledge:* Focused on classroom practice and the design and delivery of instruction.
- *Subject knowledge and pedagogy:* Focused on design and delivery of instruction specific to a subject domain.
- *Critical reflection/beliefs/orientation:* Focused on changing teachers' beliefs and/or approach to instruction, and on encouraging reflective practice.
- *Aligning curriculum with standards:* Focused on the implementation of curriculum standards developed by a district, state, or subject-matter authority such as NCTM.
- *Skill/efficiency:* Highlighted the mastery of skills that could be applied across disciplines and pedagogical methods, such as learning some new hardware and software or developing skills for communicating effectively online.
- *Teacher leadership:* Cultivated teachers' capacity to serve as change agents or to practice research in a school setting.
- *Teacher discourse/collaboration:* Built teachers' capacity to discuss practice and to collaborate on curriculum development, planning of instruction, or other school matters.

TABLE 1   Focus of TPD Interventions as Enablers of Improvement

Aspect of Teacher Knowledge, Skill, or Practice

Study*	Subject Knowledge	Pedagogical Knowledge	Subject Knowledge and Pedagogy	Critical Reflection/Beliefs/Orientation	Aligning Curriculum with Standards	Skill/Efficiency	Teacher Leadership	Teacher Discourse/Collaboration	Practice Community	Teachers' Learning	Students' Learning	Better TPD or oTPD Design	Better Research Design
Barab et al. (2004)		•							•	•		•	
Barab et al. (2002)			•						•	•		•	
Barnett (2002)		•	•					•		•		•	
Broady-Ortman (2002)	•				•					•			
Brown and Green (2003)										•		•	
Clarke and Hollingsworth (2002)		•								•	•		
Curtis and Lawson (2001)									•	•		•	
Derry et al. (2004)		•	•							•			
Desimone et al. (2004)				•						•		•	
Dutro et al. (2002)			•	•			•			•			
Fishman et al. (2003)		•	•	•						•	•		•
Harlen and Doubler (2004)		•	•						•	•			
Harris and Grandgenett (2002)		•								•	•		
Hawkes and Good (2000)		•	•							•		•	
Hawkes and Romiszowski (2001)			•					•		•			
Herring (2004)								•	•				•
Job-Sluder and Barab (2004)									•	•		•	
Kabilan (2004)					•					•		•	

* See Notes section, page 265, for full list of sources

Aspect of Teacher Knowledge, Skill, or Practice

Study	Subject Knowledge	Pedagogical Knowledge	Pedagogy and Subject Knowledge	Critical Reflection/Beliefs/Orientation	Align Curriculum with Standards	Skill/Efficiency	Teacher Leadership	Teacher Discourse/Collaboration	Practice Community	Teachers' Learning	Students' Learning	Better TPD or oTPD Design	Better Research Design
King (2002)			•					•		•		•	•
King and Dunham (2005)			•					•		•		•	
Koku and Wellman (2004)								•		•		•	
Leach et al. (2004)		•								•	•		
McKeown and Beck (2004)		•								•		•	
Mouza (2002)	•					•			•	•			
Neale et al. (1990)		•	•							•	•		
Nemirovsky and Galvis (2004)		•	•							•			
O'Connor and Ertmer (2003)								•		•		•	
Picciano (2002)	•							•		•			
Porter et al. (2000)			•							•	•	•	
Renninger and Shumar (2004)									•	•		•	
Richardson and Swan (2003)									•			•	
Riel and Polin (2004)				•						•	•		
Schaverien (2003)		•	•							•	•		
Schlager and Fusco (2004)									•	•		•	•
Sherer et al. (2003)									•	•			
Turner et al. (2004)			•		•			•		•			
Wang et al. (2003)									•	•		•	
Wearmouth et al. (2004)				•			•		•			•	
WestEd (2000)			•	•				•	•	•	•		
Yang and Liu (2004)	•								•				

- *Practice community:* Created or supported a community of practice (usually using online communications), for reasons often not clearly specified beyond community building itself.

Note that all of the programs in these studies focused on multiple enablers. All but four of the studies were primarily concerned with teachers' learning. The four that did not specifically address teachers' learning were studies more intent on improving the design, delivery, or facilitation of professional development for any population (not specifically teachers), or else on developing research methods for studying professional development.

Table 1 also indicates which studies stated that the improvement of professional development programs (either online or not) or the development of new methods for studying TPD was a primary research goal. It is notable that only five of the research studies we reviewed attempted to determine the effect of teacher professional development on student learning or educational outcomes.

FINDINGS ABOUT CONTENT AND SKILLS TAUGHT

As shown in figure 2, the professional development in the 40 studies we reviewed addressed a number of content areas (such as math, science, language arts) and professional skills (such as instructional design, peer coaching). Some addressed more than one primary topic (for instance, both math and science, or cross-disciplinary exchanges). Six of the studies did not describe a particular content focus or skill.

FIGURE 2 Content and Skills Addressed by Online Teacher Professional Development

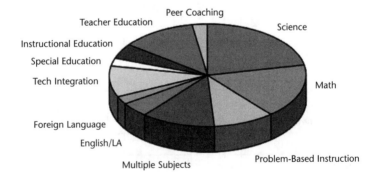

FINDINGS ABOUT PEDAGOGICAL APPROACHES

Rudestam and Schoenholtz-Read write that "electronic teaching developed from advances in communications technology, not from innovative changes in pedagogy."[26] On the other hand, Bruckman argues that technological design and pedagogy have the potential to coevolve, and recent research in oTPD supports this idea.[27] The TPD programs described by the empirical research included in this chapter were designed and implemented on the basis of explicit and implicit pedagogical assumptions held by the designers and instructors about the ways teachers can learn when the capabilities of new information technologies are utilized. The diverse range of pedagogical stances adopted by the designers of these TPD programs illuminates the current state of pedagogy in online TPD.

A common theme emerged across the range of pedagogies we reviewed—most describe a "social constructivist" or "communities of practice" stance, albeit often with a very cursory definition of the meaning of these terms in their research context.

Figure 3 gives a sense of the influence of these pedagogical theories on oTPD research and design—for example, the social constructivist approach appears to have influenced nearly every study, with communities of practice theory following closely. Most of the studies we looked at derived their pedagogical approach from more than one theory (for example, many used both social constructivist principles and communities of practice approaches), so the percentages reflect the landscape, not a cumulative count of every pedagogical theory referenced in each study.

FIGURE 3   The Influence of Pedagogical Theory on oTPD Research and Design

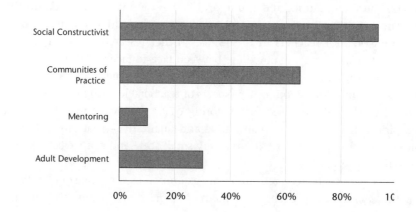

Most of the findings from empirical studies related to pedagogy were concerned with interactions among individuals and groups participating in the programs studied and the contexts or conditions that appeared to foster those interactions. Other findings included claims about what kinds of design components facilitate learning in oTPD, and still others offered comparisons between face-to-face and online interactions. Few of the studies included empirical evidence of teacher change or of student improvement, although most recommended further research to address these concerns.

Of the many studies that investigated the nature of interactions online, overall there are indications that meaningful ways of engaging in dialogue can emerge and that desirable thinking skills can develop through online interaction. Online discussions and individual contributions can be reflective, interactive, collaborative, or community-building. Their emergence, however, is hardly guaranteed by the provision of a space to develop those discussions and skills; support structures are required to overcome participants' unfamiliarity with technological environments or with the experience of communicating primarily in writing.

The next section analyzes the kinds of research methods used to derive the types of findings above. We depict how research approaches are evolving as new models of TPD emerge.

FINDINGS ABOUT RESEARCH APPROACHES

Research methods for analyzing oTPD have evolved over time.[28] In the early years of online teacher professional development, new ground was broken in research methodologies on efficacy, learning, and pedagogy by researchers who were also designers and instructors. Two research teams—Harasim, Hiltz, Toles, and Turoff, and Palloff and Pratt—were very influential in this research with their descriptive and prescriptive qualitative studies of learning networks for teachers in the 1990s.[29] Other researchers used quantitative methods to compare outcomes between face-to-face and online courses, often finding "no significant difference," yet these methods raised many intriguing questions about other aspects of teachers' learning online.[30] Now, the research methods used for exploring oTPD have expanded to include empirical methods—both quantitative and qualitative—that are replicable, although most studies are still on a very small scale and not robustly generalizable across contexts.[31]

A majority of the research studies we examined used a range of qualitative methods in their approach. These methodologies ranged from using qualitative software packages to grounded methods in coding audio or video inter-

FIGURE 4   Research Methods in Graphic Organizer

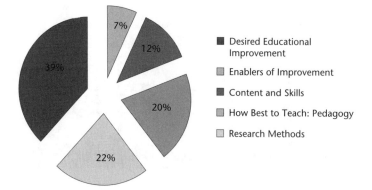

views, observations, and documents by hand. Quantitative research methods were used in some larger scale studies, primarily at the district level. However, many of the quantitative analyses used mixed methods. In those cases, qualitative data, such as interviews, were often coded and used to support the quantitative findings; or, contrarily, statistical analyses of survey responses or data frequencies (for example, the number of postings to an asynchronous discussion forum) were used to support qualitative coding methods. Several of the studies included are more conceptual in nature—they develop an argument and produce a particular analytical framework for aiding the design of oTPD or for gaining a better understanding of group and individual interactions. In fact, most of the studies we could find to review were focused on the nature of the interactivity in the program or participants being studied.

Figure 4 places the research methods in the more abstract context of our graphic organizer. Overall, the research methods terrain revealed rich findings on the design and nature of online interactions, but is much thinner on the depth and durability of teacher learning, teacher change, and impact on student learning. These findings are also reflected in the density gradient depiction of our graphic organizer.

In figure 5, we present a density gradient that summarizes where this research falls in our organizer. The shading represents what percentage of the reviewed articles considered the topic, with light colors representing a low percentage, and darker colors representing a higher percentage.

As can be seen in figure 5, the intensity of research differs by area. For example, 40 percent of our reviewed articles studied purely online methods of delivery, while the remaining articles were nearly evenly split between hybrid and face-to-face delivery methods. In contrast, only 15 percent of the

FIGURE 5   The Density of Reviewed Research on oTPD, by Area

Darker colors represent more research

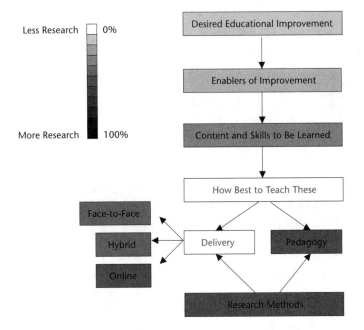

articles addressed the "enablers of improvement," with even fewer, 8 percent, attending to the overall desired educational improvement. However, we should be cautious in drawing conclusions from this density gradient, as each of the buckets of research covers a large area, and areas that appear poorly covered in toto might have sub-categories that are more fully covered, as was detailed elsewhere in this chapter.

LOOKING AHEAD: FURTHER STUDY NEEDED

As we stated at the beginning of this chapter, organizers come with several liabilities; a key one is their potential for limiting thinking to the categories presented. Our organizer presents oTPD more from the perspective of design and implementers and less from the standpoint of the participants. To guide future work, we present below an organizer with two additional categories: engagement and participant evaluation. Engagement covers research on how to get teachers to commit to TPD programs and how to keep them involved throughout the program. Participant evaluation comprises research on teachers' evaluations of the program, including whether it met their expectations. One final piece of analyzing research on TPD needs to include studies on taking small programs to scale. Since this affects every aspect of the program's design from initiation through delivery and engagement, we have encircled the entire organizer with this field. Figure 6 shows a revised organizer that can guide future, related studies.

FIGURE 6   Revised Graphic Organizer (including Sections on Teacher Engagement, Evaluation, and Scaling Up)

As new ideas and connections come to light, evolving this organizer to fit these new conceptions is an ongoing challenge.

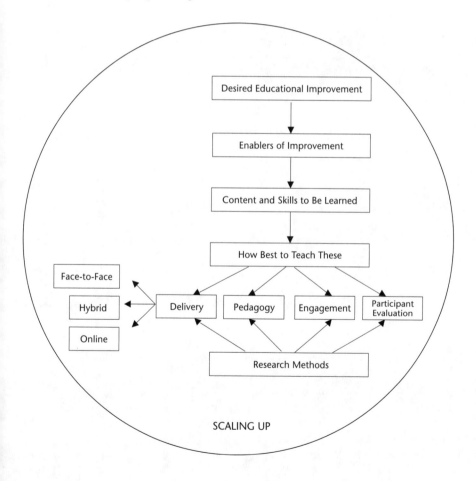

CHAPTER 2

EdTech Leaders Online

Building Organizational Capacity to Provide Effective Online Professional Development

Glenn M. Kleiman and Barbara Treacy

The EdTech Leaders Online (ETLO) program at Education Development Center, Inc. (EDC) began in 1999 with initial seed funding from the AT&T Foundation. From the start, the ETLO approach focused on enabling clients to develop their own organizational capacity to provide effective online professional development (OPD) to K–12 teachers and administrators. Since then, ETLO staff have worked with more than 120 client organizations in 35 states, training more than 1,200 educational leaders to be online professional development specialists, and those specialists in turn have provided online workshops for more than 20,000 educators. These client organizations include school districts, state departments of education, regional education centers, universities, and other providers of professional development for K–12 educators.

ETLO's capacity-building approach was, from the beginning, quite different from that offered by other OPD providers. This approach has had many implications for how the program was designed and implemented and how ETLO has worked with clients. For example, success is measured by clients' abilities, typically developed over a two-year period, to offer their own robust programs of online professional development workshops to meet the needs of their teachers and administrators. ETLO staff focus on the quality of the implementation of clients' programs and the quality of the online workshops they offer. In addition, ETLO focuses on how each client's OPD program is integrated into overall professional development plans, how it will be sustained, and how it helps the client meet teacher-quality goals. In this chapter, we describe the key elements of the ETLO program and the strategic approach underlying its success.

COMPONENTS OF THE EDTECH LEADERS ONLINE PROGRAM

A typical client organization is a school district interested in providing OPD to its teachers. The district selects a leadership team, usually composed of six individuals who may be staff developers, curriculum area coordinators, media specialists, technology directors, lead teachers, or others who have professional development responsibilities in the district. These individuals are trained to serve as OPD specialists for the organization.

Online Facilitator Program

Each team begins by participating in a ten-session course called Facilitating and Implementing Online Professional Development. This course is conducted entirely online, with teams from a district participating alongside participants from other districts around the country. The course explores recent developments in educational technology and online learning and provides participants with specialized training to facilitate OPD workshops for K–12 teachers and administrators. Course participants gain direct experience with online course tools, asynchronous discussion environments, and specific facilitation techniques as they learn to integrate online components into their professional development programs. The course also addresses critical issues such as access, universal design for learning, and course and program evaluation. Specific course topics include building an online learning community; addressing standards; equity and access; skills, strategies, and techniques of online facilitation; integrating face-to-face meetings; maintaining momentum in an online course; assessment and evaluation; technical issues; and connecting with classroom curriculum. ETLO facilitators model effective strategies and techniques for teaching online, and course participants are able to experience the online environment as learners, gaining critical preparation for teaching online. As a final product, participants collaborate with their colleagues to create their own plan to offer online workshops for local teachers and/or administrators.

Online Teaching Practicum

Following completion of the Facilitating and Implementing Online Professional Development course, the trained OPD specialists engage in a practicum during which they implement and facilitate online workshops provided by the ETLO program, while receiving ongoing support from ETLO staff and the opportunity to participate in the ETLO Forum (workshops and forum both described below). During the training course, participants, working individually or with partners, select one of the 30 ETLO online workshops to implement during their practicum, become familiar with its contents, and plan all the details of offering it locally, including how they will recruit participants, what incentives the district will provide, and how the course will be evaluated.

ETLO Online Workshops

ETLO offers a catalog of 30 online workshops that are available both as part of the facilitator training program and on an ongoing basis after the training period is over. Access to the workshop catalog allows local organizations to use their trained facilitators to continue their online program by offering a selection of workshops based on their needs. The workshops are also available for licensing by other organizations with their own trained facilitators. Options include workshops for all teachers, such as Transforming the Classroom with Project-Based Learning, Universal Design for Learning, and Differentiating Instruction; workshops for teachers of specific subject areas and grade levels, such as Using Patterns to Develop Algebraic Thinking, Inquiry in the Science Classroom, and Improving Reading and Writing in the Content Areas; and workshops for school and district leaders, such as Data-Based School Reform and Safeguarding the Wired Schoolhouse.

ETLO workshops are developed by teams of online instructional design specialists and content experts and are kept up to date through an ongoing process of content and link review. Each workshop contains an introductory orientation session followed by six content sessions designed for delivery over a seven- or eight-week period, with participants spending about four hours per week on coursework. Each session contains online readings, multimedia resources, interactive activities, and focused asynchronous discussions, with all course content provided online in the workshop website. One goal of the design is to engage participants in focused, asynchronous interactions in which they support one another's learning. The ETLO workshop catalog is available at http://www.edtechleaders.org/programs/workshops/catalog.asp.

ETLO Forum

To provide ongoing support, ETLO offers a national online forum in which OPD specialists share resources, questions, materials, and reflections with other trained online specialists and ETLO staff. The forum is a robust, interactive online community that has grown and developed to include over 1,200 online specialists trained in the ETLO program. Forum components include facilitated asynchronous online discussions, a rich collection of resources and materials developed by participating organizations, a library of references about online professional development, and a series of topical synchronous chats.

Planning and Implementation Support

In addition to the forum, ETLO staff provide ongoing individualized planning and consultation to participating teams through e-mail and telephone support while local organizations are planning and implementing their programs. ETLO also offers optional face-to-face onsite workshops for participating organizations at any point during their program, although most requests for onsite sessions occur at the start of the program.

Online Course Developer Program

Some OPD specialists move on to a second training program to learn to develop their own online courses (some who are already familiar with online learning go directly into this course). The course developer program includes a ten-session online training course, Online Course Design and Delivery, for teams from participating organizations. Participants learn to design and deliver online courses that address the specific needs of a selected audience. As they begin to develop their own courses, participants are guided through the process of defining their course goals, readings, and activities; creating provocative discussion questions; aligning their content to state and national standards; developing online assessments; and incorporating strategies for building an e-learning community. Specific course topics include organizing course content for online delivery, online instructional design strategies and techniques, incorporating Web-based resources, differentiating instruction, online assessment, developing online discussion questions, building participant collaboration, and addressing technical issues. In addition to the facilitated online discussion in the course, participants receive extensive individualized feedback from the ETLO instructor on the courses they are developing. ETLO provides a course development checklist of the key design elements, which is available at http://edtechleaders.org/documents/OCD/Course_Dev_Check.htm.

During the year following the end of their training, online course designers engage in a practicum during which they complete and pilot their courses with ongoing support from ETLO instructional design staff, along with additional support from other designers and ETLO staff through the ETLO forum.

Graduate Credit

Through a partnership with Antioch University begun in 2001, ETLO offers credit for each of the training courses and their associated practicum courses. Participants who complete all four courses receive a Certificate in Educational Technology and Online Learning offered jointly by Antioch and EDC. The four courses include the facilitator training course, a practicum in which trained facilitators run an ETLO workshop, the course developer training course, and a second practicum in which participants pilot the workshop they developed.

Technology and Technical Support

ETLO utilizes the Blackboard course management system for delivery of its training courses and workshops. ETLO can also host the pilot OPD workshops for participating teams, which allows an important way for educational organizations to explore online learning options without having to first license their own course delivery system. If an organization has its own course management system and wants to host its programs locally, ETLO can export workshops into compatible systems. In the past year, ETLO workshops and courses have been run in both the Desire2Learn and the ANGEL course management systems, as well as in Blackboard. ETLO provides technical support to participants in its training courses and expects local organizations to provide technical support to their local online program participants.

ETLO'S ORIGINS AND EXAMPLE PROGRAMS

The first OPD workshops grew out of the Leadership and the New Technologies (LNT) Institutes, a collaboration between EDC and the Harvard Graduate School of Education's Programs in Professional Education. These intensive, weeklong Institutes for district leadership teams were held each summer from 1997 to 1999. The Institutes were built around the same education and leadership development approach that underlies the ETLO program: engaging educators in professional communities of learners; focusing on authentic, context-based learning; providing hands-on experience followed by reflection and discussion; using case-study approaches; bridging research and practice; and supporting each individual in constructing his or her own understandings and strategies relevant to individual goals.

As part of planning the Institutes, EDC staff began to explore ways in which online components (the Internet was still new to most educators in 1997) could be used to begin the exchanges before the group came together at Harvard, to support and document the presentations and discussions so they would be available after the Institutes, and to provide opportunities for follow-up exchanges. The participants and presenters found that these uses of technology, innovative for their time, added a great deal to the Institutes, and they often used the online resources to share information when they returned to their districts. Following the 1998 Institute, EDC implemented its first online workshop in order to continue exploring how the Internet could enhance K–12 education, with both LNT participants and others participating online. Several workshops on other topics of interest to the LNT participants were offered, including the potential of multiuser virtual environments and of geographic information systems in K–12 education. These were very new ideas just seven years ago.

One of the online participants, Leinda Peterman (now on the staff at EDC), invited EDC to participate in a Technology Innovation Challenge Grant to work with a consortium of five rural school districts in northeastern Louisiana. This consortium, called America 2000 and centered in Concordia Parish, Louisiana, partnered with EDC to design and deliver a series of online workshops for project teachers as a way to offer consistent training and resources across the large geographic area served by the grant. The online workshops and capacity-building training EDC developed during this period laid the groundwork for the ETLO program.

A key milestone in ETLO's growth was a partnership with the Louisiana Department of Education, which grew out of the work with the America 2000 Consortium. With visionary leadership at the Louisiana Department of Education and a growing commitment to spread online professional development throughout the state, a cohort of Department of Education staff was trained as OPD specialists in the summer of 2001. The success of this training led to the expansion of online learning within many of the Department's core programs, including their new teacher induction and principal certification programs.

The Louisiana programs led to a partnership with the Southern Regional Education Board (SREB), a compact of 16 southern states, to offer pilot training to state-level educational technology staff. This initiative, supported by the AT&T Foundation, the Bell South Foundation, and the individual states, led to the formation of the Multi-State Online Professional Development Initiative (http://www.sreb.org/programs/EdTech/toolkit/onlineindex.asp) and a commitment by the SREB states to collaborate with EDC to expand online professional development opportunities across the region.

Building upon the approach developed through these initial projects, ETLO has enabled educational organizations across the country to build successful local online learning programs, some examples of which are described below.

South Carolina Online Professional Development (SCOPD) Program[1]

The purpose of the SCOPD program is to provide South Carolina educators with high-quality, accessible, online professional development opportunities in the area of technology integration. SCOPD is the primary delivery method for all technology integration professional development provided by the South Carolina Department of Education.

When faced in 2002 with severe budget cuts that reduced the size of the South Carolina Instructional Technology staff by half, while the number of districts to receive instructional technology training remained the same, the South Carolina Department of Education began exploring options to provide its training through online delivery. Recognizing that this would move staff into unfamiliar territory, they established three guidelines: leverage the existing instructional staff, build supporting course management infrastructure, and create or lease high-quality content. Since all of the staff had subject-area knowledge and the required instructional skills, the key professional development need the Department of Education identified was training in course design and online facilitation. To meet this goal, the Department of Education researched a variety of options, ranging from college courses to onsite seminar programs.

During the same time period, ETLO began its collaboration with SREB to prepare OPD specialists in member states. Grants provided scholarships for pilot SREB state teams to complete training during the 2003 and 2004 school years. State departments were able to supplement the pilot teams by funding additional participants. The South Carolina Department of Education decided that ETLO provided the necessary components to help it launch a successful online professional development effort. Therefore, it participated in the ETLO/SREB training and funded 17 additional participants beyond their four grant-funded slots.

In March 2003, a group of South Carolina Department of Education staff completed course design training and began developing a core set of entry-level online courses focused on integrating Microsoft Office applications into the curriculum. During the following 13 months, the online specialists finalized their course designs and piloted them for state educators. Department of Education staff also completed facilitator training and gained additional experience by facilitating ETLO workshops.

Parallel to the professional development efforts, the South Carolina Department of Education began a lengthy process to acquire its own course management system, in order to provide flexibility and scalability for its online programs. In December 2003, the state selected the Blackboard course management system and awarded Blackboard a contract.

In April 2004, the South Carolina Online Professional Development program went live with a catalog of 44 courses, including a combination of ETLO workshops, workshops developed by the South Carolina designers, and workshops from other sources. During that first year, 368 classroom teachers successfully completed online courses. In March 2005, SCOPD entered its second year with 50 course offerings. Enrollment has steadily and consistently increased an average of more than 8 percent each month. Additional information is available at the SCOPD website (http://www.myscschools. com/scopd/index.html).

The success of SCOPD led the department to cosponsor and host a national ETLO/SREB Institute for Online Facilitators and Designers as part of its South Carolina EdTech Conference in January 2005, followed by a half-day online learning symposium in September 2005.

Tennessee Generating Equal Access to Rural Areas (GEAR) Grant

EDC collaborated with the Tennessee Department of Education to develop a competitive grant program using No Child Left Behind Title IID Educational Technology funds. The goal of this program is to build capacity for online learning in rural districts across the state. Participants from 14 rural districts were selected to undertake online facilitator training and to deliver at least two online workshops for their teachers and administrators. Over 350 teachers were impacted during the first year of this program, and GEAR districts have continued to expand their online professional development programs.

Virginia Regional Consortia

Building on a strong collaboration with the Virginia Department of Education and the Wise County, Virginia, schools since the start of the ETLO program, ETLO was invited in January 2004 to provide training, consulting, and support to two large Virginia consortia funded through NCLB Title IID funds: the North Technology Integration Education Region Partnership (http://culpeperschools.org/TIER/), encompassing 13 school divisions, and the Blue Ridge West Consortium (http://www.scsb.org/etlo_workshops.htm), encompassing 19 school divisions. Each consortium is now in its second year of training, with a combined total of 125 trained online facilitators and 75 online course designers who are offering online workshops to teachers within the consortia. The consortia have arranged graduate credit for these workshops from local colleges and universities, and teachers are also awarded recertification points for completing the workshops.

Milwaukee Public Schools

ETLO also works closely with many large urban school districts, including Milwaukee Public Schools. Through a partnership with Harvard Graduate School of Education and initial funding from the Joyce Foundation, ETLO began work with Milwaukee Public Schools in 2002 to help them incorporate online learning into their professional development program, with the goal of improving teacher induction and retention. ETLO trained over 75 online facilitators and course designers, who have since offered approximately 200 online workshops for nearly 1,500 participants. The program has been highly successful, as demonstrated by a participant course completion rate of 94.5 percent. Many of the teachers receive graduate credit through a partnership with Cardinal Stritch University. Now in the program's fourth year, Milwaukee Public Schools continues to offer a robust program of online workshops.

Los Angeles Unified School District

Los Angeles has also worked with the ETLO program since the initial round of training, with over 30 professional development specialists trained to design and deliver online workshops aligned to district standards. In the fall of 2003, LAUSD expanded use of online learning to students by launching the Los Angeles Virtual Academy, and ETLO has offered several rounds of online instructor training for their virtual course teachers.

EVALUATION DATA

ETLO staff place a priority on learning from the feedback they get from participants. The program and courses are regularly updated based on evaluation data that are collected on an ongoing basis. The ETLO program includes pre- and postcourse surveys in each of its training courses, and data collected through these surveys are carefully reviewed by the ETLO team at the end of each training cycle. Local online specialists also complete an online survey after they implement their workshops, which provides additional feedback on the training and the workshops. ETLO maintains a strong commitment to continuous improvement and being responsive to local needs, modeling this approach for its participants.

ETLO workshops also include pre- and post-workshop surveys, and the ETLO training courses prepare facilitators to use and/or revise these surveys when they are running their workshops. In addition, ETLO teams are expected to develop a plan for evaluating their local online professional development program as part of the ETLO training process.

ETLO has also organized two studies of its program. The first was conducted during the 2002–03 school year, and the second is currently under way in 2005, with some preliminary results available.

2002–03 Study

ETLO conducted two evaluation surveys between October 2002 and May 2003. One survey was directed at ETLO-trained facilitators, and the other was directed at the educators who participated in the local online workshops these facilitators offered. Four geographically diverse organizations that had participated in ETLO since its inception were included in the survey: Gardiner Public Schools, Maine; America 2000 Technology Innovation Challenge Grant, Louisiana; Worcester Public Schools, Massachusetts; and Los Angeles Unified School District. Highlights of the results include the following:

Facilitator Survey (N = 34)
- 97 percent reported the ETLO training course met their needs and was of high quality
- 90 percent reported ETLO helped them learn new skills
- 100 percent felt supported by ETLO when facilitating their local workshops
- 82 percent reported workshops they facilitated met or exceeded goals

Participant Survey (N = 120)
- 92 percent said they benefited from and enjoyed learning online and would be interested in online learning in the future
- 91 percent reported increased collaboration with colleagues
- 84 percent reported increased knowledge of inquiry- or project-based lessons
- 91 percent reported increased understanding of technology's ability to support curriculum
- 86 percent completed a classroom project based on their locally facilitated ETLO workshop

- 88 percent reported feeling more confident integrating technology into the curriculum

Milwaukee Study

A more recent set of two studies is being conducted on the ETLO implementation in the Milwaukee Public Schools (described above) during the 2002–04 school years. These include a facilitator study, based on aggregate pre- and post-survey data from 32 facilitators and a follow-up focus group with six of these facilitators, and a workshop participant study, based on aggregate pre- and post-survey data from 62 workshops (including 16 different ETLO workshop titles), with a total of 698 workshop participants, as well as a follow-up focus group with six of these participants.

Preliminary results from the facilitator study showed that 83 percent reported that the facilitator-training courses either met or exceeded their expectations, and 87 percent reported that their ETLO instructors were either effective or very effective. Facilitators also reported that the training course provided new opportunities for collaboration, very valuable feedback from the instructor, useful resources, new skills and content knowledge, the ability to address important district goals, and the development of a cadre of teachers working toward a common goal.

Preliminary results from the workshop participants show that ETLO workshops had a positive impact on workshop participants' content knowledge, pedagogical practices, and approaches, with 89 percent reporting that the workshops either met or exceeded their expectations. In addition, the number of participants who reported feeling confident about designing classroom projects based on the content goals of the workshop they completed grew from 40 percent on the pre-workshop surveys to 90 percent on the post-workshop surveys.

GUIDING PRINCIPLES OF THE ETLO PROGRAM

From its inception, ETLO has been grounded in a core set of guiding principles that have served the program well and have evolved and been refined as the work proceeded. A brief summary of the current guiding principles for the ETLO program is provided below.

Align with the general principles of high-quality professional development. The ETLO program is aligned with a set of principles of effective professional development, based on the belief that these apply to the online environment as well as to face-to-face activities. These principles are summarized by Sparks and Hirsh, who describe a "paradigm shift" in staff development, away from one-day in-service presentations and toward professional development as an integral, ongoing part of teachers' lives.[2] The principles, elaborated by the National Staff Development Council and others, are summarized in the white paper *Meeting the Need for High-Quality Teachers: E-Learning Solutions*[3] prepared for the secretary's July 2004 leadership summit, which states that high-quality professional development is most effective when it

- fosters a deepening of subject-matter knowledge, a greater understanding of learning, and a greater appreciation of students' needs;
- centers around the critical activities of teaching and learning—planning lessons, evaluating student work, developing curriculum, improving classroom practices, and increasing student learning—rather than on abstractions and generalities;
- builds on investigations of practice through cases that involve specific problems of practice, questions, analysis, reflection, and substantial professional discourse;
- values and cultivates a culture of collegiality, involving knowledge and experience sharing among educators; and
- is sustained, intensive, and continuously woven into the everyday fabric of the teaching profession, through modeling, coaching, and collaborations.[4]

Provide a capacity-building approach. A key factor in ETLO's growth and success is its capacity-building approach. ETLO is designed as a program, not a course, and it includes training, services, and ongoing support over an extended period of time. ETLO's practicum experience is a key element of this approach that lays the groundwork for a successful program launch and provides the foundation for sustainability beyond the initial funding and implementation period.

Develop leadership teams. ETLO's capacity-building team approach involves building new leadership and preparing leaders to address the basic components of successful program implementation, including marketing, incentives, credit, scheduling, quality control, and evaluation. ETLO trains a core team within a local educational organization to collaborate on managing, implementing, and sustaining the program. For this reason, ETLO does not permit the participation of individuals who are not sponsored by an educational organization.

Employ a learning community model. ETLO focuses on a learning community model in which participants are part of a cohort of online colleagues, completing readings and assignments and engaging in facilitated discussions and collaborative activities with other participants. Each session includes a focused discussion question designed to lead to reflection and discussion related to the key learning goals. Participants are required to post a reflective response to the discussion prompt at the start of the session and then return to the online discussion several times during the weeklong session to read the responses of their colleagues and respond thoughtfully to at least one or two of them.

The learning community model is dependent on the active and careful guidance of a skilled online facilitator, who is a constant presence in the online discussion and who is prepared with strategies to keep the discussion moving. In addition to course discussions, the facilitator uses e-mail to interact with participants regularly and engages in other "behind-the-scenes" individualized e-mail and phone contact with participants, providing feedback, answering questions, or resolving specific issues. At the end of the session, the facilitator posts a summary of key themes to document the key points, provide closure to the session, and help participants move forward as a group. The ETLO learning community approach is further described in its "Ten Tips for Effective Online Facilitation" (http://www.edtechleaders.org/documents/opd/ETLO_Ten_Tips.htm).

Offer flexible approaches to meet local goals and needs. ETLO program elements are flexible and modular, and they can be aligned to specific professional development needs. ETLO works closely with each client organization to customize the model to meet its particular goals. For example, in Oregon ETLO is working with a statewide NSF-funded math project, and project staff are being trained to facilitate a specific series of ETLO math-focused workshops for participating teachers. In New Hampshire, ETLO collaborated with the Department of Education to train online specialists through their Regional Educational Service Center Network to design and deliver online courses aligned to state curricular goals for teachers across the state. As described previously, ETLO training helped the South Carolina Department of Education Office of Technology develop a series of face-to-face instructional technology workshops into a series of online courses. Each implementation is unique by design, and this flexibility supports local teams in planning whether to integrate face-to-face meetings with the online courses to create a hybrid program, taking into account the travel and schedule requirements of the participants.

Address technical and accessibility issues. ETLO provides technical support to its participants and local technical staff, who are then prepared to support their local participants. ETLO training also includes attention to access and accessibility. Local teams are required to address these issues as part of their implementation planning. By helping local teams be proactive on these issues, ETLO training enables local programs to be inclusive and broad in their reach, leading to increased opportunities for impact, support, and sustainability. ETLO courses and workshops are designed so that all materials are provided online and work well even when participants are connecting to the Internet via slow phone lines, since many teachers use these courses from home and do not have broadband access available.

Establish clear expectations and guidelines. A key element for effective professional development (and good teaching in general) is the establishment of clear expectations and guidelines. This is especially important in the online environment, where the opportunities for ongoing clarifications are more limited than in face-to-face contexts. ETLO's course and participation guidelines are shared with participants at the beginning of the training. ETLO has also developed a set of online discussion guidelines that establish the expectations and criteria for effective online discussion participation, which are available at http://www.edtechleaders.org/documents/tipsandtricks.htm.

Engage stakeholders. In order to build stable programs beyond the initial training or grant period, it is important to include stakeholders and decision-makers in the program. ETLO encourages participation by local administrators in the ETLO training and/or local workshop delivery. It is also important that local teams share their results, evaluation data, and workshop and classroom products—through websites; through presentations to other teachers, administrators, school boards, parents, and other key parties; through local celebrations; or in other ways in order to develop necessary support to fund and maintain the program. Strategies for engaging stakeholders and building sustainable programs are central to the ETLO training program.

RELATED WORK

In 2001, ETLO staff developed a strategic plan for work in online professional development, which includes four key elements: (1) continue to expand the ETLO capacity-building program, focusing on developing state-level and other large-scale programs using a combination of grant and fee-for-service funding; (2) provide online content development services to other organizations; (3) integrate online learning into comprehensive professional development programs offered by EDC; and (4) develop a research program on online professional development. These four strategies have helped to strengthen and build upon the ETLO program. Some examples of this work are highlighted below.

Online Content Development

EDC has developed about 30 online courses for the PBS TeacherLine program; four online courses for mathematics teachers in Department of Defense Education Agency schools; courses for administrators in collaboration with the Consortium for School Networking; a teacher leadership course in collaboration with Virginia Commonwealth University; and a variety of courses for other clients.

Integrating OPD into Comprehensive Professional Development Programs

EDC provides the professional development program for middle-school mathematics teachers throughout Maine. This program, tied to the Maine Learning Technology ("laptop") Initiative, provides every middle-school student and teacher with an iBook computer and wireless access throughout the schools. This two-year professional development program combines face-to-face workshops, online courses, peer coaching, and mentoring components, with each teacher taking two online courses. EDC has also provided a Leading in Technology program for members of the State Education Technology Directors Association that combines face-to-face and online components.

Research

The impact of the Maine professional development program on teachers' content knowledge, classroom practices, and uses of technology, and on their students' mathematics achievement, is the subject of a randomized control research project being conducted by the Maine Department of Education; the Center for Education Policy, Applied Research, and Evaluation at the University of Southern Maine; and EDC, with funding by the U.S. Department of Education. In addition, in collaboration with Mike Russell at Boston College, EDC has received funding from the NSF to conduct research on alternative models of online professional development and on the comparative impact and cost-benefits of face-to-face and online approaches. These research projects are providing solid evidence that online professional development can impact teachers' content knowledge and professional practices. They are also enabling EDC to refine the professional development approaches incorporated into the ETLO program and other work.

NEXT STEPS

As the program continues to evolve in response to educational needs and lessons learned, ETLO is beginning two new initiatives: a Virtual Schools Program and an E-Learning for Educators initiative funded by a U.S. Department of Education Ready to Teach grant.

Virtual Schools Program

The Virtual Schools Program includes training courses to enable teams to design and deliver virtual courses for their students. The programs include Implementing and Instructing Virtual School Courses, which prepares online instructors for virtual courses for students; Designing Virtual School Courses, which trains participants to design online courses for middle or high school students; and additional offerings, which include Online Mentor, Student Orientation, and Planning and Implementing Virtual School Programs workshops. The ETLO online professional development catalog is also available in order to provide ongoing professional development for course instructors in content, pedagogy, and technology integration.

E-Learning for Educators Initiative

In fall 2005, ETLO began a five-year partnership with Alabama Public Television and a consortium of nine state departments and public television stations that were awarded a U.S. Department of Education Ready to Teach grant. ETLO will provide the core training for a comprehensive capacity-building program to establish a statewide online professional development program in each of the participating states. States will also collaborate to develop a set of standards for online course design and delivery, and a series of model online courses will be developed for use among all participating states.

The E-Learning for Educators initiative will also include a series of large-scale, randomized control treatment research studies on the impact of the online professional development workshops on both teachers and their students. A series of intensive studies at various grade levels and in various subject areas will be conducted to assess the impact of online learning on teachers who participate in a series of three online workshops over a two-year period.

CONCLUSIONS

The ETLO program has come a long way since it began seven years ago with a few initial exploratory online workshops. For many educators, online learning can provide powerful opportunities for professional growth, and in fact a good number of educators report that they prefer online learning to other types of professional development. ETLO staff have been pleasantly surprised at the ease with which educators engage in supportive professional inter- actions online, sharing ideas and concerns, learning from each other, and, in some cases, forming ongoing relationships. The ETLO story demonstrates that with committed staff, careful planning, and good training and support, many organizations can successfully build their own online professional development programs to address local and regional needs. The ETLO team has also become convinced, along with others working in this area, that it is the quality of the content, educational design, and instruction that deter- mines the value of professional development experiences for educators, not whether they are offered face to face or online.

CHAPTER 3

Piaget Goes Digital

Negotiating Accommodation
of Practice to Principles

Martha Stone Wiske, David Perkins, and David Eddy Spicer

Helping teachers improve their practice so that students learn better is a perennial goal of education.[1] Laudably, it is one thoroughly studied, but regrettably, it is also one rarely achieved on a wide scale. The largest fault line is all too familiar: Most professional development consists of transmitting information to teachers, a strategy that does not work significant changes in their practice.[2] Even when teachers learn how to enact new strategies, they typically do not change their accustomed practice very much.[3]

The reality is that substantial changes in professional practice involve "sailing against the wind." Countervailing forces at both the individual and the institutional levels tend to maintain the status quo. With teachers, as with other professionals, individual beliefs and habits commonly hinder taking in new ideas or applying them in practice. Institutional factors such as pervasive norms, policies, and organizational structures constrain individuals who want to change.[4] To invoke one of Swiss developmentalist Jean Piaget's most familiar conceptions, teachers—and institutions—often *assimilate* into their existing patterns what they learn in professional development rather than *accommodating* their practice to new principles.

This chapter describes an online program for educators that directly addresses the challenges of professional development on a wide scale. The WIDE World program offers online professional development courses specifically intended to foster changes in teachers' practice, not just to transmit information. We chart the challenges of professional development, explain the theory of change underlying the design of the WIDE World program, and articulate in some detail how WIDE World operates in relation to this theory. Included are results of research on the process and effects of the WIDE World program. We conclude with a summary of findings, remaining questions, and recommendations.

THE CHALLENGES OF PROFESSIONAL DEVELOPMENT FOR EDUCATORS

Bridging the Knowledge-Action Gap

Understanding principles that inform practice is one hurdle, adapting and accepting them as worthwhile is another, and enacting them flexibly on a regular basis is yet a third. Academic learning normally focuses on the first of these, asking for changes in neither belief nor behavior beyond engaging in intelligent and informed discussions and writing papers. In contrast, professional education aims to change the learner's everyday mindset and conduct in the context of professional practice.[5]

Professional learning also contrasts with technical training, which calls for the learning and consistent employment of standardized procedures. A hallmark of teachers' work, as with other professionals, is that it requires judgment, interpretation, and expertise in response to varying and uncertain conditions.[6] Awareness of "best practices" is not the same as having the will and skill to adapt such practices to one's own priorities, requirements, constraints, and resources.

Although theorists of professional learning may debate the relationship between understanding principles and enacting expert practice, they agree that some integrated connection is required. Schön characterizes the desired relationship as "knowledge-in-action" and advocates that professionals need to learn how to reflect on their practice in relation to principles.[7] Eraut regards professional learning as deeply embedded in its context of application: "Learning knowledge and using knowledge are not separate processes but the same process."[8] In sum, a key challenge in professional education is promoting participants' commitment and capability to interpret and apply principles of effective practice in flexible ways tuned to their own practical circumstances.

Assimilation versus Accommodation

As mentioned earlier, two key concepts from the work of Jean Piaget illuminate the hurdles of professional development: *assimilation* and *accommoda-*

tion.[9] Usually applied to fundamental shifts in the child's conceptualization of the world, these ideas also inform the challenges of professional development.

Piaget used the term *assimilation* to describe the process of acquiring information within established frameworks and modes of thinking. Piaget mapped this process in his study of young learners. Even infants must negotiate new learning in relation to their prior understandings. There is great power in making sense of novel experiences by seeing relationships and making analogies to prior knowledge. The risk, however, is that underlying concepts and interpretive frameworks may become fossilized and impervious to adaptation rather than renewed to take genuine account of the new data.

Piaget used the other term, *accommodation,* to describe adjusting established frameworks and modes of thinking in light of new data and ideas not fully and richly assimilable into existing repertoire. Accommodation is the organism's deeply adaptive response to the fundamentally novel. However, excessive accommodation also has its downside. Wisdom built up through prior experience may be neglected rather than used effectively to interpret new information or perceptions.

The forces of assimilation and accommodation are at work with teachers involved in professional development, just as they are with all learners. A frequent source of vexation for would-be school reformers is teachers' excessive tendency toward assimilation, as described memorably by David Cohen in his case study of Mrs. Oublier.[10] Mrs. Oublier believed that her attendance at a professional development workshop had transformed her views of teaching mathematics. Cohen observed that her classroom practices were a complex mix of new approaches and traditional ways. She filtered the new curriculum through her more traditional beliefs about teaching, learning, and mathematics. The presumed educational value of the new approach was diluted or lost entirely.[11]

There are considerable differences between typical cases of assimilation versus accommodation in Piaget's work and here. Piaget's studies emphasized conceptual development, with the child achieving different levels of complexity in understanding the world. In professional development, the characteristic challenges are not primarily conceptual—like Mrs. Oublier, most teachers can fairly readily grasp the ideas that typically figure in professional development. As noted earlier, the main challenges lie more in the areas of sustained commitment and revised practice, integrated effectively with the many exigencies of professional life. Nevertheless, the contrast between assimilation and accommodation proves telling. One may, like Mrs. Oublier, talk a bit of the talk, undertake some adjustments here and there, and pretend or even believe that one is "doing it" without making significant change—or one may find ways to make distinctive personal meaning of new ideas and come to more fundamental shifts of mindset and practice.

Sailing against the Wind

The tendency toward assimilation in teacher development is all too understandable. Revising one's practices amidst the complexities of professional life is a perpetual process of "sailing against the wind," which, from a number of personal and institutional sources, blows in the opposite direction from the way one is headed.

At the individual level, teachers' established beliefs about what is good and possible regarding curriculum and pedagogy constrain the ways they interpret or experience new ideas. Habits of practice, tried and true strategies that seem to have served well in the past, are not easily foregone. Attitudes, such as pride in one's own expertise or a sense of self-respect that generate "reactance" against being "volunteered" or coerced by administrators, may also make teachers reluctant to enact "the latest great new thing."[12] Also, simple preoccupation with competing agendas may limit teachers' capacity to remember to try a strategy they learned, even if they thought it seemed promising.

Institutional forces combine with teachers' individual traits to hold existing practices in place and to work against the implementation of new strategies. Policies and available materials related to curriculum and assessment of students' achievement shape what teachers feel able and inclined to teach, and may discourage interest in the "learner-centered" curriculum and methods recommended by many educators.[13] Norms and teacher evaluation procedures influence perceptions of what constitutes effective classroom procedures. Students' and parents' expectations about roles, responsibilities, and learning activities constrain teachers' tendency to implement new regimes. While some school cultures value faculty innovation and creativity, in others such out-of-the-box endeavors generate mistrust and resentment from colleagues and administrators.

TOWARD NEGOTIATED ACCOMMODATIONS

If professional development is to help teachers make significant changes in their practice so that student achievement improves in noticeable ways, it must help teachers sail against the wind. It must support them in achieving a negotiated accommodation with new ideas and strategies. By *negotiated* we mean that, in contrast with typical Piagetian conceptual tasks, there is no one perfectly correct accommodation to be attained. Rather, teachers need to work out individually and collectively what genuine steps forward make sense for them in their distinctive contexts. Accommodation may involve various elements: *replacement* of old practices and ideas with new ones, *compromise* through gradual or partial integration of new practices, and *synthesis* by emphasizing and extending existing practices that are consistent with the new model.

Negotiating an appropriate configuration depends on finding ways to support new ideas and practices while challenging the initial mix of ideas, experience, and countervailing forces at both the individual and institutional levels.[14] One dimension of support for negotiating accommodations looks to teachers' individual inclinations, strengths, and constraints. Engaging teachers in analyzing the relationship between their accustomed practice and the new approach, trying out new strategies that seem within reach, and reflecting on the results are all ways of helping teachers to sail against the wind of individual factors.[15]

Another dimension of support involves helping teachers learn how to manage institutional factors that may limit their progress. For example, teachers may be helped to review the new approach in relation to required curriculum and assessment mandates to find ways of meeting both sets of criteria at once. Another strategy is to help teachers identify allies—colleagues and administrators—with whom they can collaborate to build a conducive professional community.[16]

Yet a third dimension concerns the institution itself. It is a sound homily that professional development typically requires institutional development. Indeed, institutions structurally and culturally display the same patterns of assimilation and accommodation one finds at the individual level. Accordingly, working with leaders in a broad sense—administrative leaders, instructional leaders, and others—becomes an important aspect of thriving professional development, with the goal of fostering negotiated accommodation at the institutional level resonant with the hoped-for shifts in classroom practice.[17]

A THEORY OF CHANGE FOR PROFESSIONAL DEVELOPMENT

The WIDE World (WIDE stands for "Wide-scale Interactive Development for Educators") online teacher-development initiative responds to this set of challenges by taking advantage of networked technologies. The theory of change underlying the design of WIDE World programs focuses on supporting teachers in making smart accommodations with principles of effective pedagogy.[18] The theory includes the following elements. None of them is surprising, but each is tremendously important for discouraging outright assimilation and supporting negotiated accommodation.

- *Model the principles:* Make the target principles of effective teaching explicit and public, keep these continually up front in the learning process of the professional development itself, and systematically use the principles as the basis for guiding and assessing teachers' practice. Nothing would undermine a negotiated accommodation more than the perception that the professional developers themselves do not walk the talk. Also, in this way, teachers experience effective practices as learners even as they study them in a more conceptual way.
- *Support application and reflection during the course:* Build in multiple opportunities for teachers to plan and enact applications of the new principles to their own practice *during* the professional development course so that teachers have time to negotiate their accommodation before the course ends. Encourage them to analyze and interpret the abstract principles in relation to their own knowledge, expertise, and circumstances. Help them anticipate implementation challenges and plan ways to address them. Give teachers practice in sailing against the wind while they are still in the supportive environment of the course.
- *Provide coaching:* Provide multiple rounds of supportive coaching that include modeling good teaching practice, engaging the participants in relationships with the coach and fellow participants, and offering specific assessments of draft work in relation to principled criteria along with suggestions for improvement. Effective coaches offer suggestions about ways of surmounting hurdles that teachers anticipate and then comment on teachers' reflections about their implementation experiences. The aim of coaching is to support teachers as they modify their practice, without either trying to be overly ambitious or diluting the principles excessively.
- *Foster reflective, collaborative professional communities:* Support learning from and with peers by establishing norms that encourage risking not knowing, acknowledging vulnerability, posting draft work, exchanging ideas, offering peer feedback, and sharing expertise. Promote dialogue by telling stories, reflecting on experience, and building relationships. These forms of dialogue and exchange help teachers surface, express, and examine tacit knowledge that either can support or may undermine steps toward new practices. Through these processes, teachers learn from peers about how to negotiate sensible accommodations for themselves. They also begin to

develop professional skills and relationships that can help them continue to understand and apply research-based practices after the course ends.

- *Negotiate institutional accommodation:* Help to address and, if possible, reduce institutional forces that undermine teachers' negotiated accommodation to the new practices. Encourage participants to discuss countervailing institutional factors—such as educational goals and policies, prevailing routines of pedagogy and assessment, technological resources, and organizational structures and culture—and how they might adapt the new ideas and practices to these conditions, and vice versa. Once expressed, doubts, concerns, and strategies can become the focus of dialogue among participants and coaches who exchange ideas about sailing upwind. In addition to helping teachers adjust to these forces, build a conducive context through working with local administrative and instructional leaders as well as support personnel.

WIDE WORLD'S GENERAL GOALS AND STRUCTURE

The WIDE World project attempts to apply this theory of program change primarily through online professional development courses with some limited face-to-face elements. Here we summarize briefly the goals and structure of WIDE World with a focus on its scaling model, material that is presented more fully elsewhere.[19] Subsequent sections address how WIDE World enacts the foregoing theory.

WIDE World offers online professional development courses designed to foster teachers' application of research-based strategies in planning curriculum and fostering and assessing students' learning. These strategies include the Teaching for Understanding framework discussed below, applications of Gardner's theory of multiple intelligences, and the synthesis of these models in differentiating instruction for diverse learners and integrating new technologies to improve student performance.[20] Some courses offered by WIDE World focus on using such strategies to improve teaching in particular subjects, such as mathematics, reading, and writing. WIDE World courses do not advocate the use of any particular curriculum content. Instead, they help teachers define curriculum goals and select and adapt materials and methods that focus on promoting students' understanding.

WIDE World's primary format is online asynchronous professional development courses and interactive tools. Learners access these online components through a website (http://wideworld.pz.harvard.edu) created by the program's technology team. This site includes a platform for course delivery and administration that integrates registration forms, an online teaching/

learning environment designed to reflect the Teaching for Understanding framework elements, a threaded discussion tool customized from a commercial product called Web Crossing, a resource library that instructors and participants stock with recommended files and websites, and tools that coaches and instructors use to monitor and record participants' progress.

The WIDE World site links to two supplementary websites (http://learn-web.harvard.edu) that are freely available to the public and that provide a range of related resources including a collaborative curriculum design tool. This tool is an interactive workspace for designing curriculum that includes scaffolding shaped by the Teaching for Understanding framework and a built-in message board for collaborating with coaches and colleagues.

A central component of the WIDE World model is tailored support from an expert online coach for every participant. Before the course begins, instructors review the list of participants and cluster them into study groups of approximately ten individuals or small teams, then assign them a coach who shares their interests. WIDE World encourages people to enroll in courses with two or three colleagues, to form a team that functions effectively as one participant, rotating responsibility for posting responses in each session. The team then serves as a local work group for dividing labor and reflecting about accommodation to the local context. Some team members meet face to face, although others collaborate entirely online.

To help participants derive maximum benefit from their online experiences, WIDE World also provides onsite services or synchronous online experiences upon request from institutional customers. However, the online components of the program are central in achieving the core purpose of WIDE World, providing high-quality professional development on a wide scale for large numbers of teachers.

WIDE WORLD IN ACTION AT THE PERSONAL LEVEL

The WIDE World initiative embodies in a number of ways the program's theory of change outlined earlier. Let us consider the first four elements here, capped by examining the affordances of networks for this approach to learning. We will save the complex discussion of "negotiating institutional accommodation" for the section after.

Model the Principles

WIDE World courses are explicitly designed to reflect a research-based educational model called the Teaching for Understanding framework. This framework was developed by a team of researchers based at the Harvard Graduate

School of Education in collaboration with teachers of various subject areas recruited from a range of middle schools and high schools in Massachusetts. This project, led by Howard Gardner, David Perkins, and Vito Perrone, set out to identify teaching moves that promote students' understanding.[21]

Members of the project embraced a performance-based conception of understanding: Understanding is the flexible capability to think creatively with one's knowledge and to apply it appropriately in a range of circumstances.[22] Then the project identified teachers of four different areas—science, mathematics, social studies, and language arts—who were effective in fostering this kind of understanding in their students. Project members prepared case studies of curriculum units taught by these teachers and analyzed cross-cutting patterns in the cases in relation to theories of effective learning and teaching. Through sustained collaboration, the researchers and teachers synthesized their empirical and theoretical findings into a set of four elements that define effective teaching for understanding: (1) provocative, inquiry-oriented *generative topics*—central to the subject matter, students' experience, and teachers' passions; (2) *goals for understanding*—articulating publicly what learners are to come to understand in a coherent, connected way; (3) *performances of understanding*—episodes of active learning that build on students' initial knowledge and stretch it further around the topic and goals; and (4) *ongoing assessment*—frequent assessments focused on the understanding performances that generate insight and improvements both for learners and teachers.

Educators who have worked with this framework and with new educational technologies recently added another element to the framework: (5) *reflective, collaborative communities* of learners whose members take diverse perspectives into account and promote respect and reciprocity around communal accomplishments, as well as individual performances.[23] Educators noted that the original framework implied interactive and reflective aspects of learning without emphasizing them. Recent research demonstrating the importance of social interaction in learning, coupled with the opportunities provided by the new technologies that are increasingly available in schools, prompted the inclusion of this fifth element.[24]

Considerable experience with Teaching for Understanding has shown that it serves negotiated accommodation well. The framework is a roomy one. While it takes a strong position on the nature of understanding and the characteristics of teaching and learning for understanding, that position is a broadly principled one with ample latitude for individual teachers to adapt the framework to their personal styles, subject areas, students, and institutions.

Because Teaching for Understanding is a pedagogical framework aimed at changing performance, it is well suited to guide professional development, not only to teach academic subjects. WIDE World professional development courses aim to develop understanding as a performance capability in teachers and to help them foster this kind of understanding with their own students. WIDE World courses explicitly model the elements of this framework in five ways: (a) course topics are formulated in ways that will be generative for teachers and relevant to their concerns and goals; (b) understanding goals for participants are publicized in the course syllabus, and each session explicitly states understanding goals related to the course-long goals; (c) the course activities include various kinds of understanding performances supported by coaches who provide tailored guidance to each participant; (d) ongoing assessments of participants' work use public criteria related to goals and include feedback from coaches, peers, and learners themselves; and (e) coaches and course activities foster reflective, collaborative professional communities among participants.

Support Application and Reflection during the Course

WIDE World courses take place over six sessions, each of which lasts two weeks during winter and spring terms and one week in the condensed summer term. Course activities include learning about new concepts or principles from readings and/or studying model cases, but also, in the spirit of negotiated accommodation, applying the principles to one's own practice through designing and/or implementing instructional and assessment activities, and sharing and assessing draft work in relation to explicit criteria. A session typically requires approximately seven hours of work on course-related activities (reading, designing, posting comments in the online forum, and reading and responding to others' comments), not counting time devoted to implementation in the classroom.

Many courses support progressive development of a course-long project, such as the design or revision of a curriculum unit or carrying out a unit developed in a previous course. Alternatively, courses may consist of several smaller assignments that involve applying a concept or strategy from the course in one's own classroom and reflecting on the experience. Although the instructor sets the general guidelines for an assignment, participants have an opportunity to adapt the assignment to their own goals and context. Coaches help participants conduct a project that provides good opportunities to apply principles taught in the course to their own practice. The project or other work is coupled with online discussions in which participants reflect on how the new approach compares and contrasts with their accustomed practice and how they can find support within the resources and constraints of their local context.

One learner who completed a survey after taking two WIDE World courses emphasized the program's focus on practical application in the following way: "The courses were designed to apply directly to students' learning. While theory was always a part of the courses, application in my classroom was a key part of my understanding."

Provide Coaching

Coaches help participants feel comfortable in the online environment and ensure that their logistical and technical concerns get addressed. Most importantly, coaches provide personalized assistance to all participants or teams to help them negotiate their personal accommodation of the course concepts to their own individual framework and institutional context. Coaches respond to each participant's work in relation to a clear "reflection guide" or rubric and provide suggestions for revising the work as the course proceeds. They encourage participants to conduct assessments of their own work, using the same assessment rubric that coaches use.

Coaching for WIDE World is a serious professional commitment. Coaches are experienced educators who undertake work with WIDE World as a second job and receive compensation for their involvement. WIDE World provides courses and an apprenticeship program for coaches. Online coaches figure critically in the scalability, cost-effectiveness, and sustainability of the WIDE World model while simultaneously ensuring a high-quality experience for participants. The coaching role also provides a rich form of professional development for lead teachers.

Most coaches are recruited from the pool of WIDE World participants. Instructors may invite successful graduates of the courses to take WIDE World's online course for coaches. Graduates of the coaching course may become apprentice coaches, observing an experienced coach who supervises as the apprentice supports one or two participants in a study group. The coaching course helps teachers learn how to become leaders and mentors to their peers.

Foster Reflective, Collaborative Professional Communities

WIDE World courses are designed to promote the development of norms, expertise, and relationships that support reflection and collaboration among members of professional communities, helping them to achieve a negotiated accommodation with their own existing frameworks, their colleagues, and their institutions. Like all learners, teachers' understanding advances through dialogue with others who share similar goals and a common language for analyzing their evolving insights. Principles of pedagogy are much more likely to make their way into practice when teachers work with colleagues who are similarly engaged and with whom they can exchange ideas, puzzles, strategies, and materials.

As we've noted, WIDE World fosters reflective, collaborative professional relationships through several structures. First, WIDE World encourages participants to enroll as part of a team of colleagues with whom they will work closely during the course. Second, participants are clustered into online study groups of ten individuals or teams who share similar interests, guided by a coach with expertise in those interests. Third, besides providing coaching per se, the coach strives to build a community. The coach helps each participant provide information about his or her own background, goals, and expertise and demonstrates how to promote collegial exchange in the online discussion forums. Assignments in the online courses include sharing work, responding to colleagues, and learning how to use a rubric to analyze work and participate in peer feedback. Coaches model these behaviors, help participants develop relationships with fellow learners, and guide participants in learning how to give and receive reflective feedback with colleagues. Some of the online courses use a particular protocol developed at Project Zero. Called the Ladder of Feedback, it specifically supports effective peer assessment.[25]

How the Affordances of Networks Help

Networked technologies play an important role in providing the means for integrating the four elements examined above. Face-to-face interactions have long been the gold standard for professional development, and the WIDE World model includes a limited role for them. However, we have found that faith in a pure face-to-face approach is somewhat misplaced. First of all, however desirable in principle, face-to-face contact with developers or even among participating teachers is difficult to sustain on a regular basis amidst the complex realities of school settings.

Second, online development turns out to have its own distinctive advantages. Each participant's work is readily visible to all the others. Written communication in threaded discussions promotes a level of deliberation and reflection that is less likely in oral conversation. Comments and files captured digitally are preserved in a form that can easily be reviewed, revised, and constructed collaboratively by multiple colleagues. Coaching around reflection and collaboration that may be provided to one participant can be seen by other members of an online study group, so that coaching efforts are instantly amplified to all participants. Whether participants in WIDE

World courses develop relationships with local colleagues through the online course or only interact with distant peers, they begin to understand strategies for and benefits of participating in reflective, collegial professional communities.[26]

WIDE WORLD IN ACTION AT THE INSTITUTIONAL LEVEL

Negotiating Institutional Accommodation

So far in this chapter, we have mostly discussed the process of supporting individual accommodation, but institutional factors are also part of our theory of change. Individuals ultimately negotiate their professional development experiences within their workplaces, where institutional norms, structures, resources, and relationships may support or constrain this process.

At WIDE World, we pursue two general strategies for moving beyond assimilation into negotiating accommodation at the institutional level. One strategy supports individuals in working with their own institutions, and the other works directly with institutional leaders.

Accommodating in Context

For the first, WIDE World courses help individuals respond to contextual factors. Instructors remind participants to consider the realities of their own setting—policies, resources, schedules, relationships—as they make decisions about applying what they learn in the course to their own practice. Assignments and discussion prompts throughout the courses encourage participants to identify ways to negotiate their own accommodations with these realities.

For example, participants review their required curriculum standards, and coaches help them to define understanding goals that also address those standards. WIDE World also encourages participants to enroll in courses as part of a team of local colleagues who can then serve as a source of onsite support for one another. Together they may be able to identify and address institutional factors that limit or undermine their negotiated accommodation. For instance, members of teams may work together on an interdisciplinary curriculum unit that enables them to formulate a more generative topic and design a richer range of learning activities than they would be able to accomplish without collegial collaboration. Developing a cohort of colleagues with whom one shares a common language for analyzing and discussing the improvement of practice may create a supportive microcontext that buffers the countervailing forces of the larger institutional context.

The following quote from a WIDE World learner highlights the value of working with colleagues to promote a supportive school context:

> I've found the courses exceptionally valuable in learning through a learning community with other colleagues all over the world. It broadens my thinking and understanding of focused questions. This time we are fifteen persons from our school and that is the most powerful force I've experienced to develop understanding and progress about our praxis. We are building a community of understanding and words for that understanding when we are forced to write it down and share it with other people all over the world. We get to know each other as practicing teachers in a way that we never could accomplish on our own. The confrontation in the prompts with specified issues in full sight of other people is remarkably effective in getting us to think in the same direction. We are educated together and we need each other for the education as we can talk to each other between the sessions and build a community in our school.

Developing Supportive Contexts

WIDE World also attempts to work directly with educational institutions and their leaders to create more supportive contexts. Beginning in fall 2004, WIDE World shifted the focus of its outreach efforts from individual to institutional arrangements. We framed WIDE World as a suite of programs and resources, both online and onsite, designed to help schools, districts, and other educational organizations promote a sustained process of instructional improvement.

The WIDE World outreach staff works with institutional decisionmakers to clarify their organization's goals, resources, existing programs, and constraints as they consider which WIDE World programs might support their priorities. WIDE World is developing materials and experiences to support local facilitators and leaders of professional development as well as administrators engaged in systemic school improvement. Through interaction with local leaders, WIDE World staff aim to devise a program that is individually tailored for the organization and that will promote accommodation at the institutional level. For example, the institutional plan might include some onsite workshops to augment the online program, direct engagement of local instructional leaders and administrators in online courses so that they learn how to support teachers who take the courses, plans for participants to enroll in a coherent sequence of online courses well matched with district priorities, and a process whereby some members of early cohorts become coaches to subsequent cohorts.

Onsite events, or synchronous events mediated by technology such as a videoconference, introduce a large number of local participants to the principles that will be studied during the online courses. These events help to develop awareness and support at the institutional level. The content of the online courses can also be adjusted slightly, through coaching in the study groups, to support specific institutional requirements. By clustering participants from a single institution into study groups and assigning coaches with particular expertise in dealing with the institution's realities, WIDE World negotiates mutual accommodation with the institution.

Several other strategies have been helpful in this process. One is working with a local facilitator who becomes a liaison between WIDE World and the local institution. For example, WIDE World worked with the Namibian Institute for Educational Development in a multiyear effort to support the Namibian educational reform initiative. The local facilitator worked onsite in Namibia, serving effectively as a two-way mediator between Namibia and WIDE World. She helped WIDE World staff and coaches understand and adjust their support for the Namibians while helping the Namibian participants and their administrative leaders interpret the WIDE World program in relation to their own norms and goals.

The local facilitator identified several strands of support that she provided toward a negotiated accommodation: pedagogical support (explanation and coaching for both participants and their administrative leaders on the pedagogical content of the online course), technical assistance (arranging for access to both the necessary technology and technical support), political interventions (advocating with political leaders and assisting them in providing leadership and administrative support), cultural mediation (interpreting norms, values, and connotations for both participants and WIDE World coaches to help them avoid misunderstanding and confusion), administrative support, and social support (convening meetings, promoting relationships among participants, and supporting teamwork).[27] WIDE World is working to understand these strands and to identify, prepare, and support local facilitators.

WIDE World also attempts to negotiate accommodation with institutional contexts by working directly with local educational leaders. We encourage institutions to enroll leaders in the online courses so that they can provide direct support to their local colleagues. One district, for example, has chosen to enroll principals in online courses along with teachers from the district. WIDE World will cluster the principals with one another in a study group and provide coaching tailored to their particular interests. The principals will focus their work in the online course on devising effective ways of supporting teachers around the course content.

In its work with the Cambridge, Massachusetts, Public Schools, WIDE World worked closely with the leadership team of Project COOL (Collaborative Online/Off-line Learning) to support the development of teachers' abilities and attitudes in curriculum planning, professional collaboration, and technology use. The project involved online course work and face-to-face mentoring for 24 teacher teams in schools throughout the district. Seventy-five teachers and administrators from Cambridge enrolled in five different WIDE World courses over four terms. Those completing the spring and fall courses were, on average, very positive about their experience. The vast majority reported in the end-of-course surveys that the course had led to "significant" improvement in their teaching practice. In spring 2004, 16 out of 17 agreed, 9 strongly, that through the course they learned guidelines to help them better assess their teaching. Members of three of the four teams in spring 2004 noted that the online course provided an external structure and timeline for accomplishing their task of curriculum design. Others noted that contacts with educators beyond Cambridge and around the world who were enrolled in the course helped them see their particular challenges with students and curriculum in a broader context.[28]

Members of the COOL leadership team repeatedly noted the contribution their online experience brought to their ability to lead the project as a group. The leadership team reported that they were able to support each other better and mentor the teachers with whom they worked more effectively.[29] Importantly, the team also allowed and encouraged its members to build trust about the project and its elements among their supervisors who, in turn, deployed district resources for a related initiative aligned with specified district needs. The district's initiative, then, built on the expertise developed within the COOL–WIDE World project, which spread to affect greater numbers of Cambridge faculty and the students they teach.[30]

WIDE World is also engaged with professional development leaders in the International Baccalaureate North America (IBNA) program, which offers a range of programs in international education. IBNA identified leaders in their cadre of professional development providers and invited them to be part of the first cohort of participants enrolled in a sequence of two WIDE World online courses. Successful candidates from this cohort were invited to participate in WIDE World's coach development program, and some of them became coaches for subsequent cohorts of professional developers from IBNA.

These participants will incorporate what they learned in the online course into the designs of professional development programs that they provide for IBNA teachers. In this way, IBNA can develop an expanding cadre of professional development leaders who are sustained in their own learning through online courses while they foster similar learning in their colleagues through the face-to-face professional development activities they provide. Building and maintaining a network of local leaders promotes accommodation at the institutional level.

TAKING STOCK OF PROGRESS

WIDE World began with a focus on individual teachers.[31] Developing institutional relationships has led to our own accommodation as an organization. We have restructured some of our own administrative systems, including financial administration as well as technical and customer support. We devised new methods for marketing and sales and for sustaining relationships with institutional customers. We modified WIDE World online courses and other offerings in response to customers' needs.

Quality Assurance

The increasing number of relationships with institutions led WIDE World to systematize and standardize operations that were initially led by individual course developers/instructors. WIDE World evolved through an ongoing design/research process that entailed iterative cycles of design, implementation, and assessment.[32] This effort included defining standards of quality based on previous program research and on external standards, yielding an array of tools for evaluating program processes and personnel. For example, a course design and assessment guide used by course developers, reviewers, and instructors helps to ensure that all our courses enact the theory of change described earlier. A coach assessment tool supports the development of WIDE World coaches by guiding evaluations of coaches by instructors and WIDE World's education manager and by coaches' ongoing self-assessment.

Program Evaluation

Internal evaluation has also focused on formalizing assessment and evaluation practices to provide evidence of effective learning. Performance assessment guides provide the instructional team for each course with a structured yet customized instrument to guide feedback to course participants and facilitate summative assessment of their work.[33] Research in constructivist learning and teacher evaluation has informed our design of a classroom observation protocol for assessing teachers' use of constructivist practices. Each term we invite enrollees to complete surveys at the start of the course, at midcourse, upon completion, and at a follow-up time about six months later, to help us both improve our courses and gauge their impact. We maintain an extensive database, currently holding information on 2,650 participants from the past seven semesters; this facilitates data analysis as well as contacts for additional surveys or observations. We design and review all of these evaluative tools using multiple sources of input, paying close attention to validity and reliability issues.

What follows is a brief summary of results from our evaluation efforts.[34] As of summer 2005, WIDE World had provided services to about 3,700 educators in 81 school districts or educational institutions within the United States and 63 abroad. This fiscal year, WIDE World's enrollments and revenues grew by more than 80 percent over the previous year, and projected growth rates sustain this pattern in the near term, keeping WIDE World on or ahead of schedule with its business plan. We have significant initiatives in North and South America, Africa, and China. According to surveys conducted after WIDE World courses, most participants report that the courses have an impact on their teaching and their students. In the past three years, more than two-thirds of participants found that the program generated improvement in their teaching practice; one-third saw this improvement as substantial, while one-third considered this improvement to be moderate. The changes they reported include improvements in design of curriculum and lesson plans, assessment of students, and communication with students. A similar distribution is found in participants' reports about the impact on their students' learning, with positive changes in attentiveness, the types of questions asked, and depth of understanding.[35]

Beginning in spring 2004, the WIDE World final course survey asked course participants to respond to several statements that gauge the degree to which their WIDE World course work helps build a sense of professional community, both online and in their own contexts. Close to 700 learners have responded to the following statements over four semesters, and the averages across semesters given below are very close to the averages for any specific semester:

"This course helped me connect with
a community of professionals."   Agree or strongly agree: 83%

"I have learned concepts and terms
that will help me exchange ideas with
other professionals."   Agree or strongly agree: 88%

"I feel better able to participate in a
reflective community of educators."   Agree or strongly agree: 79%

Also, in surveys conducted before and after WIDE World courses during the last three semesters, participants showed significantly enhanced attitudes toward computers and online communication.[36] In addition, a group of our enrollees showed marked improvement on Massachusetts' state-mandated Technology Self-Assessment Test after taking a WIDE World course.[37]

CONCLUSIONS AND RECOMMENDATIONS

We believe that networked technologies offer significant advantages that diminish the drawbacks of traditional professional development. By creating means of modeling effective teaching, allowing educators to learn while they actively apply new ideas in their own work settings, providing sustained coaching and feedback, and cultivating reflective and collaborative professional communities that survive after the course, online professional development can help educators negotiate effective accommodation to research-based pedagogies. Networked technologies also promote coherent communication and joint efforts across levels of educational organizations, so that individual and institutional accommodations are mutually supportive.

Clarifying the nature of these processes and verifying their impact depends upon further rounds of design research. This research requires clarification of treatment variables, of direct outcomes of professional development (such as impact on teaching practice and on professional relationships and attitudes), and of desired indirect outcomes (such as improvements in student performance). It also depends upon the development of valid and reliable instruments to gauge these processes and results. We pursue these challenges as part of our ongoing mutual accommodation between improved educational research and improved educational practice.

CHAPTER 4

PBS TeacherLine and Concord Consortium's Seeing Math Secondary

Scaling Up a National Professional Development Program[1]

Rob Ramsdell, Raymond Rose, and Mary Kadera

BACKGROUND

PBS TeacherLine and Concord Consortium's Seeing Math project are five-year grants supported by the U.S. Department of Education with funding initiated in 2000 and ending in 2005. Both projects, funded through the Ready to Teach program, provide high-quality professional development for K–12 teachers, with the goals of improving teacher quality and increasing student achievement. While both projects focus on mathematics teaching, PBS TeacherLine has also coordinated the development of online courses in the areas of reading, science, curriculum and instruction, and the integration of technology to enhance student learning.

During the five-year grant, PBS subcontracted with such producers as the Education Development Center, Indiana University, McREL,[2] and Thirteen/WNET, resulting in the development of more than 100 Web-based, facilitated courses. The Concord Consortium produced its own courses and is now using PBS TeacherLine as the distribution channel for Seeing Math courses for teachers of secondary-level algebra. All courses were developed with input from K–12 education leaders and research experts, and the courses target areas in which a high percentage of teachers lack content knowledge or teaching skills.

Working in partnership with nearly 80 local PBS stations, whose involvement is described more fully later in this chapter, PBS TeacherLine has run more than 2,800 course sections, fulfilling nearly 30,000 enrollments in all 50 states. Approximately 27 percent of participants and a quarter of its facilitators work in Title I schools. In 2004–05, 8,154 course enrollments were generated by 6,469 individuals enrolled in 90 distinct courses.[3]

Program content is hosted by PBS, and courses are delivered by both PBS and its member station partners. Skilled facilitators substantially influence the experience of course participants, and more than 600 facilitators have been trained.

The quality of courses, the experience of participating educators, and potential impact on student achievement have been measured extensively by external, independent evaluators. We believe that our experiences with program evaluation, detailed more fully later in this chapter, provide important food for thought about the outcomes we are trying to achieve with online professional development; the best protocols for measuring these outcomes; and the expectations we have about the time and effort required to effect meaningful change, particularly in the area of increased student achievement.

The Collaboration between PBS TeacherLine and the Concord Consortium

The collaboration between these two projects began in 2002, and the projects combined a number of strengths. The Concord Consortium brought a tradition of innovation in the development of online courses, and by 2002 the facilitation model they developed had already been adopted and adapted by PBS TeacherLine. PBS brought its own experiences in distance learning and teacher professional development, as well as an extensive dissemination operation through its member stations' longstanding relationships with state agencies and local districts.

At the time the projects began to collaborate, both had been working at the elementary and middle-grade levels but neither had developed materials that specifically targeted high school teachers of mathematics. The two organizations agreed to collaborate on the development and distribution of a series of courses for algebra teachers.

Focus for Educational Improvement

The U.S. Department of Education's Ready to Teach program has the stated goal of improving teaching in the core curriculum areas, ultimately enabling students to meet challenging academic achievement standards, particularly in reading and math. In order to meet these goals, PBS and the Concord Consortium first focused on ensuring that the quality of the course content and the learning experience would support changes in teacher attitudes and behaviors. Thus, much of the work over the first three years of the project centered on intensive advisory input while courses were developed, as well as ongoing, formative evaluation of the courses and the learning environment (for instance, quality of online discussion). Advisors have included experts in online learning; content area professionals from NCTM, IRA, and other groups; and district leaders and K–12 classroom practitioners.

Development of new courses usually begins with an identification of those "hard-to-teach" concepts that may be addressed in the courses, as well as a review of the appropriate academic content standards. Courses developed by PBS TeacherLine and the Concord Consortium address both content knowledge and the teaching strategies that research suggests will foster student learning. Courses aim to strengthen the ability of participants as they work to identify gaps in student knowledge, and the course assignments include information about appropriate methods of instruction and suggested strategies to help develop student understanding.

Furthermore, courses are designed to promote a teacher's reflection on his or her own classroom practice. The courses provide opportunities for teachers to assess the current capabilities and potential misconceptions of their students, with the goal of supporting teachers as they make decisions that improve their teaching strategies. To ensure that the teacher's new knowledge, understanding, and skills are applied in the classroom, most courses include assignments prompting teachers to develop activities or instructional units they will try in their classrooms.

Research by independent evaluators suggests that these are high-quality, engaging courses that participants perceive as valuable to their improved teaching. In 2004–05, 95 percent of participants in courses distributed nationally by PBS TeacherLine reported that the course met or exceeded their expectations. More than two-thirds of the participants surveyed indicated that instructional strategies and content area knowledge covered in PBS TeacherLine courses had already been incorporated into their instructional practice. The evaluators concluded that the large majority of the survey responses revealed that, upon course completion, users had good command of the course content and instructional strategies covered.

In 2003, as an outgrowth of No Child Left Behind, the Department of Education requested that PBS and the Concord Consortium develop rigorous, scientifically based measures to evaluate the impact of the professional development courses on student achievement. These evaluation activities, described more fully later in this chapter, represent some of the earliest efforts to assess the causal link between online professional development and student achievement through randomized, experimental studies. The experimental evaluation recently concluded by Hezel Associates does not confirm the link between participation in these online courses and increases in student learning as measured by teacher-administered tests.[4] It does, however, provide important learning about the evaluation protocols that will be employed in the future as we work to effect changes in student achievement. It also raises valuable questions about the expectations we have for teacher professional development, as well as the relative value of the outcomes to which we are attuned.

Expectations of Participants and the Appeal of the Online Courses

Through the external evaluation conducted by Hezel Associates, extensive data have been collected from course participants. The expectations of participants and the appeal of the online courses distributed nationally by PBS TeacherLine provide an interesting backdrop to a discussion of the courses themselves.

In 2004–05, a total of 8,197 preparticipation questionnaires were submitted by 6,648 individual respondents. Noticeable changes were demonstrated in participants' main learning expectations and their expectations regarding how TeacherLine courses could enhance their teaching practice. The most-cited learning expectation has been the same over the years: to gain insights about different approaches to instruction. However, as shown in figure 1, strong evidence shows that users have become more course oriented and less technology oriented. The second most-cited learning expectation, course content, is the only learning expectation that has increased over time. Technology-oriented learning expectations, such as becoming more comfortable with technology, understanding how online learning takes place, and helping students with technology, have declined gradually over the years.

Participants continued to expect that TeacherLine courses would offer new instruction strategies and enrich lesson plans. Thirty-five percent of the respondents, an increase of 5 percent from the previous year, reported that participants counted on TeacherLine courses to enhance teaching practice by training others in the subject matter. In contrast, only 57 percent of the responses suggested that TeacherLine courses were expected to enhance teaching practice by helping participants handle technology more effectively, compared with 64 percent in 2003–04 and 70 percent in 2002–03.

FIGURE 1   Learning Expectations

Question: What statement best describes your main learning expectation for this course? (Check all that apply.)

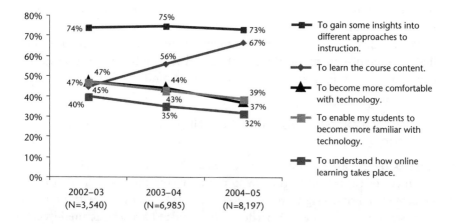

- To gain some insights into different approaches to instruction.
- To learn the course content.
- To become more comfortable with technology.
- To enable my students to become more familiar with technology.
- To understand how online learning takes place.

FIGURE 2   Appeal of TeacherLine Courses

Question: What attracted you to TeacherLine courses? (Check all that apply.) (*N*=7,038)

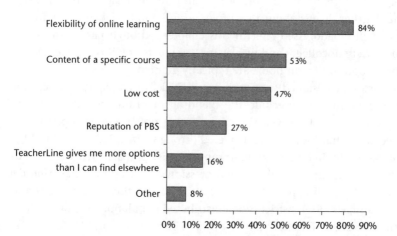

This year, participants in courses distributed nationally by PBS Teacher-Line were asked what attracted them to TeacherLine courses. As shown in figure 2, a large majority of the responses identified the flexibility that online courses allow. Specific content and low course cost were also noted.

The high percentage of teachers who are attracted to the flexibility of online learning suggests that the audience has a preconceived idea about this approach and is attracted to it. Survey respondents showed a good sense of their learning style and a high level of comfort with nontraditional or collaborative learning situations, further suggesting that participants are self-selecting this particular model.

While considering the structure of courses, technical requirements, and design principles in the sections that follow, it may be useful to keep the expectations and motivations of participants in mind.

OVERVIEW: COURSE STRUCTURE, TECHNICAL REQUIREMENTS, AND SUPPORTS

Courses developed by the Concord Consortium and PBS TeacherLine are designed for cohorts of learners who typically commit 30–45 hours to participate over a six-to-eight-week period. Cohorts typically run with no fewer than 8 and no more than 25 participants. Courses have a structured weekly schedule, and participants are expected to progress through the weeks of the course together, communicating asynchronously during each week. Courses are facilitated by an educator who has participated in a training program designed by the Concord Consortium and further adapted by PBS Teacher-Line. Further details about this program and additional supports for facilitators will be addressed later in this chapter. Through partnerships with a wide variety of colleges and universities, graduate credit is available for most courses, and two credit hours are typically granted.

Courses are designed so that they can be delivered purely online, though there is nothing to preclude the blending of online activities with face-to-face activities. However, the courses have not been developed with the expectation that they will be delivered through a blended model, and therefore there is limited scaffolding to support this approach. The Concord Consortium's elementary-level online professional development has been delivered in a blended approach, but the audience for those courses has always been a single school district, not a distributed population as is often the case with courses distributed nationally by PBS TeacherLine. In PBS TeacherLine's approach during its new grant period (beginning in September 2005), the current model will be refined to include blended approaches, which will be discussed later in the chapter.

Beginning in 2005, all courses distributed by PBS TeacherLine will be delivered through the Desire2Learn platform. TeacherLine has also developed custom applications to manage many of the registration, course management, and e-commerce functions. This development has been necessary because of PBS TeacherLine's unique combination of locally and nationally offered courses and the important role played by a distributed network of PBS member stations across the country. The technology platform, which is hosted by PBS, provides assistance to participants to alleviate certain technology issues they may face. Before a course begins, a software wizard can check a participant's computer for the necessary plug-ins, operating system, and browser capabilities. Web-based "help desk" tools offer further assistance, as does telephone support from PBS staff. Finally, local PBS stations may also provide technical assistance to participants in their communities.

Guiding Design Principles

Grounded in the research literature as well as standards published by organizations such as the National Staff Development Council, the courses reflect principles of high-quality professional development. The last two principles below are very closely tied to the use of multimedia in online learning environments and to the application of facilitated online discussions.

Tie to classroom practice. Courses are designed to keep classroom practice in mind by providing opportunities for teachers to immerse themselves in real classroom situations, through the viewing of video clips and the use of interactives that illustrate challenging teaching concepts. Participants are encouraged to improve and adapt course materials, to create their own teaching resources, to modify their teaching practice, and to discuss results with peers. The goal of this approach is to ensure that the professional development experience is relevant and tied directly to each teacher's specific classroom context. The introduction of new teaching strategies in the classroom is an expected outcome of the course experience.

Use actual student work. Online videos incorporated in the courses show students at work. Digitized versions of student work are often provided as examples, and participants are encouraged to present examples of their own students' work. Students' thinking as illustrated by their work becomes a basis for discussions providing context and insights for analyzing student performance and informing instruction.

Link content to standards. Courses link content to local and national standards, providing a consistent and coherent framework for change. Given the national scope of PBS TeacherLine's distribution network, ties to local standards are made by PBS member stations who offer courses tailored to local needs and state content standards. When courses are offered to a national audience, the course content is always directly linked to national standards. Courses include the expectation that teachers will customize and create materials to support state and local standards, and online discussions encourage teachers to explicitly address and reflect on curriculum standards.

Promote reflection in teaching. Courses are designed to provide opportunities for teachers to reflect on their own teaching and learning. This reflection helps teachers grow from their experiences, understanding the process of learning, solidifying areas of strength, and determining areas for growth. All courses provide opportunities for reflection through journaling activities, reflection papers, and online discussions, as well as pre- and post- activities regarding expectations, goals, and self-assessment.

Model effective teaching. Courses use strategies for active learning and multiple modes of representation to engage teachers in learning, just as they should be engaging their own students. The course design and content, as well as the role of facilitators, aim to promote active learning through practical, classroom-relevant activities.

Create a safe and productive learning environment. Courses are designed to build communities of practice and to use asynchronous online discussions as the vehicle for collaboration and problem-solving. Online discussions are carefully organized, structured, and facilitated so they are productive and support risk-taking. Facilitators are responsible for managing interactions, providing feedback, and asking questions that will deepen online discussions.

Promote effective use of technology. Courses are developed to help teachers become familiar with different models for integrating technology into the curriculum to support instruction. Courses also illustrate best practices through the use of the medium in ways that will engage participants and provide access to information and communication in forms that are unique to the medium. For example, the use of video, Web-based interactives, and asynchronous online discussion are central features of the courses. These principles are guiding the creation of materials by PBS TeacherLine and the Concord Consortium, as well as professional development activities in schools and districts across the nation. The application of these principles in turn shapes the experiences of course participants.

Use of Facilitated Online Discussions and Multimedia

Many of the principles described above are reflected in features that provide important context for learning.

Use of facilitated online discussions. In order to foster a collaborative community environment and counter teacher isolation, courses are scheduled so that cohorts of teachers proceed together through course assignments. Online discussion among participants is a required element of course participation and counts significantly toward the final assessment of course participants. Participant feedback shows that teachers find the support and insight gained from these discussions particularly valuable.

Although the facilitators have a background in the subject matter of the course, they are not presented as subject-matter experts or as instructors. Subject-matter expertise is captured in the design of the courses and in the course developers' content. This approach increases the need for defined objectives, well-conceived activities, and scaffolding of the course experience. For example, online discussions are typically initiated by carefully conceived prompts tied closely to the objectives for each section of the course. The use of facilitators rather than instructors is also necessary to support efforts to scale the program nationally. Given the number of courses operating in any given term, it would be nearly impossible to staff these with instructors with special expertise in content and pedagogy.

Comprehensive guides for the facilitators accompany every course, and prospective facilitators are required to complete the Online Facilitator Training Program (OFT)—a six-week online course. The OFT comprises six topic areas and takes 30 to 46 hours to complete.

Course Section	*Time*
Part 1 – Learning Communities	4–6 hours
Part 2 – Adjusting to Online Learning	5–8 hours
Part 3 – Building Online Community	6–9 hours
Part 4 – Offering Feedback and Seeding Discussions	6–8 hours
Part 5 – Developing Strategies for Delivering and Localizing Courses	5–8 hours
Part 6 – Celebrating Your Work Together and Planning Next Steps	4–7 hours
Total Time	30–46 hours

In 2004–05, 35 percent of OFT participants reported the training met their expectations, and 63 percent felt the training exceeded their expectations ($N = 247$). After facilitating an online course, 90 percent of facilitators who completed a post-course debrief survey ($N = 158$) reported the OFT training effectively prepared them for their roles as facilitators. For certain courses, including Algebra I courses developed by the Concord Consortium, additional training was highly recommended for facilitators because of the challenging nature of the content presented.

PBS TeacherLine coordinates and manages ongoing support for a corps of national facilitators through the Facilitator United Network (FUN). The FUN provides support to facilitators in an asynchronous online environment with activities including the following:

- A brief training event offered online four times a year to ensure that all facilitators are informed on most recent best practices
- Course-specific forums in discussion board format
- A monthly discussion forum for current issues
- A monthly newsletter
- A mentoring program for those embarking on their first course
- A course resource area with supporting documentation and course-delivery materials
- A monthly course update highlighting recent course improvements, revisions, and upgrades

Evaluation activities have validated the success of efforts to create a safe and productive learning environment for course participants. Hezel Associates' study of TeacherLine's online discussion and facilitation determined that facilitator quality related directly to participants' ability to apply course content to their classroom practice, to their satisfaction with course discussion, and to their overall satisfaction with the course.[5] In 2003, the evaluators provided feedback to further strengthen facilitator–participant interaction and to create higher-level dialogue among participants, feedback that PBS TeacherLine has since implemented.

The overall completion rate for TeacherLine courses in 2004–05 was 77 percent, which compares favorably with completion rates typically reported for online learning. Eighty-six percent of program participants indicated they would be "very likely" or "somewhat likely" to enroll in additional TeacherLine courses. Both of these measures are likely influenced by a range of factors, but it is believed the role of online discussions and the guidance of a skilled facilitator are very significant in attaining these positive results.

Use of video. Most courses include approximately five video clips that are three to five minutes in length. In a course requiring more than 30 hours of a teacher's time, the videos may seem like a small part of the learning experience. However, the use of video provides a powerful stimulus for online discussion of teaching strategies and class organization. Video offers the lux-

TABLE 1   Perceived Helpfulness of Course Components
by Percentage of Participants

Course Component	N	Very Helpful	Moderately Helpful	Neutral	Minimally Helpful	Not at All Helpful
Reading course-related content	4,172	57.4%	34.5%	3.5%	4.3%	0.3%
Participating in online discussions	4,168	53.8%	34.3%	5.5%	5.0%	1.4%
Working on my assignments and/or projects	4,175	72.4%	24.0%	1.9%	1.3%	0.4%
Consulting other resources (Web links, applets, etc.)	4,108	60.4%	31.2%	6.1%	1.9%	0.4%
Multimedia activities	3,798	40.3%	40.2%	14.0%	4.3%	1.3%
Videos	3,784	28.0%	38.3%	19.6%	9.9%	4.2%
Reflecting in my journal	3,773	22.2%	34.6%	22.9%	12.0%	8.4%
Peer review work	3,729	45.3%	36.1%	11.5%	5.3%	1.9%

ury of multiple chances to listen, to review, and even to study transcripts of what teachers and students say. Often student thought is highly original; in a classroom, in real time, it may be difficult to understand. By going into real teachers' classrooms and presenting the problems they face and the solutions that emerge, the clips provide a rich source of insight that all teachers can use to develop their practice.

Video commentaries have also been a useful supplement to classroom-based videos. For example, in the Seeing Math Secondary professional development courses produced by the Concord Consortium, commentaries provide views of a featured classroom from different perspectives. Sometimes this includes a video that captures the teacher reflecting on the lesson that she was teaching when she was previously videotaped. Listening to a fellow teacher reflect on her practice offers a way for participants in the online course to identify with another professional encountering similar challenges.

In addition to documenting classroom situations, some courses include videos of nationally recognized education specialists who comment on the challenging concepts, student thinking, and instructional practices shown in the classroom videos. The perspectives and experience of these education specialists help participants see beyond a single experience to understand other approaches to the same problem. Video commentaries have proved to be a strong vehicle for eliciting additional perspectives that in turn serve as catalysts for online discussions.

Although video has proved useful, realizing the potential of this medium as a support for high-quality professional development can be difficult. As shown in table 1, course participants perceived video as less helpful than some other course components.[6] This finding may reflect technical challenges associated with using the videos, which are streamed over the Web. Or it may be that additional training and structure are needed to make the videos seem more useful to participants.

Some educators have expressed concern about the use of video that is produced in other school districts. These educators would prefer a connection to the local environment to strengthen the relevance for teachers participating in a local professional development program. In response to this interest, the Concord Consortium has revamped the Video Paper Builder, a multiplatform software package originally developed at TERC in Cambridge, Massachusetts. Video Paper Builder (http://vpb.concord.org) facilitates the production of a multimedia document that can contain digital video, text, and still images including PowerPoint slides, allowing districts to show local practice.

Video Paper Builder was used in pilot sites during the Seeing Math project, when particular school sites decided they needed a local connection in the videos. Instead of using the video produced for the course, these school sites used the production of video papers by teachers as part of a larger professional development experience.

Use of interactives. Almost all courses distributed nationally by PBS Teacher-Line include Web-based interactive applications that target particular teaching challenges. The interactives provide an easy way to work with multiple representations of specific concepts. There is power in looking at specific concepts in different representations—verbal, numeric or tabular, symbolic, and graphic—and understanding that a change in one is mirrored by a change in the others.

For example, the Concord Consortium's interactive tool called the Ready to Teach Linear Transformer (figure 3) gives participants the ability to change representations of a function and then instantly observe what happens. This provides a rich learning activity for teachers, and many teachers in turn use these same interactives with their students. This interactive helps users see something that is difficult to show on paper.[7] For example, a fundamental difference between linear and quadratic functions is the x^2 term—the defining attribute of quadratic functions. Observing the relationship between graphic and symbolic representations can increase the user's familiarity with the characteristics of quadratic functions and improve her or his general understanding of functions and the relationships that functions can describe.[8]

FIGURE 3   Linear Transformer

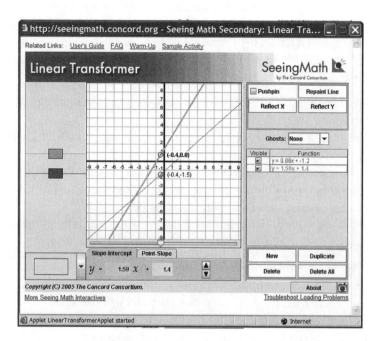

SUSTAINABILITY EFFORTS

Professional development in K–12 education remains a highly fragmented endeavor, and there is not yet a track record of financial success for national providers of online professional development. This is particularly the case if *high-quality* professional development is the standard and if impact on student achievement is the ultimate measure of success. PBS TeacherLine evolved over time to build toward a sustainable model that will ensure consistent access to the content that has been developed through grant support from the U.S. Department of Education.

Transition from Pilot Stage to National Launch

In its initial pilot stage of 2000–03, 32 PBS member stations received grant funding to support the promotion and implementation of PBS TeacherLine courses. A variety of models were implemented at different costs, utilizing a range of course offerings, marketing programs, and levels of support. The courses were subsidized by grant funds and often provided free of charge to teachers and school districts. As TeacherLine approached the midpoint of its grant period, PBS and the Department of Education both felt it was necessary to take further steps to support a sustainable model. Lessons learned from the first three years of the grant provided critical data as PBS TeacherLine developed and refined a strategy for national dissemination and sustainability.

Transitioning from its pilot stage and building toward a more sustainable model led to the following developments in 2004:

- Establishing a pricing model, currently based on a per-seat price of $199 for a 30-hour course[9]
- Establishing a fee structure for licensing relationships with PBS member stations and other organizations
- Increasing access to TeacherLine's course catalog by continuing to support members stations as they offer local courses, while simultaneously offering additional courses on a nationally coordinated schedule
- Establishing a coordinated postsecondary relationship program that provides a basis for graduate credit on the local and national levels[10]

Our five years' experience as a national program suggests that grant funds will remain important to support research activities, product innovation, and subsidies to high-need districts. However, PBS will continue to move the national program toward a goal of having ongoing operating expenses covered by the marketplace, which has its own resources to support programs such as PBS TeacherLine. Central to PBS TeacherLine's strategy is its tiered partnership model involving member stations across the country.

National Dissemination through Partnerships with PBS Stations and Other Local Agencies

Local PBS stations have played an important role in the dissemination and implementation of PBS TeacherLine across the nation. Stations have been essential contributors to TeacherLine's promotion and marketing efforts by reaching out to individual teachers, schools, districts, state departments of education, and other professional organizations in each area. Stations have recruited and supported local educators as course facilitators and have worked with these local facilitators and other key stakeholders to customize and administer local course instances. Furthermore, stations have been instrumental in securing graduate credit for the courses through an array of colleges and universities across the country.

Local PBS stations have provided a significant conduit to decision-makers in their areas. Often this is due to longstanding institutional affiliations between local public television stations and state or local educational entities. In some cases, as with KLVX in Las Vegas or WHRO in Norfolk, Virginia, local PBS stations are owned and operated by a local K–12 school district or consortium of districts. These stations have a particular mandate to provide educational services and programming to their local teachers. In other cases, close relationships have been nurtured over time, as in Buffalo, where local station WNED hosts the offices and training facilities of the local school system's professional development unit. Many PBS stations have historically played an important role in local professional development, offering services such as the National Teacher Training Institute and Intel's Teach to the Future and engaging in the U.S. Department of Education's Teaching American History initiative.

Still, local PBS stations vary widely in their institutional relationships with school systems and state departments of education, their number of education staff, their specific knowledge of K–12 issues and needs, and their expertise in digital content production and delivery. The PBS TeacherLine dissemination model is designed so that member stations within a state or region can serve as coordinators of PBS TeacherLine and in this role tap the potential of additional partners.

Texas provides a good example of the success of PBS's local station partnership model. Local stations KLRN (San Antonio) and KLRU (Austin) coordinate the activities of the 11 other Texas PBS stations, who help market the service as PBS TeacherLine of Texas. These stations conduct special outreach to Title I schools; for example, KLRN's Urban Systemic Program provides math and science professional development to nine districts in its area. Partners promote the service through local websites and on-air announcements. They also schedule and attend district-level meetings with the PBS TeacherLine of Texas state director, an education staff member at KLRU.

This unified statewide demonstration of commitment led by the two coordinating stations allowed PBS TeacherLine of Texas to launch a formal partnership with the Texas Computer Educators Association (TCEA). The partnership has resulted in special placement at the statewide TCEA conference, promotion to TCEA's 8,000 members, recruitment of additional facilitators from TCEA membership, and pending approval from the State Board of Educator Certification to endorse TeacherLine courses toward the state's master technology teacher certificate. PBS TeacherLine of Texas is also currently formalizing a partnership with the Texas Association for Gifted and Talented that will enable TeacherLine courses to count toward the state's gifted-teacher certification and renewal process.

At the national level, PBS manages the work of coordinating stations, manages distribution of PBS TeacherLine where there is not yet a coordinating station identified, and leads all national marketing efforts. While reaching sustainability was not an objective identified in the original proposal to the U.S. Department of Education, it has become an increasingly important goal. This dissemination model and the interplay between local and national activities lay the foundation for sustainability.

EVALUATION

Evaluation findings, particularly those gleaned from survey results, are interspersed throughout this chapter. What follows is an overview of evaluation activities, along with initial indications from summative studies that will be released in the fall of 2006.

Overview of Activities

Both PBS and the Concord Consortium are committed to the rigorous evaluation of materials developed under the Ready to Teach grant, and they have engaged external evaluators since the beginning of the grant period for formative and summative evaluation. Within the past two years, the U.S. Department of Education has set new priorities for educational evaluation and research, which include conducting experimental research where possible and high-quality quasi-experimental research where experiments are not feasible, and the use of other scientifically rigorous methods in other circumstances. With their evaluators, PBS and the Concord Consortium have responded to these priorities by developing experimental and quasi-experimental designs in the summative components of their overall evaluations.

PBS contracted with Hezel Associates to evaluate TeacherLine beginning in 2002, the third year of the initiative. The evaluation has investigated TeacherLine's model of online professional development, with particular attention to the learning environment and the learning outcomes associated with the students of teachers who participate in TeacherLine's online courses.

Since 2003, the evaluation has examined patterns of course enrollment and completion, collecting data nationwide on teacher expectations as they began TeacherLine courses and teacher-reported outcomes as a result of their participation. The evaluation has also involved an expert panel review of selected TeacherLine courses, an assessment of the quality of online discussion board communications, and focus groups of course facilitators and participants. In addition, in the 2004–05 year, the evaluation developed a randomized experiment to test a sequence of TeacherLine mathematics courses targeted to elementary teachers. Experimental results have shown an increased belief in standards-based teaching and learning principles, though

FIGURE 4   Knowledge of Teachers' Participation

Question: Who of the following are aware that you are taking this course? (Check all that apply) (N = 7,038)

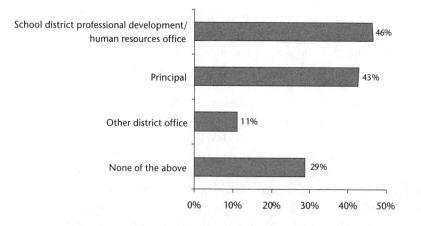

early tests have not found a significant change in practice or demonstrable improvement in student performance.

The Concord Consortium has engaged separate evaluators for the formative and summative components of their program evaluation. Edcentric has provided ongoing formative studies of courses in development, and Hezel Associates has conducted summative studies of Seeing Math Algebra course modules. Findings suggest that teachers learn primarily in pedagogy as opposed to specific content areas, and that subsequent to taking the course, teachers continue to learn (in some content areas and in pedagogy) as they incorporate into their instruction Seeing Math materials and resources provided to them by the program. As with PBS TeacherLine, a link to improved student performance has yet to be established.

Finding: Insufficient Tie to Systemic Change Efforts

During the past five years, the Concord Consortium and PBS have focused primarily on developing exemplary models of online professional development content. Still to be explored, however, are the possibilities of crafting professional development interventions that use online content within a comprehensive professional development program. For the most part, courses have been offered to individual teachers; and, even when offered through schools or districts, they are often not part of a comprehensive initiative at the local level.

Findings from the 2004–05 Hezel evaluation validate the concern that many participants are taking courses independently, outside of a coherent plan within their school or district. As shown in figure 4, almost three in ten of the teachers responding to preparticipation surveys indicated that neither school district professional development offices, nor human resources offices, nor principals knew of the teacher's participation in TeacherLine courses.

Professional development in general can make a difference, but only if it is part of a school's or district's overall plan, one involving specific achievement goals and squarely focusing on instruction, assessment, and school- and district-based curriculum initiatives. Without these ties, professional development will not have a deep, systemic impact—and furthermore, as Dennis Sparks of the National Staff Development Council warns, online professional development "may provide a centrifugal force that moves teachers away from daily collaboration with colleagues in professional development learning communities within their schools."[11] Tying online professional development to school-based activities can deter this unintended outcome.

Another tie to school- and district-based professional development initiatives is also important in supporting the goal of making the program financially sustainable. In its K–12 professional development forecast, Eduventures notes that districts plan to focus on internal capacity-building, drawing on and building internal capacity before seeking outside knowledge and support.[12] Thus, it is essential that online professional development providers use design and delivery models that complement locally based modes of professional development to ensure that their online offerings support district- or school-based initiatives.

NEW FUNDING AND REFINED DIRECTION

In August 2005, PBS received notice that it will be awarded another five-year grant. PBS TeacherLine will use this opportunity as a means to develop new ways of packaging professional development content and to refine and test different distribution models. PBS will continue to collaborate with course producers during the coming grant period, and it will also work closely with Indiana University, Learning Point Associates, and a design team of advisors. The design team, comprising educational experts in online and face-to-face professional development, will integrate their expertise with PBS Teacher-Line's past experience and new research data gathered by Hezel Associates. The team will guide the evolution of the current model (focused on courses) to modes of delivery that more specifically support local professional devel-

FIGURE 5   A Path to Maximum Growth and Improvement

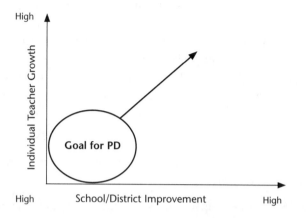

opment activities, among them coaching and mentoring programs and learning communities.

A cross-departmental team from Indiana University's School of Education and the School of Informatics will develop prototypes of these new models. Prototypes will be evaluated and refined, and PBS will use the design team's recommendations and Indiana University's development specifications to build on and extend existing materials in TeacherLine's current array of courses. These activities will provide PBS TeacherLine with new, more flexible delivery models.

However, we believe that impacting student achievement also requires effective implementation strategies and support, particularly to high-need districts. Learning Point Associates (LPA) will partner with PBS to offer implementation assistance that specifically targets Title I and high-need schools. LPA will provide direct implementation assistance to at-risk schools that need support in order to develop comprehensive professional development plans tied to local needs and to integrate PBS TeacherLine content and tools into that comprehensive plan. LPA will also provide referral services to connect at-risk schools with appropriate local agencies that can provide consultative support.

By creating additional and more flexible delivery models, PBS TeacherLine will be in a better position to support interventions that are significantly embedded in comprehensive professional development plans. As illustrated in figure 5, the goals are to design and test models that have a high level of impact on individual teachers and also to substantially influence school and district improvement efforts. We believe that this link between teacher growth and school improvement is essential if the goal is to tie online professional development to student achievement gains. However, we also believe that a national program that is dependent on this link will be very difficult to scale and may face ongoing financial challenges. Herein lies the challenge of developing high-quality professional development that is scalable and sustainable and that impacts student learning.

CONCLUSION

Reflecting on our experience of the past five years, we find that several questions deserve our continued and special attention.

1. *Sustainability.* Educators deserve consistent and dependable sources of high-quality professional development. What models will best meet this challenge? What is the "right" scale? How do we balance the desire to innovate and the need to steadily operate?
2. *Integration of online professional development in comprehensive school improvement efforts.* As external providers of products and services, we need to remain mindful of our place in school improvement efforts. How do we best complement local efforts? What is the most effective way to package and present solutions that are transparent: serving as catalysts and adding value, but fitting naturally within local improvement efforts?
3. *Evaluation of online professional development and expected outcomes.* The field faces pressure to demonstrate measurable results on student achievement. In what time frame may we reasonably expect to see changes in student achievement? What other changes do we hope to foster? How can we best evaluate these anticipated outcomes? If a direct causal link to any single intervention will be difficult, what strategies can we utilize to build faith in the legitimacy of our work?

As we continue to innovate and perfect models of professional development, these questions are important to consider. Together they encompass many of the issues that will shape the direction of our field and the outcomes of our work.

CHAPTER 5

EMentoring for Student Success

Online Mentoring and Professional Development for New Science Teachers

Roberta Jaffe, Ellen Moir, Elisabeth Swanson,
and Gerald Wheeler

Large numbers of veteran teachers are retiring, class sizes are being reduced, and more children are entering our schools every year. More than half of the teachers in our nation's classrooms will be hired during the coming decade. At the same time, districts are facing demands from the No Child Left Behind Act of 2001 to have a "highly qualified" teacher in every classroom. Unfortunately, teachers new to the profession often do not have the skills and knowledge to meet these standards.

This challenge is particularly poignant in science education, where significant numbers of science teachers do not have degrees, or even college coursework, in the science they are assigned to teach.[1] Furthermore, teacher-preparation programs do not appear to be doing an adequate job of providing the content knowledge that science teachers need.[2] High-quality science teaching demands a unique set of skills—from addressing student misconceptions about scientific ideas to managing a laboratory environment. Increasing student achievement in science hinges on keeping mentees in the profession and giving them the knowledge and skills they need to help students learn science.

The National Science Teachers Association (NSTA); the New Teacher Center at the University of California, Santa Cruz (NTC); and the Science/Math Resource Center and Burns Telecom Center at Montana State University

(MSU) have formed a partnership to meet this challenge. The eMentoring for Student Success (eMSS) project, funded by the National Science Foundation (NSF), is designed to increase student achievement in science by providing early-career middle and high school science teachers with science-specific mentoring and professional development through an online learning community.

A NEW APPROACH

Many programs for new teachers focus on "nuts and bolts" issues like classroom management, school organization, obtaining resources, and communication with parents and colleagues.[3] Widely used resources on mentoring emphasize supporting and encouraging mentees, familiarizing them with the school community, increasing their cultural proficiency, and coaching them to be reflective, confident, and self-reliant.[4] Though these activities are all important for any new teacher program, when the goal is to increase student achievement in science, they are not enough. New science teachers have needs that cannot be met by generic induction programs.

Content-based mentoring that extends new teachers' understanding of science and discipline-specific pedagogy is important for early-career science teachers.[5] Yet only 13 states recommend that new teachers be paired with a mentor in the same field, and only a handful of states require it.[6] Furthermore, programs that support sustained interactions between new science teachers and subject-matter experts are not required in any state. From the beginning, we worked from the premise that new teachers need help for their *science* teaching, and that the best help would be provided through facilitated and sustained interactions with experienced science teachers and scientists. And, because the single biggest challenge all teachers face is lack of time, we wanted to build an online system that would allow access freed of scheduling constraints.

Essential Characteristics

The eMSS model is based on evidence that effective professional development programs place high priority on student learning.[7] The project emphasizes facilitated inquiry into science content and into the ways students think and learn about science—two elements conspicuously absent in many mentoring and induction programs. The eMSS model facilitates discussion and collaboration among novice science teachers, experienced science teachers, and research scientists. All inquiries and discussions are guided by a commitment to the content and instructional principles in state and national standards and to the research on student learning and best practices in science education.

Each new teacher receives support from a mentor who has experience teaching the same content at the same grade level. Mentors receive extensive training in online interactions, content and pedagogical coaching skills, and best practices in science education to ensure that they can apply effective coaching skills in an asynchronous online learning environment. Mentees are paired with a mentor from the same state so that conversations about standards, assessment, and curricula take account of local contexts. Perhaps most important, this one-on-one relationship is embedded within a larger community of science teachers and scientists.

A coordinated curriculum of inquiries and discussions serves as a conversation guide for the learning community. Experienced mentors are trained as facilitators who start, steer, and summarize the dialogues that take place. Inquiries on topics from effective labs to using data in the classroom allow the mentor and mentee to work together and apply new ideas directly to the mentee's classroom. At the same time, mentors and mentees can draw on the expertise of scientists as they struggle with new ideas.

The scientists, who also receive training in pedagogical issues and online interactions, play a critical role in the community discussions. They do not simply answer questions; they also establish relationships with the teachers and engage them in exploring, questioning, and learning about the key principles and current research in the discipline.

Logic Model

The model for this project is based on a chain of causal assumptions that begins with training facilitators and scientists so that they understand the needs of teachers and their own role in guiding online dialogue. The next critical component is training for the mentors. That training enables the facilitators, scientists, and mentors to provide the mentees with a range of professional development experiences. Mentees receive one-on-one mentoring, facilitated inquiries into content and teaching issues, interactions with scientists, and access to resources. These experiences increase teacher retention and improve their knowledge and skills, which in turn increases student achievement. A graphic of the logic model is provided in figure 1.

Putting It Online

During the early pilot phase, we used a blended approach of online and face-to-face meetings in order to answer some basic structural questions. The project is designed, however, to be entirely online. Participating states may

FIGURE 1   Logic Model for eMSS

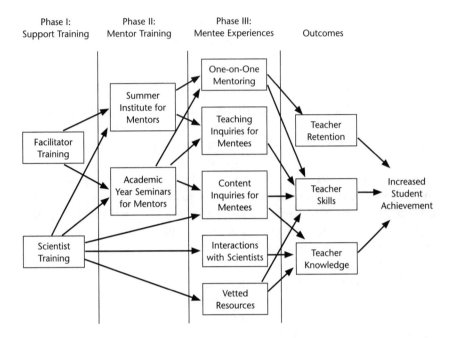

arrange face-to-face meetings, and mentors and mentees are matched within a state to allow for this, but the program does not require it. Furthermore, all of the interactions are designed to be asynchronous—that is, they do not require participants to log on at the same time. The professional literature and our experience suggest that online professional development, including e-mentoring, can be highly effective with careful design and follow-through.[8] Because activities and interactions are asynchronous, professionally active teachers, mentors, and scientists can maintain communication and interaction despite pressing schedules.

The online environment allows pairings of mentors and mentees based on teaching assignments rather than proximity or convenience. A mentor in a different town with the same teaching assignment has more to offer a mentee than a mentor in the same building who teaches a different subject. Face-to-face mentoring works well when schools and districts are close to one another, or when trained mentors are available in the same school, but appropriate science mentors are not always available. In rural areas, where schools are far apart, the opportunity for personal contact between a mentor and mentee is obviously restricted.

While the primary relationship in the eMSS program is that of the mentor-mentee pair, this relationship is enhanced by being embedded within a larger community of learners. The online environment allows the mentoring relationship to be integrated into other professional development experiences. Thus, there is a dynamic back and forth between the larger group and the mentor-mentee pair that would not be possible in face-to-face meetings.

The online environment affords other benefits as well. For example, the needs of individual teachers vary considerably. By virtue of offering a range of activities online, we can provide mentees with a choice of experiences so they can choose how to focus their energy and time. Online interactions also promote anonymity, creating a safe place for mentees to ask questions that they might not be willing to ask at a department meeting. In addition, the writing and reading process of asynchronous online learning encourages reflection in a way that face-to-face experiences do not. And finally, online interactions enable us to record dialogue and track participant experience, allowing us to refine the facilitation techniques we use and the kinds of experiences we offer.

IMPACTING SCIENCE TEACHERS

We believe that we can impact student achievement in science by improving the retention of new teachers and the quality of their classroom practice. The connection between student achievement and high-quality science teaching is clear.[9] Several studies reveal a positive correlation between student achievement and teachers' science content knowledge.[10] By meeting the specific needs of teachers at different stages of their development, we can have a positive impact on teacher quality and on student learning in science.

Teacher Quality

Our intended impact on teachers is guided by our vision of teacher quality. We were guided by a continuum of teacher quality—"profiles" of a beginning teacher, an established science teacher, and a highly professional science teacher—from a matrix of rubrics that combines the work of three groups: the Interstate New Teacher Assessment and Support Consortium, the National Council for Accreditation of Teacher Education (developed by NSTA), and the National Board of Professional Teaching Standards. The matrix covers ten domains of teacher quality, ranging from content knowledge to pedagogical skills (see Appendix A). This matrix has guided our thinking about teacher needs at different career stages and has helped us design learning experiences (including training for mentors) that support development along this continuum.

Differentiated Experiences

The continuum of teacher quality provides a way to create differentiated inquiries and dialogues for participants based on how many years they have been teaching. Discussions and inquiries for first-year teachers focus on planning instruction aligned to standards, selecting and applying strategies for all students, and creating a science learning environment. Second-year teachers build their capacity to modify instruction based on known misconceptions and assessments of their students' thinking. They also learn how to increase student conceptual understanding by focusing on the central principles of the discipline, conducting open-ended investigations, and involving students in analyzing and interpreting data. By the third year, we expect the teacher to have gained experience in using effective strategies to meet content standards. While the discussions and inquiries within eMSS continue to emphasize the relationship between content and pedagogy, they also extend to the application of science to the everyday life of students and the use of community resources and data for science teaching.

It is important to note that within these general stages, teachers will have idiosyncratic needs and interests. Throughout this three-year process, new teachers become an active part of a community of learners that helps them to further their personal and professional growth. Through the selection of different inquiries and discussions, supported by a one-on-one mentoring relationship, mentees can choose a learning pathway within the differentiated curriculum that meets their individual needs.

Meeting Immediate Needs

The eMSS program also addresses the immediate concerns of new teachers—classroom management, the school culture, and student communication—in an effort to keep teachers in the field. With close to 40 percent of new teachers leaving the profession after five years, many quit before acquiring the skills that produce the strongest learners.[11] First-year teachers often request lessons and materials early on, then seek out more reflective and deeper learning experiences later. We strive to meet mentees' immediate needs while simultaneously advancing their practice. For example, we can provide mentees with access to resources through NSTA programs—such as SciGuides, a collection of vetted, Web-linked lesson ideas—then engage them in conversation about how to use the lessons in their classrooms. In this way, the mentee's immediate need for "stuff" is addressed, but it is placed in the context of talking about teaching goals and students' learning needs. By meeting the immediate needs of mentees while enabling them to experience promising levels of student achievement, we can increase their career satisfaction and desire to remain in education.

Developing Leadership

Both research and the experience of NTC and MSU with mentoring and induction programs suggest that ongoing professional development is essential for all participants, including mentors. It is important to have the mentors continue in the project from one year to the next. To support this, mentor training is differentiated into beginning and advanced seminars, and mentors are given support throughout the year through a mentor forum. In this way, their skills improve over time, and their leadership responsibilities can increase from mentoring more than one beginning teacher to becoming a facilitator for a discussion group. At the same time, this pathway leads to the development of a leadership cadre in science education.

The program will also provide third-year mentees with leadership training and firsthand experience in engaging other teachers, administrators, and community members in inquiry, discussion, and decision-making around issues important to science students' success. This transformation in the mentees' self-perceptions and activities occurs gradually as they progress from simply coping, to recognizing and addressing students' learning needs, to becoming involved in local leadership.

THE CONTEXT

To understand our approach and the eMSS model, it is important to consider the context of the program. This includes the prior experiences and local contexts of the participants and the demands we make on them in terms of time and use of technology.

Mentees

The mentees in this project are new to teaching—either recent graduates, career-changers, or experienced teachers who are new to the assignment of teaching science. Thus, their content background and general teaching experience vary greatly. They are also exposed to a wide range of amounts and types of professional development within their local contexts. The two states that were piloted in the first years of the project—California and Montana—provide a good example of the range of opportunities available to mentees. California has a highly structured and financially well-supported induction program with a mentoring requirement for all beginning teachers, while Montana has no such program. As eMSS adds new states, the goal is to be adaptable to the diversity of teacher backgrounds and the state contexts that determine professional development opportunities. We believe that the unique characteristics of eMSS make it a complementary addition to most local situations. For example, a first-year mentee with no access to a district induction program may participate in the eMSS inquiry on managing student behavior, focusing on management of science lab activities. Another mentee may decide that all of her general pedagogy needs are met by her district program and consequently go directly to content discussions about the physics topics she teaches.

Mentors, Scientists, and Facilitators

It is also important to consider the background of the mentors, scientists, and facilitators. Mentors are science teachers who have demonstrated content expertise and leadership, but they often do not have mentoring experience, and very few have had training focused on online mentoring. Scientists have content expertise, but they often lack an understanding of the classroom situation, best practices in teaching, and the science standards. Both mentors and scientists have little experience with facilitating dialogue as a learning strategy. The eMSS facilitators are expert mentors who have a track record of leading online conversations and the ability to steer discussions in a way that promotes learning. We consider the training of mentors, scientists, and facilitators of paramount importance to the success of the project.

Participant Commitments

The mentees are expected to invest about three to five hours over one week for an online orientation, and they are expected to check in several times during the week for a total of two to three hours per week during the school year. The mentors must commit to ten to fifteen hours per week over three weeks for the online summer institute, and they must check the website three or four times per week during the school year, for a total of three to four hours per week. Scientists are expected to commit three to four hours per week because they are involved in some design work and conference calls in addition to being online. During summer institutes, facilitators are required to put in 20–25 hours per week, and during the school year they are engaged for five to ten hours per week.

Infrastructure and Technology

All participants need to have Internet access. The Internet software platform is WebCT, a course-based content management system that is a popular courseware package at many universities. WebCT was chosen because it is easily available and because MSU has had extensive experience using it in the context of professional development for science teachers. While technologies exist that could provide more interactive and exciting opportunities—for example, the use of streaming video could be helpful in the sharing of classroom experiences—many of them demand higher-level Internet connections for participants. Our use of emerging technologies is limited by the technical infrastructure at the user end and the resulting demand for more training. Participants are teachers with a full-time job; they are not necessarily technologically savvy, and many are connecting to the network through a modem from home.

TEACHER LEARNING

The central method of learning in this project is guided and facilitated dialogue. Mentees are engaged in dialogue with their mentor and with a larger community that has a carefully designed balance of expertise. These conversations, reflections, and discussions are driven by inquiries focused on both content and teaching issues that engage participants throughout the year. We also believe that teacher learning is most effective in collaborative environments and that instructional changes are most likely to occur when teachers assess their practices against recognized professional standards.

Rationale

The underlying theory of learning for eMSS draws on the experiences of NTC and MSU with different mentoring and induction programs in California and Montana, and on a large-scale study by the American Institutes for Research. That study reports on six key components that make professional development effective. These include

- *innovative forms*—such as teacher networks or study groups;
- *duration*—preferably sustained and intensive programs rather than shorter ones;
- *collective participation*—preferably activities designed for teachers in the same school, grade, or subject area are best;

- *content focus*—substance and subject-matter focus being key to deepening teachers' knowledge of their subject area and how to teach specific concepts;
- *active learning*—getting teachers actively involved in analysis of teaching and learning;
- *coherence*—experiences that fit teachers' local context and goals and are aligned with state standards and assessments.[12]

These different aspects of effective professional development play out in different ways within the eMSS program.

Mentor and Facilitator Training

The literature on online programs shows that the quality of dialogue, and thus participants' learning and development, depends heavily on facilitation.[13] We have two summer online seminars for mentors—one for beginning mentors and one for returning mentors, scientists, and new facilitators. The online seminar for beginning mentors has several objectives. We provide mentors experience in working with the WebCT platform and introduce them to the eMSS curriculum and philosophy of best practice. In addition, we help them establish techniques for building trusting relationships and for developing effective listening and responding strategies in the online environment.

The advanced online seminar uses readings from *Facilitating Online Learning* to prepare returning mentors, scientists, and facilitators for work in the online environment.[14] They receive training in introducing, maintaining, and deepening online dialogues in ways that advance the professional practice of the mentees. They employ a variety of conversation analysis tools, adapted from those developed for researchers, to examine how participants build relationships and construct knowledge about science teaching online.[15] Participants gain skills and strategies in topics ranging from creating reflective behaviors to understanding the eMSS philosophy and their role in the project.

Mentoring

The mentoring relationship is central to the eMSS model. Each mentee is matched with a mentor who has teaching expertise in the mentee's content area and grade level. Each pair has a private discussion space, called "Pair Place," where they can interact one on one. This relationship is key to the engagement of the mentee with the program. The pairs will generally visit other areas of the site together (though asynchronously) and work together even when part of a larger discussion community. Project statistics show that the biggest concentration of interactions is in Pair Place.

Facilitated Inquiries

Mentors and mentees work together in selected "inquiries" throughout the school year. These inquiries are offered during specific times so that a community of mentor-mentee pairs can be involved in the same topic. In every inquiry the mentors and mentees plan together, the mentees implement the plan in their classrooms, and the mentors and mentees reflect and revise the plan together. While the mentor and mentee work together in Pair Place, they also share their questions, concerns, and new ideas with other mentor pairs and scientists, in topic-focused discussion areas guided by a facilitator.

Mentees participate in inquiries that they select in consultation with their mentors. For example, a first-year teacher might select inquiries focused on classroom procedures, lesson design, and effective labs. In the second year, that teacher might select inquiries centered around developing design challenges, looking at student understanding, and using technology in the classroom. For the third year, the teacher might choose topics such as using real-time data, integrating science articles, and teaching diverse learners. Through these inquiries, eMSS engages the mentees in exploring topics relevant to their classrooms and in conversations that develop their understanding of best practices.

Content Discussions

The eMSS network includes discussion areas specific to different disciplines (chemistry, physics, life sciences, and earth sciences) where scientists, mentors, and mentees can engage in content dialogues. During these content-focused discussions, the scientists are learning how to best integrate content and pedagogy for student learning. Interactions may include responding to content questions, clarifying common misconceptions, connecting lesson ideas to standards and conceptual understanding, and discussing current areas of research. Content experts have found that through presenting dilemmas regarding how to teach a concept, teachers engage in exploring both the content and effective pedagogy. Each content area also has a teacher facilitator to serve as a liaison between scientists and teachers and ensure ongoing flow of the dialogue.

ENSURING HIGH-QUALITY ENACTMENT

In the eMSS project, dialogue is the key. We ensure the high quality of project enactment by looking very carefully at the online dialogue and by looking at artifacts of mentees' practice. By formatively assessing these elements and measuring them against project goals, we are continually working to ensure that the project is providing high-quality professional development.

Measures of Quality

We use the dialogue record both to evaluate our success in helping mentees be more reflective and to help the mentors develop their dialogue skills. Horizon Research, Inc. (HRI), our program evaluator, has developed a rubric for assessing the quality of the dialogue between mentors and mentees. To evaluate the extent to which dialogue is likely to enhance the capacity of the participant to provide high-quality science instruction, the following elements are considered:

- The purpose of the conversation is clear, and participants are addressing the specific question or discussion item.
- The content within the conversation is accurate or made accurate through the discussion.
- There is a positive culture within the conversation (including willingness to share, evidence of trust, collegial relationships, and sensitivity to the needs of participants).
- There is evidence of participants' reflecting on their practice.
- The issues are perceived as relevant by participants (mentees' questions are answered, and common pitfalls are addressed).
- The topics are important for classroom practice, made relevant to classroom practice, and explicitly discussed.
- There is sense-making within the conversation (common ideas are pulled out, summarized, and fit within a larger context of teaching).
- The conversation is taken to a higher level (generalized to larger themes and connected to promoting student learning).

We have also developed indicators of the quality of artifacts from mentees' practice. For example, we examine lessons to see whether (1) they are structured to provide opportunities for students to access the content; (2) their instructional strategies and activities reflect attention to students' experience, preparedness, prior knowledge, and learning styles; (3) they provide opportunities for students to build on their present understanding; (4) they provide sufficient pathways for students to build understanding of the content; and (5) there are opportunities for the teacher to assess student understanding.

Formative Evaluation

The evaluation by HRI has provided valuable feedback to the project. A number of formative data-collection activities were conducted, including interviews with mentors and mentees, observations of project activities, and analyses of dialogue and conversations. Feedback from HRI was provided to eMSS in a report in March 2005, as well as informally through conference calls and during planning meetings.[16]

The interviews and observations indicate that mentors and mentees view eMSS primarily as a source for resources and advice—activities, lesson plans, useful websites, and opportunities to communicate with experienced teachers or to ask questions of content experts. Analysis of conversations supports these findings: Roughly a third of the conversations were about resources or sharing lesson plans, while less than 10 percent related to deepening participants' content or pedagogical knowledge. One of the unique aspects of this project is our ongoing analyses of the dialogues. We are finding that we can garner evidence of reflective practices and evaluate the depth of dialogue. In this way, we can determine how well the content of the dialogues matches project goals and whether those dialogues are likely to lead to participant learning.

EXTENDING THE MODEL

To have a significant national impact on student achievement in science, we must reach more teachers. This means both expanding access to new states and ensuring that the program can be sustained beyond the funding period. It is important to note, however, that extending our model requires engaging a large number of schools, teachers, and scientists. And such engagement requires a viable business model and a measurable impact.

Increasing Reach

The project started with two states—California and Montana. As we enter year four, six additional states have been selected to join eMSS in a pilot for scaling the program to a national audience. These states were selected to establish a diversity of rural and urban settings representing all regions of the nation. As an overall mix, we were also looking for states that had a range of induction offerings for beginning teachers. Each state was required to provide a program coordinator. The key role of this person is to recruit participants, match mentor-mentee pairs, monitor the site, and provide ongoing communication and support. As we continue to expand, we must answer several questions: How does the eMSS curriculum adapt to different state contexts? What is needed to effectively administer the program in each state? What are the costs of administering the program?

Our method of delivery (online, asynchronous) removes some of the major barriers to scalability by reducing time constraints and serving a large enough population to allow us to address individual needs. The remaining challenge for expansion is the need for a viable business model. We must determine who pays, who is paid, how much they are paid, and how we can get active research scientists to devote the time to be trained and be responsive.

Sustainability

We do not have the final price points, but our initial plans call for a business-to-business strategy with school systems. This plan includes a blended approach for general induction activities onsite and science-specific mentoring online. NTC is involved in national professional development efforts with school districts to prepare mentors for teacher induction. MSU has extensive experience providing distance-learning courses and graduate degree programs to a national audience of science and mathematics teachers. This partnership can form the groundwork for developing a self-supporting national model.

RESEARCH AND SUMMATIVE EVALUATION

Research and summative evaluation are focused in two areas. First, we are establishing the efficacy of creating a national network that will facilitate dialogue between beginning teachers, mentors, and scientists. In the second and third years of eMSS, the external evaluation began collecting preliminary evidence of impacts on mentees and mentors.

Project Research

The project research team includes faculty, graduate students, and staff from eMSS, NTC, and the NSF Center for Learning and Teaching in the West (at MSU). Several studies have been undertaken by members of this group. One team member has completed a study of changes in beginning teachers' understandings of pedagogy, pedagogical content knowledge, and strategies for supporting the learning of diverse students through participation in discussion areas.[17] Other members of the research team have completed a study of the evolving relationships between mentors and mentees as the mentees shift from "survival to professional practice."[18] Both studies involved extensive analysis of dialogue posted by participants, as well as interviews with mentors and mentees.

Measuring Effect

The first yardstick of effectiveness is whether the science teachers use the system. In numerous reports and interactions we have found that mentees are so overwhelmed that even just their presence online is an indication that they value the experience. We have been engaged in a "numbers game" at this stage, deciding which structures and activities are most attractive to all participants. In the future, we will look for changes in teacher practice, increases in retention, and gains in student understanding. The easiest of these impacts to measure is retention: Do mentees in this program have better retention rates? The next measurable impact will be to learn if the artifacts of practice (student assessment instruments, lesson plans, and so on) become more aligned with best practices in science teaching. The most difficult measurement will be detecting gains in student achievement and determining whether those gains are attributable to this project. HRI is currently developing an assessment procedure that will examine this.

Findings

We have gathered findings from HRI's preliminary evaluation and from our project research. At the end of the year, HRI found that mentees rated themselves better prepared in terms of ability to work online and basic teaching and management skills, but not better prepared with respect to their content-specific pedagogical skills. While mentees' overall preparedness in their content-specific pedagogical skills did not change, one particular skill—identifying and developing lessons aligned to address student needs—did change significantly. With regard to this skill, 76 percent of mentees rated themselves at least "fairly well prepared" at the end of the year, compared to 46 percent prior to their involvement with the project. Because eMSS offered an inquiry that directly addressed lesson design, this change could be the result of mentee participation in that inquiry. When we have enough participants, we will perform disaggregated analyses that take participation in particular inquiries into account. We also plan to assess the impact of the content-focused aspects of the program on the mentees as their numbers increase.

The way this project thinks about and carries out online professional development has been influenced at a fundamental level by a cluster of evaluation and research findings regarding the nature of the dialogue occurring online, and the likelihood that such dialogue can lead to the changes in mentee practice. The HRI dialogue rubric provided the project with a reality check regarding the online discussions. The analysis performed by HRI revealed that the percentage of posts pertaining to science content, pedagogical content knowledge in science, or even thoughtful reflections on general pedagogy was quite low. At the same time, an abundance of messages requested or provided quick lesson ideas, with little attention to challenges associated with teaching the content, or to how the lesson might need to be adapted to different learners. These results also revealed that the majority of postings did not request or elicit a response. HRI has developed a second dialogue analysis tool now being used to provide the project with information about the quality of entire online conversations rather than of individual posts. When trying to transform beginning teachers' practice through online professional development, dialogue really matters. This is perhaps the most important lesson learned in this project.

We are also intrigued by initial evidence that "invisible learners"—those who are on site but not posting—are still getting value out of their experiences. These participants may read and think deeply about dialogue without necessarily posting many responses themselves. User reports provided by the Burns Telecom Center at MSU revealed that all participants, and especially mentees, were doing far more reading than responding. Distance-learning research tends to focus on visible interactions among participants and facilitators, but we have noted that attention to frequency of posting may obscure measures of learning through reading and processing.[19] Program participants read 141,297 messages in the second year of the program, but posted only 9,307 messages; in other words, for every 47 messages read by a participant, they would post three times. And in large group discussions, the mentees posted far less frequently than the mentors. Yet interviews with mentees revealed that they were reading and thinking about the discussions regularly and that they could describe specific ways they applied the information in their classrooms.[20] One particular mentee read over 1,100 messages in one year, rarely posted, and was able to describe in specific terms how she benefited from her experience.[21] The distance-learning community sometimes minimizes the potential benefits of "lurking." Our findings lend support to studies showing the idea that invisible learning is an important phenomenon, and our research team is investigating the phenomenon further.[22]

Refining the Model

Since the start of the project three years ago, its leadership has continually assessed the effectiveness of different components and has revised and added components to meet new-teacher needs, mentor professional development, and project goals. To maintain high participation numbers we have had to change some of our presentation materials. Beginning teachers, having just graduated from college, are not attracted to activities that look like we are placing them back into a classroom. In the third year of the project, we changed the structure of the inquiries to increase relevance to the mentees' practice by following a plan-practice-reflect cycle, and we put more definition into the mentor-mentee dialogues by suggesting they follow a "start-steer-summarize" structure. Finally, we introduced the use of teaching dilemmas (similar to minicases) to increase the interest level for the mentees.

The project is also working to develop strategies that balance attention to mentees' immediate needs and concerns with engaging the mentees in experiences that will support their ongoing development as effective science teachers. Beyond these plans, the project leaders recognize that maintaining this balance will likely be a continuing challenge, requiring ongoing monitoring and continuing support for mentors and facilitators. By virtue of our continued investigation into the dialogues taking place, the project is also developing strategies that facilitators can use to capitalize on opportunities within discussions and to help guide conversations toward more fully supporting teachers' learning.

The ongoing dialogue analysis by HRI, the studies by the project's research team that used dialogue analysis to examine conceptual growth and change, and our subsequent response may be our most important contribution to the field of online learning. For example, the findings contributed to our decision to introduce formal training for all online facilitators, including project staff, scientists, and returning mentors.[23] Project facilitators are currently required to complete this training, including an initial seminar and ongoing participation in a discussion area for facilitators. The project is continuing to study and refine this training, now in its second year. Preliminary evidence from HRI's evaluation suggests that the relevance and quality of participant dialogue is improving across the site, a trend that we expect to continue as our skill in training facilitators improves.

CONCLUSION

As we enter the third year of eMSS and expand the project to include eight states, we are seeing the enormous potential of online, asynchronous mentoring embedded within a learning community that is focused on the discipline-specific needs of beginning teachers. Collaborative, dialogue-driven environments centered around science and student learning can be a powerful tool for both novice and veteran teachers. It is clear that providing effective training for facilitators and balancing the needs of mentees with longer-term professional goals are both critical to ensuring that this kind of professional development is effective. Dialogue is central, and encouraging exchanges that promote reflective practices is the paramount challenge. If we can overcome these challenges and keep finding better ways to encourage meaningful interactions among new teachers, experienced teachers, and scientists, we will fill a critical gap in professional development for new science teachers. Ultimately, we will keep more new science teachers in the profession, help them improve their practice, and increase student achievement in science.

APPENDIX A
A RUBRIC FOR STANDARDS FOR TEACHERS OF SCIENCE

Introduction

The following rubrics have been compiled from the work of three groups: The left column—the expectations of what a beginning teacher of science can do—comes from the Interstate New Teacher Assessment and Support Consortium. The middle column represents the attributes of an established teacher of science. These standards are derived from the National Science Education Standards and the essential core of the NSTA document that has been adopted by the National Council for Accreditation of Teacher Education for use in evaluating and accrediting science teacher preparation programs. The last or right-hand column comes from the work of the National Board for Professional Teaching Standards.

These standards more directly target secondary science teacher preparation than elementary teacher preparation, though these ten Standards are relevant for all who teach science from preK to college, for graduate and workplace education, and for the educators who prepare teachers.

Standards for the Education of Teachers of Science: Content

Content refers to:

- Concepts and principles understood through science.
- Concepts and relationships unifying science domains.
- Processes of investigation in a science discipline.
- Applications of mathematics in science research.

1.1 Examples of Indicators

1.1.1 Preservice Level	*1.1.2 Induction Level*	*1.1.3 Professional Level*
A. Demonstrates strong and significant understanding of the major concepts in all fields for which licensure is sought, consistent with the National Science Education Standards, recommendations of the NSTA, and an assessment of the needs of teachers at each level of preparation.	A. Exhibits a conceptual understanding of concepts in all fields taught and demonstrates a progressive ability to identify and link major organizing concepts.	A. Presents a strong, flexible understanding of the major conceptual interrelationships in the field, identifies recent significant changes in the field, and applies this understanding to planning and instruction.
B. Demonstrates ability to develop a thematically unified framework of concepts across the traditional disciplines of science in keeping with the National Science Education Standards.	B. Thematically unifies concepts from the different traditional disciplines of science in a relevant and appropriate manner.	B. Regularly unifies science concepts from diverse disciplines of natural science, facilitating development of an interdisciplinary understanding of science.
C. Conducts limited but original research in science, demonstrating the ability to design and conduct open-ended investigations and report results in the context of one or more science disciplines.	C. Significantly incorporates design and use of investigation and problem solving as the context for instruction in the classroom; engages students in research projects.	C. Regularly incorporates, designs, and uses investigation and problem solving as the context for instruction in the classroom; engages students in research projects.
D. Provides evidence of the ability to use mathematics and statistics to analyze and interpret data in the context of science.	D. Uses activities employing mathematics and statistics to develop fundamental concepts in science and to analyze and explain data as appropriate for the teaching field and the level of the student.	D. Actively and regularly employs mathematics and statistics to develop fundamental concepts in science, to analyze and explain data, and to convey the nature of science to students.

Standard for Education of Science Teachers: The Nature of Science

Nature of science refers to:

- Characteristics distinguishing science from other ways of knowing.
- Characteristics distinguishing basic science, applied science, and technology.
- Processes and conventions of science as a professional activity.
- Standards defining acceptable evidence and scientific explanation.

2.1 Examples of Indicators

2.1.1 Preservice Level	*2.1.2 Induction Level*	*2.1.3 Professional Level*
A. Plans activities to convey the nature of basic and applied sciences, including multiple ways to create scientific knowledge, the tentativeness of knowledge, and creativity based on empirical evidence.	A. Uses activities and lessons designed to convey the nature of basic and applied sciences, including multiple ways to create scientific knowledge, the tentativeness of knowledge, and creativity based on empirical evidence.	A. Consistently integrates activities and lessons to convey the nature of basic and applied sciences, including multiple ways to create scientific knowledge, the tentativeness of knowledge, and creativity based on empirical evidence.
B. Compares and contrasts rules of evidence and distinguishes characteristics of knowledge in science to rules and knowledge in other domains.	B. Involves students regularly in comparing and contrasting scientific and nonscientific ways of knowing; integrates criteria of science in investigations and case studies.	B. Designs effective lessons distinguishing science and non-science and referring to the continuum of criteria for evidence; provides case studies that allow students to analyze knowledge and actions against the tenets of science.
C. Explains and provides examples of conventions for research, evidence, and explanation, distinguishing laws, theories, and hypotheses.	C. Shows how research questions and design, and data interpretation, are guided by contemporary conventions of science and concepts of the nature of knowledge.	C. Designs lessons showing how research questions and design, and data interpretation, are guided by contemporary conventions of science and concepts of the nature of knowledge.
D. Provides examples of changes in science knowledge over time, referring to the historical development of foundational concepts in the teaching field.	D. Regularly refers to historical events to illustrate fundamental aspects of the nature of science, including the durable but tentative character of knowledge.	D. Systematically involves students in inquiries pertaining to the nature of science including historical and philosophical changes that have shaped subsequent knowledge and the social interpretation of knowledge and events.

Standards for the Education of Teachers in Science: Inquiry

Inquiry refers to:

- Questioning and formulating solvable problems.
- Reflecting on, and constructing, knowledge from data.
- Collaborating and exchanging information while seeking solutions.
- Developing concepts and relationships from empirical experience.

3.1 Examples of Indicators

3.1.1 Preservice Level	*3.1.2 Induction Level*	*3.1.3 Professional Level*
A. Plans and implements data-based activities requiring students to reflect upon their findings, make inferences, and link new ideas to preexisting knowledge.	A. Regularly requires students to collect, reflect upon, and interpret data, to report the results of their work, and to identify new problems for investigation.	A. Consistently engages students in critical discussion about the results of their inquiry, interpretations of their results, the implications of their conclusions, and possible new problems.
B. Plans and implements activities with different structures for inquiry, including inductive (exploratory), correlational, and deductive (experimental) studies.	B. Involves students in diverse investigations, analysis of investigative structures, and discussion of criteria for analyzing outcomes.	B. Systematically integrates investigations with different formats into classroom work and relates student work to research traditions that typify the various sciences.
C. Uses questions to encourage inquiry and probe for divergent student responses, encouraging student questions and responding with questions when appropriate.	C. Regularly uses divergent and stimulating questioning to define problems and stimulate reflection; leads students to develop questions appropriate for inquiry in a given area.	C. Skillfully facilitates classroom discourse through questioning, reflecting on, and critically analyzing ideas, leading students toward a deeper understanding of the inquiry process itself. Uses questions to define problems and potential solutions.
D. Encourages productive peer interactions and plans both individual and small group activities to facilitate inquiry.	D. Systematically provides students with opportunities to engage in inquiry with peers using a variety of formats.	D. Skillfully meshes opportunities for science-related inquiry with critical reflection on the role of the individual as an inquirer in a collective context.

Standards for Teachers of Science: The Context of Science

The context of science refers to:

- Relationships among systems of human endeavor including science and technology.
- Relationships among scientific, technological, personal, social, and cultural values.
- Relevance and importance of science to the personal lives of students.

4.1 Examples of Indicators

4.1.1 Preservice Level	*4.1.2 Induction Level*	*4.1.3 Professional Level*
A. Engages students in activities and projects in which they examine important social or technological issues related to their discipline(s).	A. Regularly engages students in examination of local issues related to applications of scientific and technological knowledge.	A. Makes substantial and continual use of local and national problems, issues, and concerns as a context for teaching scientific and technological concepts and processes.
B. Analyzes values and processes of decision-making about science and technological issues and applications.	B. Engages students in discussions of how values affect scientific knowledge and its applications in technology and society.	B. Integrates discussion of value relationships among science, technology, the individual, and society to form thematic strands that connect concepts throughout the course.
C. Relates science to the personal lives and interests of students, to potential careers, and to knowledge in other domains.	C. Personalizes science where appropriate and works with teachers from other fields, including social science and technology education, to incorporate interdisciplinary activities into instruction.	C. Shows skill in creating a context for science, which includes the students' personal worlds and knowledge from other fields, to create a comprehensive educational framework for learning.

Standards for Teachers of Science: Skills of Teaching

Skills (Pedagogy) refers to:

- Science teaching actions, strategies, and methodologies.
- Interactions with students that promote learning and achievement.
- Effective organization of classroom experiences.
- Use of advanced technology to extend and enhance learning.
- Use of prior conceptions and student interests to promote new learning.

5.1 Examples of Indicators

5.1.1 Preservice Level	*5.1.2 Induction Level*	*5.1.3 Professional Level*
A. Plans and incorporates science teaching strategies appropriate for learners with diverse backgrounds and learning styles.	A. Plans for and regularly includes alternative activities to teach the same concept; is able to identify primary differences in learners in the student population.	A. Demonstrates a command of alternative strategies to meet diverse needs and systematically provides activities that meet those needs.
B. Demonstrates the ability to effectively engage students in learning science, both individually and in group work of various kinds.	B. Regularly includes group as well as individual activities to teach science, allowing learners latitude in organizing groups according to their age and background.	B. Addresses the role of social and group interactions as a basis for conceptual learning and inquiry, and uses strategies to facilitate student abilities to form and organize their own groups.
C. Identifies goals and provides a well-reasoned rationale, based on student needs, for choosing particular science teaching strategies.	C. Shows flexibility in planning and applying teaching strategies, and uses ongoing observation and assessment to determine subsequent actions.	C. Readily articulates sound reasons for actions and is able to switch strategies quickly to take advantage of "teachable moments" and sudden insights.
D. Uses appropriate technology, including computers, to provide science instruction.	D. Regularly incorporates available technology into instruction. Involves students in the use of technology for investigating, retrieving information, and processing data; relates technology to the process of inquiry.	D. Identifies information technologies as fundamental to teaching, learning, *and practice* of science and engages students both in use of technologies and understanding of their use in science and learning.
E. Uses diverse teaching methods to address important concepts from different perspectives; uses learning cycles for some instruction.	E. Builds a repertoire of teaching materials and learning cycles to address a concept from several perspectives.	E. Has a well developed set of thematically related materials and learning cycles used to teach concepts from different perspectives.
F. Identifies common student misconceptions or naive conceptions in the teaching field, their source, and an appropriate teaching response.	F. Begins to systematically identify and anticipate student misconceptions or naive conceptions and plans activities and discussions to address and modify them.	F. Regularly anticipates misconceptions and naive conceptions and uses assessment as the basis for constructing more scientifically acceptable concepts and relationships.

Standards for Teachers of Science: Curriculum

Science curriculum refers to:

- An extended framework of goals, plans, materials, and resources for instruction.
- The instructional context, both in and out of school, within which pedagogy is embedded.

6.1 Examples of Indicators

6.1.1 Preservice Level	*6.2.2 Induction Level*	*6.2.3 Professional Level*
A. Relates instructional goals, materials, and actions to state and national science education standards, analyzing strengths and weaknesses in a particular classroom context.	A. Systematically develops a framework for instructional goals, materials, and actions consistent with state and national science education standards.	A. Has a well-defined rationale for instructional goals, materials, and actions in relation to state and national science education standards and student achievement.
B. Assembles a diverse set of potentially useful instructional materials in the teaching field from a variety of sources, including the World Wide Web.	B. Continuously searches for potentially useful instructional materials from commercial and professional sources, including meetings, journals, and colleagues.	B. Participates in the development of new and unique resources for colleagues in the school and in the science education community.
C. Develops and implements long-range and unit plans, with clear rationales, goals, methods, materials, and assessments.	C. Interrelates concepts and experiences among units to create courses with thematic elements and well-defined goals in the teaching field.	C. Links experiences in the classroom to the broader world beyond; takes advantage of events and topics of interest; can redefine goals skillfully.
D. Understands the role of technology in education and can define a rationale and long-range strategy for including technology in science education.	D. Begins to plan and implement a long-term strategy and plan for incorporating technology into science teaching.	D. Has a developed inventory of technology to use effectively to develop interest and excitement during inquiry and learning, and uses technology to enhance student understanding of the relationship between science and technology.
E. Designs and implements learning activities that thematically relate science with other school subjects and community resources.	E. Adapts learning activities to consistently and systematically connect science with other school subjects and community resources.	E. Creates a curriculum that integrates concepts, ideas, and skills from many subject areas and the community, allowing students to take advantage of their strengths and interests in other fields to learn science.

Standards for Teachers of Science: The Social Context

The social context of science teaching refers to:

- Social and community support network within which occur science teaching and learning.
- Relationship of science teaching and learning to the needs and values of the community.
- Involvement of people and institutions from the community in the teaching of science.

7.1 Examples of Indicators

7.1.1 Preservice Level	*7.1.2 Induction Level*	*7.1.3 Professional Level*
A. Identifies people and institutions in the community who are willing to assist in teaching certain topics, and plans for their involvement in teaching.	A. Involves members and institutions of the community with appropriate expertise or relevance in science instruction.	A. Develops a network of community members and institutions to call upon to help in science instruction.
B. Uses data about a community, its culture, and its resources to plan science lessons that are appropriate for, and relevant to, students from that community.	B. Collects data about the community, its resources, and the students; experiments with ways to use those data to plan science lessons that are most appropriate for those students.	B. Regularly uses information about the community, its resources, and the students to plan relevant and appropriate science instruction.
C. Plans activities that involve families in the science teaching/learning process and communicates effectively with families of students.	C. Selects or designs activities to involve family members in the teaching and learning of science, and communicates systematically and effectively with parents or guardians.	C. Designs and employs a range of activities to cultivate a relationship with families in support of science instruction.

Standards for Teachers of Science: Assessment

The program prepares candidates to use a variety of contemporary assessment strategies to evaluate the intellectual, social, and personal development of the learner in all aspects of science. Assessment refers to:

- Alignment of goals, instruction, and outcomes.
- Measurement and evaluation of student learning in a variety of dimensions.
- Use of outcome data to guide and change instruction.

8.1 Examples of Indicators

8.1.1 Preservice Level

8.1.2 Induction Level

8.1.3 Professional Level

A. Identifies and uses the most appropriate methods for gathering information about student learning, based on student needs and characteristics and the goals of instruction.

A. Employs multiple methods to systematically gather data about student needs, abilities, and understanding and reflects upon goals of instruction.

A. Creates new methods for helping students demonstrate knowledge, and uses results to alter classroom practices.

B. Aligns assessment with goals and actions, and uses results to alter teaching.

B. Guides students in formative self-assessment, relating each tool to a specific learning outcome.

B. Regularly and consistently provides students with varied opportunities to demonstrate their individual learning.

C. Demonstrates the ability to use multiple strategies to assess teaching and learning authentically, consistent with national standards and goals for science education.

C. Uses multiple resources for assessment and can cite changes in practices made because of assessment.

C. Continuously experiments with new assessment techniques, including those suggested in the literature, and reflects on their meaning for altered practice.

D. Engages in reflective self-assessment and develops a system for self-assessment as a practicing teacher.

D. Engages in reflective self-assessment and uses a system for self-assessment, modifying practice and the system of assessment as required.

D. Regularly modifies and informs practice through multiple self-assessment indicators.

Standards for Teachers of Science: The Environment for Learning

The program prepares candidates to design and manage safe and supportive learning environments reflecting high expectations for the success of all students. Learning environments refers to:

- Physical spaces within which learning of science occurs.
- Psychological and social environment of the student engaged in learning science.
- Treatment and ethical use of living organisms.
- Safety in all areas related to science instruction.

9.1 Examples of Indicators

9.1.1 Preservice Level	*9.1.2 Induction Level*	*9.1.3 Professional Level*
A. Identifies and promotes the elements of an exciting and stimulating science learning environment; plans and develops opportunities for students to learn from resources, events, and displays in the environment.	A. Creates a classroom that reflects a commitment to science inquiry and learning, and gives students the opportunity to learn on their own.	A. Provides many opportunities for students to engage in inquiry in a variety of ways, through learning centers, exhibits, printed materials, displays, posters, aquariums, terrariums, etc.
B. Understands and sets up procedures for safe handling, labeling, and storage of chemicals and electrical equipment, and knows actions to take to prevent or report an emergency.	B. Exercises safe practices in classroom and storage areas, and demonstrates that safety is a priority in science and other activities; can take appropriate action in an emergency.	B. Systematically ensures safety in all areas and takes whatever steps are necessary to ensure that the school science program is conducted safely.
C. Understands liability and negligence, especially as applied to science teaching, and can take action to prevent potential problems.	C. Takes action to prevent hazards and communicates needs and potential problems to administrators.	C. Stays informed of potential hazards and legal concerns, and communicates with other teachers to maintain a school environment free of potential problems.
D. Knows the standards and recommendations of the science education community for the safe and ethical use and care of animals for science instruction.	D. Adheres to the standards of the science education community for ethical care and use of animals; uses preserved or live animals appropriately in keeping with the age of students and the need for such materials.	D. Adheres to the standards of the science education community for ethical care and use of animals; uses preserved or live animals appropriately in keeping with the age of students and the need for such materials.

Standards for Teachers of Science: Professional Practice

Professional practice refers to:

- Knowledge of, and participation in, the activities of the professional community.
- Ethical behavior consistent with the best interests of students and the community.
- Reflection on professional practices and continuous efforts to ensure the highest quality of science instruction.
- Willingness to work with students and new colleagues as they enter the profession.

10.1 Examples of Indicators

10.1.1 Preservice Level

A. Develops and states personal goals and a philosophy of teaching based on research and contemporary values of the science education community.

B. Understands the concept of a community of learners and interacts with instructors and peers as a member of such a community.

C. Documents personal strengths and weaknesses and seeks opportunities to improve his or her preparation to teach science.

D. Takes personal responsibility for growth and for assisting others who are preparing to teach science.

E. Demonstrates the ability to handle problems and tension calmly and effectively, and to relate to peers, instructors, and supervisors with integrity.

F. Participates in student associations, workshops, and activities related to science teaching and reads journals of professional associations in the field.

10.1.2 Induction Level

A. Regularly reflects upon his or her philosophy and goals and their relationship to actual teaching practices and adjusts practice as needed to bring them into alignment.

B. Applies the concept of a community of learners to science teaching and learning in the school environment.

C. Pursues and documents formal and informal learning opportunities, to strengthen his or her ability to teach science.

D. Takes responsibility for assigned classes and students, and works with other teachers to develop high quality learning experiences in science.

E. Treats colleagues, students, and supervisors with respect and takes action to solve problems amenable to solution.

F. Joins state and national professional associations for science teachers and regularly reads publications to improve teaching and stay abreast of current events in the field.

10.1.3 Professional Level

A. Has a well-developed philosophy consistent with the latest educational research and effective practices in science education.

B. Works with other science professionals to develop opportunities for continuous learning as members of a professional education community.

C. Shows a record of professional growth and development and demonstrates an ongoing commitment to improving science teaching practice.

D. Takes responsibility for new science teachers, student teachers, and practicum students and works with them collegially to facilitate their growth and entry into the profession.

E. Demonstrates a record of professional integrity and the respect of colleagues, administrators, and students.

F. Attends regional, state, and some national conventions, conferences, and workshops in science education; takes leadership or participates as a presenter in such gatherings.

CHAPTER 6

Science Learning and Teaching

A Case of Online Professional Learning

Susan J. Doubler and Katherine Frome Paget

The professional development program described in this chapter emerged from an initiative at TERC and Lesley University to develop a fully online masters program in science education for K–8 teachers. Our foremost challenge was to create a sustained professional experience that would "open the science door" to teachers who were tentative about teaching science and challenge skilled science teachers to improve and to reflect on their practice. In their coursework, teachers learn *science* and learn to transform their *science teaching practice*. This dual agenda is central to our discussion.

We'll begin by providing an overview of the online Masters in Science Education (MSE) program and attempting to set it in a broader theoretical context. Next we will briefly present the results of several evaluation and research studies: (1) an evaluation of teachers' science learning, (2) a comparative study of science learning online and face to face, and (3) indicators of change in teaching practice. We will then describe the ways our instructional design supports learning and argue for synergy obtained from its paired course presentation. Next we will report results from studies of online facilitation in the program. We will close by raising questions in need of answers and propose the impact data we would like to collect.

OVERVIEW OF THE MSE PROGRAM

Current frameworks for teacher learning in general, and research on science teaching in particular, informed the development of the MSE program. The affordances of the online environment provided some unique opportunities as well.

Teacher Learning

In their framework for teacher learning, Hammerness, Darling-Hammond, Bransford, Berliner, Cochran-Smith, McDonald, and Zeichner summarize the multiple challenges faced.[1] Teachers need (1) a vision of their practice; (2) a set of understandings about subject matter, teaching, and learning; (3) dispositions about how to use this knowledge; (4) practices that allow them to act on their intentions and beliefs; and (5) tools that support their efforts.[2]

Developing a vision of practice is a critical focus in our program. We attempt to build this vision in multiple ways but recognize that the common obstacles to developing such a vision of practice include "the apprenticeship of observation." Lortie describes how the universal experience of sitting in a classroom for 12 years is bound to yield many preconceptions about teaching.[3]

A second critical focus of our program is modeling best practices. But we recognize the major challenge of linking subject matter and pedagogy understandings to classroom practice. Called the "problem of enactment" by Kennedy, this major challenge of transfer to practice reminds us of Simon's observation that *knowing that* is not the same as *knowing how and why*.[4]

A third critical focus of our program is providing tools that support transforming classroom practice. We recognize, however, the important distinction between appropriating tools and mastering such tools, and we expect such transformation may very well take several years of practice.[5]

The last critical focus we want to emphasize is coherence around the way the learning experiences are organized and conceptualized. With all due respect to Emerson's observation concerning small minds and consistency, we will rely on the results of the 93 empirical studies on learning to teach that demonstrate great effectiveness of long-term professional development programs when the message and focus are consistent.[6]

Science Teaching

The seemingly straightforward agenda for teaching science—teachers need to have knowledge of science curriculum, content appropriate to it, and the pedagogy necessary to teach it[7]—belies its complexity. Recently, we have seen increased attention to "understanding how the subject matter knowledge is generated and acquiring the disciplinary tools required for lifelong learning."[8] Three bodies of work on science teaching were particularly important to us in addressing this challenging task in our development efforts: the work of Wynne Harlen, Rosalind Driver, and Stone Wiske and her colleagues in the Teaching for Understanding project.[9]

Harlen's work on the inquiry model in teaching science undergirds the course content in two of the modules: Science as Inquiry, paired with the introductory course Try Science, and Classroom Facilitation, paired with biology. In Classroom Facilitation, participants experiment with strategies designed to shift the focus from teacher-centered to more learner-centered, investigation-based instruction. Harlen's work concerning the importance of formative assessment supports the course content of Assessment for Learning, paired with ecology. Driver's work on children's alternative frameworks about science, as well as on the nature of science itself, serves as the foundation for the course content in Listening to Children's Ideas, paired with physics, in which the techniques of the semiclinical interview are introduced and tried. Wiske and colleagues' Teaching for Understanding (TfU) model provides the core framework for Curriculum Designed for Understanding, paired with earth science, in which participants analyze and redesign curriculum using the TfU model.

The Online Environment: Amplifying Learning and Implementing Quality

Duffy and Kirkley note that "distance education is forcing a closer examination of and attention to practices in higher education regardless of whether online or in the classroom."[10] Indeed, the online environment provides a unique opportunity to suspend established beliefs about teaching, to rethink what is effective and why, and to test effectiveness. Developing the online MSE was an opportunity to put into action theories of learning with particular attention to the role of inquiry and the roles of learning communities and peer-to-peer mentorship to support the development of teaching practice.[11] It also provided opportunity to shift the attention of teaching faculty from delivering content to knowing the learner and asking questions at the "cutting edge of [his or her] understanding."[12]

One critical affordance of the online environment is that the intended curriculum becomes the enacted curriculum, something that cannot be fully accomplished in face-to-face environments. In addition to contributing to consistent implementation, this congruence is a very useful quality for research.

Features of the Professional Development Program

With Hammerness' framework for teacher learning, which includes vision, understandings of subject matter, teaching and learning, dispositions, practices, and tools, we can define the expectations we had for our graduates.[13] Teachers would complete their program with a clear vision of effective science teaching and learning. They would be willing and motivated to transform their practice in the direction of teaching science through inquiry. They would continue to develop their own subject-matter understanding, as well as their instructional practice including attention to children's ideas and classroom assessment. Reflection on their practice would become a habit, and they would continue to be part of a professional community of science teaching or form such a community after the program ended. The online environment and learning experiences of the MSE program were designed to support these aims. Here are the key characteristics of the program:

- *Fully online:* All of the assignments and course resources are online, as is all of the interaction among students and between students and facilitators.
- *Hands-on investigations offline:* Students receive kits that enable them to conduct science investigations at home that they later report on and discuss in study groups.
- *Rigorous and research-based content:* Both science and pedagogy learning goals are standards-based. Content understanding develops through inquiry.
- *Curriculum of paired science and pedagogy courses:* The science courses are facilitated by research scientists and the pedagogy courses by master teachers.
- *High degree of consistency of implementation:* The specifics of the course syllabus, requirements and assessments, the learning activities, and their sequence and timing do not vary.
- *Collaborative learning:* Online discussions of investigations, findings, and teachers' ideas form the core of the learning experience. They contribute significantly to course grades.

Taken together, these features are fundamental to the design of the online masters degree program. This model also serves as the basis for a science leadership program currently under development with Tufts University. The 33-credit masters degree program in science education comprises one three-credit course and five six-credit modules. The leadership program under development at Tufts comprises three three-credit online courses and four face-to-face seminars ranging from one to five days. Both programs award university credit for their semester-long online courses, and both serve K–8 educators.

Background

The MSE program was developed by TERC and Lesley University with funding from the National Science Foundation and the U.S. Department of Education Fund for the Improvement of Postsecondary Education. It has been offered by Lesley University since June 2000 and by Walden University since January 2005. Over 500 teachers from 41 states and three countries have participated in one or more courses. Currently over 150 educators are enrolled in the full masters degree program. Program retention rates are 95 percent or higher at both universities.

Participants build their science content knowledge and teaching skills through a combination of on- and offline learning and discussions with course colleagues that take place in online study groups of five to seven. A weekly pattern characterizes the work. The assignment is posted every Friday; most teachers print out the assignment and carry out their investigations and other work at home over the weekend. They report to their study group by Tuesday evening, and between Tuesday and Thursday they read each other's posts and respond to their colleagues. The study groups are engineered to foster the development of a collective understanding.

Modules are cofacilitated by a scientist and a science educator. The scientist guides participants in their acquisition of science content, skills, and habits of mind while the science educator coaches participants as they learn about and try new teaching and assessment strategies in their classrooms. In order to prepare for teaching online, new faculty participate in a four-week online seminar designed specifically for the program.

LEARNING SCIENCE AND LEARNING TO TEACH SCIENCE

We chose two primary goals for this program: (1) to further participants' understanding of science content and the nature of the discipline through the methods of science inquiry, and (2) to develop strategies for supporting investigation-based science teaching and begin the transfer to practice.

The Importance of Subject-Matter Understanding

Professional development standards for teachers of science emphasize the importance of subject-matter understanding—for instance, "Professional development for teachers of science requires learning essential science content through the perspectives and methods of inquiry."[14] This goal is supported in the research literature.

Teachers' understanding of science influences the way they teach science. Lee, as well as Harlen and Holroyd, reports that when teachers lack knowledge and confidence, they may compensate by avoiding some topics, relying on texts, or overemphasizing practical work.[15] Asoko found that lack of subject-matter knowledge constrained teachers in many ways: in the balance between process and content, in the use of practical work, in classroom talk, in the development of explanations, and in the ability to take into account and use children's ideas.[16] Monk has reported a positive relationship between teachers' physical science coursework and their students' achievement.[17]

We adopted a broad definition of subject-matter understanding in the program, expanding understanding subject matter from knowing facts and concepts to "being able to think and act flexibly with what one knows."[18] It includes understanding the nature of the subject, taking on its dispositions, and understanding and being able to use its procedures, ideas, and skills to address real-world problems.[19] It also involves understanding the subject's social nature and efforts to build "public knowledge."[20] Becoming scientifically literate requires developing scientific ways of acting and thinking, which lead to reasoning skills and dispositions for future learning.[21]

Science, as practiced, is full of contrasts. It is theory-building as well as theory-challenging. It is intuitive and creative as well as logical. It aims for universal agreement but is able to challenge current beliefs. It is a system for producing knowledge, but the knowledge it produces is dynamic and changing. Its skills are designed to separate theory from evidence, but also to coordinate the two. It requires judgment, but at times the suspension of judgment. It is both the complex balancing and interweaving of selected activities and the collective use of those activities for learning.[22]

The Benchmarks for Science Literacy propose that "the challenge for educators is to weave these different aspects of science together so that they reinforce one another."[23] Yet many teachers have limited experience with science as a knowledge-generating enterprise. The MSE program aims to remedy this by engaging teachers in sustained science inquiry. In each science course—the introductory course Try Science and the courses in physics, biology, earth science, ecology, and engineering—teachers investigate a few carefully selected concepts in depth. They observe and predict, they collect and analyze data, they build models and generate explanations based on evidence. Online they work in study groups to compare and discuss results, look for patterns across findings, and argue the validity of each other's explanations. They engage in science both to learn science content and to become scientific thinkers.

A key question as we began our development of the program was whether teachers could learn science through inquiry in the online environment.[24] Conducting the science investigations proved surprisingly simple. Participants received a kit of materials and carried out their investigations at home, often with family members. They then reported their results in their study group forum, read each other's reports, considered the different ideas and findings of their group colleagues, and negotiated collective explanations.

This process was central to their learning experience, but was it resulting in learning science? In order to find out, we designed a pre-/post- set of embedded assessments to accompany each science course. Participants posted these assessments as part of their coursework. The results of these pre-/post- assessments from our summative evaluation and a research study conducted by Harlen and Altobello provide insight into teachers' science learning.[25]

Evaluation Results: Science Learning across the Program

A longitudinal evaluation study followed a cohort of 22 course participants over three years as they completed all courses and modules that comprised the online MSE program. Quantitative data from embedded course assessments (also called "thought experiments") were collected and analyzed in order to assess change over time in program participants' understanding of science concepts. These thought experiments were embedded twice in each of the six course modules, toward the beginning (time 1) and the end (time 2) of the module. The assignment was described to course participants as a mental exercise in which they think through a suggested experiment but do not actually conduct it. Two external science experts coded the thought experiments for biology, ecology, earth science, and engineering.

Overall, participants' performance on the embedded thought experiments provided evidence that the first program goal, to further students' understanding of science concepts, was being met. In all but one of the five modules examined, participants' scores increased significantly from the beginning to the end of the course, effectively demonstrating an increased understanding of the particular science content presented in that module.

Research Results: Science Learning Online versus on Campus

Research was conducted on the introductory module, Try Science, in order to evaluate the effectiveness of this part of the program and to provide an account of the participants' and facilitators' experience. The criteria of effectiveness were that learners would be involved in the intended active inquiry-learning processes; that they would develop their understanding of the science concepts involved in Try Science as well as their understanding of inquiry and of inquiry teaching; and that they would gain confidence in teaching science.

Data were collected during two cycles of the course. We then asked whether certain learning outcomes are more readily achieved through teaching the Try Science course online or face to face. An on-campus course was run as a temporary addition to the Lesley University professional development program.

We recognized that there were many inevitable differences in structure and interaction among facilitator, participants, and materials inherent to the formats of the two courses. Face-to-face learning is essentially synchronous, with participants being able to respond to one another immediately, while online learning in Try Science is asynchronous. The face-to-face course allows for some flexibility to move more quickly or more slowly to meet the participants' needs, while the online course was laid out from start to finish in weekly packages. In addition, the two components of the online course—for developing scientific knowledge and developing pedagogy—were facilitated by two people while, in keeping with the usual University procedures, one course leader was enlisted to run the on-campus course. Other, uncontrolled differences between the two courses were related to the experience and backgrounds of the participants.

Data collection from the on-campus course differed mainly in that direct observation and videorecording were used, in place of the analysis of messages posted by participants in the online course, to collect class experiences. Despite the uncontrolled differences between the two forms of the course, the data from the on-campus course added an important dimension to the interpretation of the online course outcomes. Results concerning learning achieved, time spent, and confidence in teaching science indicated that

- Participants in both courses increased their understanding of the science content of the course (as measured by a pre-/post- thought experiment), but the increase was significantly greater for the online participants.
- Online participants spent, on average, 7.5 hours per week on the courses, compared with 5.5 hours per week spent by the on-campus participants.
- Facilitators of the online course spent an average of 16 percent more time per week teaching the course than did the on-campus instructor—on average over nine hours per week.
- Participants in all courses expressed increased confidence in their capacity to teach science through inquiry, but the difference was significantly greater for online than for on-campus participants.

Evaluation Results: Changes in Teaching Practice

Teachers' understanding of science—its content, dispositions, and strategies—is crucial to effective science teaching, but we don't assume that if teachers understand science, then understanding will be reflected automatically in their teaching.[26] Explicit professional development is required for teachers to integrate understanding of science, learning, and pedagogy, and then to transfer that understanding to their classroom.

Studies of professional development suggest that learning science and learning how to teach science can develop concurrently in an interdependent manner.[27] Other findings indicate that the quantity of professional development in which teachers participate is strongly linked to involvement in inquiry-based teaching practice and investigative classroom culture.[28] Learning science concurrently with learning to teach science, to practice inquiry-based teaching, and to foster an investigative classroom culture were central to the program. Our aim was for teachers to develop and try inquiry teaching and formative assessment in their classrooms. Was this happening?

Print surveys and telephone interviews were developed and administered to gather self-reported information about teaching practices. Data from examination of participants' teaching and assessment styles were further analyzed via embedded teaching assignments. To develop the print survey, questions were selected from existing instruments, including the National Teacher Enhancement Network Participant Questionnaire created by Horizon Research, Inc., and the questionnaire developed by Harlen for conducting a comparison of the learning process and outcomes of the online and face-to-face versions of Try Science.[29] Telephone interviews were conducted at two points during the summative evaluation, with questions focusing on the pedagogical component of each module. In order to further examine participants' teaching and assessment styles, the embedded teaching assignments (lesson plans) that participants submitted during the Try Science and earth science modules were analyzed with rubrics developed by the project team.

Print Surveys

Several questions were designed to obtain information about participants' self-reported teaching and assessment practices and their perceived change in these practices. Questions were asked multiple times (at baseline and after up to three modules) in order to examine change over time. Due to the small overall sample size, particularly with respect to the number of participants who responded at all three data collection points ($N = 11$), advanced statistical analyses were not conducted. Generally, those activities that participants reported more frequently after having completed two to six program modules involved students taking the lead in large- and small-group discussions; students working with data, including collecting, recording, analyzing, representing, and using data in investigations; and students presenting findings to the class. The activities that participants report increasing in frequency over time and after taking further MSE courses suggest the program has influenced teaching behavior in the intended direction toward implementation of inquiry teaching.

Phone Interviews

Phone interviews, conducted at two points during the three years of data collection, were designed primarily to obtain participants' perceptions of change in their teaching in specific response to the pedagogical component of each module completed. Participants had completed at least two modules, one of which was Try Science. Participants were directed to think about "the teaching part" of the module as they described the main point of the course and gave examples of changes in their teaching. At the beginning of each phone interview, participants were asked to describe their teaching style at that moment. Nearly all described practices involved inquiry, such as focusing less on ensuring students get the "right" answer, encouraging students to think about and raise more questions, and allowing students more time to discover on their own. Participants were asked how they assess their own students' ideas about scientific phenomena. Most described combinations of informal and formal assessment, including some interviewing and discussion as well as some tests, quizzes, and lab reports. Participants' comments on two of the courses are of particular note.

Curriculum Designed for Understanding: Participants perceived the main point of the TfU approach to be that the teacher focus less on what students will know at the end of a lesson and more on what they will understand. They also saw the value of including students in the process when generating topics. They described individualizing lessons, making multiple assessments of performance, including students in setting the goals, and taking more time to be sure students understand the material.

Assessment for Learning: After this module, participants reported changes in their teaching that included different approaches to assessment in their classrooms. Most participants said that their new understanding and use of formative assessment would continue to encourage them to make changes in their classrooms. The idea of establishing criteria and basing assessment on those criteria was the one that most influenced participants' current and planned teaching practices.

Lesson Plans

Teachers in Try Science, the introductory program course, were instructed to plan a 40-minute science investigation that they would attempt with children. The lesson plans were scored with a rubric, provided by project developers, comprising four sections. Each category included from 4 to 12 criterion items; points were summed, for a total possible score of 27. The average score received by summative evaluation participants was 17, with a range from 10 to 23. On average, participants received 63 percent of the total points. Overall, more than half the participants mentioned most of the rubric items in their lesson plan. Fewer participants (15 percent) mentioned "involving students in investigating their own questions" or "applying concepts learned," and 5 percent mentioned "involving teachers in using students' ideas." In contrast, however, 90 percent of participants mentioned "involving teachers in finding out students' ideas."

In the earth science module teachers again developed lesson plans, this time using the TfU framework. The lesson plans were scored with a rubric comprising the TfU categories, each of which included from two to four criterion items. Participants received one point for each item included in their plan. Points were summed, for a total possible score of 15. Plans from 18 summative evaluation participants were analyzed; on average, participants received a score of 13 (87 percent of the total points possible).

THE CONTRIBUTION OF INSTRUCTIONAL DESIGN

The ultimate goal for teachers' science and pedagogical learning is its transfer to the classroom in the form of transformed teaching and enhanced student learning. This is encouraged in the MSE program by having teachers plan and try out new pedagogical ideas in their classrooms with their own curriculum. The MSE program accomplishes this by coupling a science and a teaching course. The science course supports the development of subject matter, but also models the inquiry teaching approaches presented in each of the program's pedagogy courses: Science as Inquiry, Listening to Children's Ideas, Classroom Facilitation, Curriculum Designed for Understanding, Assessment for Learning, and Investigating Equitable Classrooms.

In this section, we analyze the instructional design of the MSE program to consider how the program serves the dual educational agenda of *learning science* and *learning to teach science*. We focus primarily on one six-credit module—Earth Science from a New Perspective and Curriculum Designed for Understanding—to illustrate our points.

In higher education, science education programs are commonly configured as standalone liberal arts science courses and standalone education courses. With this disconnect much is left to chance; when faculty come from different academic departments with distinct cultures, communication is not easy. Schwartz, Martin, and Nasir recommend using an integrated professional learning model to support the development of both content and pedagogy.[30]

In the MSE program, we connect and also disconnect science content and pedagogy within the paired-course modules in deliberate ways. Although the emphasis shifts from science to teaching across each semester, the two learning agendas have an intricate relationship. The online environment affords the opportunity to create couplings and uncouplings to best serve both learning agendas.

How does this work? Technically, each course has its own instructor, discussion forum, expectations, and credit award. Discussion forums for science and teaching are kept deliberately separate. But both courses take place in the same online environment and share the same syllabus. This structure provides logistical and cost advantages for the university—such as mounting one course environment instead of two—while establishing clear boundaries for awarding liberal arts or education credit. For the learner, the structure means more time devoted to learning and less to logins and navigation.

Most importantly the paired-course structure provides a synergy that we believe contributes to learning. The semester's study begins with science to allow teachers to suspend their focus on teaching and engage in learning science for their own intellectual growth. Their science courses are taught through inquiry, creating a vision of what science might look like in the classroom. For example, science facilitators pose clarifying or probing questions to move teachers' thinking forward and rarely short-circuit the discussion by quickly giving the correct answer. Investigations are structured so teachers make their prior knowledge and intuitions explicit to both themselves and to others through predictions. They actively debate the results of their investigations together, generating explanations based on evidence. They reflect on their learning through journaling as well as self- and peer assessments. By these means teachers develop a "feel" for inquiry before formally learning to teach in this way.

Conversely, each teaching course draws on the content of its companion science course for examples of teaching. For instance, when teachers study Newton's second law of motion in the Investigating Physics course, the companion teaching course Listening to Children's Ideas includes interviews with children about their understanding of force and motion. The student interviews provide opportunity for teachers to revisit the science they recently studied themselves, further deepening their understanding.

In the following discussion, we take a close look at the design of Earth Science from a New Perspective and its companion course, Curriculum Designed for Understanding, to see the interplay between teachers' study of the Nile River system and their curriculum study based on the TfU framework. Using this example we'll discuss how the paired-course instructional design enhances opportunities to consider important ideas across disciplines, to model pedagogy and make its purpose explicit, to strengthen learning by presenting and revisiting central concepts, and to promote deep discussions. Our hypothesis is that the designed connections, which allow for revisiting or foreshadowing content between each pair of companion courses, provide strong scaffolding for learning and transfer to practice.

In the curriculum study teachers learn to analyze and refine their science curriculum using five elements of the TfU framework—generative topics, throughlines, understanding goals, performances of understanding, and ongoing assessments. This same framework was used in the design of the program courses. So, while teachers have not formally been introduced to TfU in the first course, they have experienced its effect on their learning. In the second semester, the framework becomes explicit and teachers put it into action in their classroom planning. In the companion earth science course, the teachers' study is about "Earth as a system" set in a specific context. The understandings developed through study of the Nile are applied to other rivers later in the semester.

Consider Important Ideas across Disciplines

In the first week of the semester, teachers are introduced to an important cross-course theme, Understanding. In the precourse announcement they read:

> Through two courses over the next 12 weeks, you'll explore what it is to learn and teach science for understanding. Understanding, as you'll see, is not just having knowledge, but using knowledge creatively, in new situations. To bolster your own understanding of Earth Science, you'll head to Africa to investigate the Nile River. On the teaching side, you'll explore a framework called Teaching for Understanding, and apply it to the science curriculum you teach.

In their study, teachers explore the issue of understanding from the perspectives of both learner and teacher. This is an example of a "bottomless" topic. Consistent with TfU's definition of generative topics, a bottomless topic connects important ideas within and across disciplines, in this case science and teaching, and can be approached through a variety of entry points.[31]

Model Pedagogy and Make Its Purpose Explicit

With the paired-course structure we can model and make explicit pedagogical approaches. Sidebars included in each earth science session bring into sharp relief how the course designers used the key ideas of the Teaching for Understanding framework—generative topics, understanding goals, performances of understanding, and ongoing assessment—in developing the course. Figure 1 shows the sidebar from the second session of the course.

Strengthen Learning by Presenting and Revisiting Central Concepts

With the paired-course structure we can introduce, revisit, and thread important ideas within and across courses. Here are three examples.

Example A: Model of Inquiry. The program's model of science inquiry (shown in figure 2) is introduced in Try Science and revisited in each of the teaching courses. This is also the model used by developers to design the investigation experiences in each of the science courses. This semester, as teachers are introduced to their curriculum project, they are reminded that their plan must be investigation-based and must align with the model of inquiry. This model is an example of a *throughline*, a key component of the TfU framework. The developers' aim is to use the pedagogical approaches presented in the teaching courses throughout the program so that there is sufficient time for an approach to become internalized.

Example B: Peer Feedback. Ongoing peer assessment takes place using identical procedures in both the science and teaching courses. As teachers develop their lessons using the TfU framework, they have access to one another's plans. All work is public—teachers are able to see how their colleagues approach the planning process and how the framework is used with a range of curriculum topics. This openness allows teachers to contrast their work with that of others and to consider strategies others have discovered, which "encourages

FIGURE 1   Session 2 Sidebar

Curriculum Design Point: Understanding Goals

The instructors are being clear about the understandings they hope you will develop in this course. These are called understanding goals, and appear in two forms:

Overarching Understanding Goals: These goals are course-long, and describe the "big ideas" you will understand. This Earth Science course has two overarching understanding goals—to understand Earth as a dynamic system and to understand how to analyze and interpret data.

Session-Specific Understanding Goals: Each session begins by explicitly naming the understanding that will be generated about the topic during the week. These goals may change from week to week, but they will always contribute to the course's overarching goals.

FIGURE 2   Model of Science Inquiry

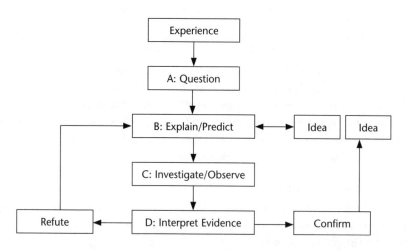

FIGURE 3   Four Steps for Giving Feedback

Clarify: First ask questions and gather information about things that aren't clear to you (e.g., about their class, the topic, what they want their students to understand, etc.).

Value: Then state what you like about their ideas, say the connections you see between their plan and the criteria for Understanding Goals and Generative Topics.

Offer Concerns: In an open manner, share with them some genuine worries you might have about their design.

Suggest: Share with them ideas about how they might improve their design. If they've shared a dilemma, offer some ideas about it.

them to view learning as an incrementally staged process, while providing them with concrete benchmarks for their own progress."[32]

Participants use four steps for giving formal feedback to colleagues, as shown in figure 3. They have used these steps in previous courses. This semester, they learn that the four steps are part of the TfU framework. They again give feedback to each other, but this time they also consider how to involve their students in giving useful feedback in the classroom.

Example C: Revisiting Science Content. Throughout the program, teachers have opportunities to revisit the science they've studied in a new context. Examples of best practice, such as video cases of classroom science and examples of lesson plans, are included in each teaching course. In these examples, the science from the companion course serves as the content. In the curriculum course, when teachers develop their own teaching plans, they refer to a model lesson—in this case, Precipitation and the Nile River System—excerpted from their science study in the earth science class.

Promote Deep Discussions

Although the connections between the paired courses and across the program provide synergy and coherence, at times we decided to deliberately disconnect the paired courses.

Discussions for science and teaching are separate, each having its own facilitator and discussion forum. The purpose is to sharpen the focus and allow conversations to deepen. Teachers make their thinking explicit, both to themselves and to others in the forums. They read each other's posts, consider each other's perspectives, and become familiar with previously unquestioned features of their own thinking.[33] Great care is taken to craft discussion questions that will result in focused debate and explicit rethinking of ideas. The intent of such engineering is to promote increasingly elaborated discussions that result in understanding.

The science course is facilitated by a practicing scientist who coaches teachers in developing their understanding of both the science content and the nature of the discipline. The teaching course is facilitated by a master teacher who understands the complexity of the classroom and who coaches teachers as they develop and implement teaching and assessment approaches. The facilitator's role is a highly nuanced one.

RESEARCH FINDINGS: ONLINE FACILITATION

The program developed a four-week seminar to help faculty become familiar with their role as online facilitators. This role is challenging and requires close attention to learners' ideas. A study conducted by Sheingold captures this complexity. In her study, Sheingold concluded:

> We learned that the process of facilitating science inquiry in the context of a well-designed course enables and requires that facilitators focus on stu-

dents' learning and thinking. . . . They must become expert at questioning, probing and encouraging students' engagement with course content in collaboration with each other, while at the same time refraining from taking center stage. They must help students take responsibility for their own learning in the course, while at the same time seeing the learning as it plays out in online conversations, and deciding whether, how and when to intervene.[34]

To begin to understand how facilitators' online behavior leads to deepening student understanding, Sheingold analyzed the posts of four facilitators and developed a coding system that characterizes facilitation, including 12 kinds of codes that fall within three general categories of intervention: (1) making the course process work, (2) helping students engage with content, and (3) teaching/telling.

Results indicated, among other things, a surprisingly high focus on helping teachers engage with content. Sheingold found that although facilitators initiated very few threads themselves, they made a surprisingly high percentage of content posts (56%). These messages were primarily in the form of questions, observations, and probes whose purpose was to help teachers engage with concepts and ideas that were central to the course. The messages also prompted teachers to take a scientific stance or to apply their understandings. For example, a science facilitator in Try Science asked, "Could you quantify that?" or "What variables would one adjust to see under what conditions this happens?" We believe that the separation of discussions into science and teaching components works to support our goal of elaborating discussions in order to deepen understanding.

We have done some soul-searching regarding the quality and quantity of this apparent coherence across courses. We believe this coherence was made possible because we had the luxury of designing the program from scratch rather than taking existing on-campus courses and converting them. With a consistent vision and a real determination to practice what we preach, we aimed to foster an understanding of subject matter, teaching and learning, the dispositions of how to use this knowledge, the practices that allow teachers to act on their intentions and beliefs, and tools that support their efforts.[35]

REMAINING QUESTIONS AND RESEARCH PLANS

While findings from the program's summative evaluation indicate that teachers who participate in the MSE program rethink their classroom practice, we have not yet investigated the nature, extent, or durability of these changes. Clearly, studying practice presents a weighty challenge, but now that the program is stable and widely disseminated, the conditions are right for studying specific and expected changes. When teachers have developed a vision of practice and a set of understandings about subject matter, teaching, and learning, and when they have appropriated the tools to support changes in practice, do they actually make these changes? If we shift our attention more fully to classroom implementation, will we see changes in practice and gain insight into the mechanisms and complexities of such transformation?

This program presents a coherent, consistent, and integrated vision for learning and teaching essential science content through inquiry. The instructional design of the paired-course presentation and the consistent facilitation prepare teachers for adopting an inquiry stance and pave the way for specific expectations for outcomes. Specifically, we expect that our teachers will

1. Use inquiry as the method for teaching science.
2. Organize curriculum around goals for student understanding and important science concepts, rather than around activities that are simply engaging or "fun."
3. Rather than provide direct instruction, facilitate student learning through science inquiry with explicit attention to developing understanding.
4. Use alternative forms of assessment, including formative approaches that support learning.
5. Probe the nature of students' understanding to ascertain prior knowledge and use these findings to guide teaching.

Each of these outcomes reflects a pedagogical emphasis of the program, highlighted in a particular course. Participants in the program complete complex projects that require them to put these pedagogical concepts into practice. Accordingly, program designers have created a clear set of rubrics by which to evaluate these projects. These rubrics can be adapted for research purposes in order to gain a window onto ongoing practice.

If we were to examine participants' classroom practice during the introductory course, at the end of their fifth course module, and in the first teaching year after completion of the program, what patterns in the transformation of practice would emerge? What methods would help us capture revealing evidence of teacher learning and its implementation in the classroom?

We imagine several methods for documenting teachers' practices at these points in time, as well as their understanding of these practices and their change:

- *Existing artifacts:* We will draw on artifacts from teachers' coursework, including lesson plans and associated examples of student work. These course products would provide information about how teachers are interpreting and implementing the course curriculum within their course assignments.

- *Simple online logs written by teachers about their teaching at regular intervals:* The logs would provide information beyond initial transfer to additional instantiations of learning. In addition to providing the teachers' perspective on the ideas and behaviors under adoption, they would provide insight into what is being given up. The logs also would reveal teachers' understanding of their current practice and the steps they are taking to improve it—their ability to monitor their own learning.[36]

- *An adapted version of Sheingold's interview protocol:*[37] Interviews would address the same five aspects of practice listed earlier—use inquiry, organize curriculum around goals, facilitate learning theory and inquiry, use alternative forms of assessment, and ascertain prior knowledge—with teacher logs helping to bring nuances associated with change forward.

- *A series of contrasting cases concerning dilemmas in teacher practice:* Bransford and Schwartz maintain that analyzing contrasting cases helps learners differentiate knowledge.[38] We believe that such cases would help us to determine the degree to which teachers' understanding of practice is differentiated. The contrasting cases would be administered in standardized written form to all participants, with follow-up probes designed to mine reasons for responses. These dilemmas would form the substance of telephone interviews targeting key issues in science practice reform, such as sharing understanding goals with students, organizing learning activities so they have multiple entry points, and using prior knowledge for classroom planning.

We are aware of the enormous challenge of studying classroom practice in all its complexity. Devising methods that are reliable but sensitive enough to capture change will not be simple. This is the challenge our field now faces. Online learning environments, with their potential for producing, replicating, and widely disseminating quality professional development (virtually being able to serve any teacher anywhere); minimizing the difference between the intended and implemented professional curriculum; and inventing new research methods that take advantage of the virtual connections in "online-ness" have an exceedingly important role to play in meeting this challenge. We look forward to joining the research community in this effort.

CHAPTER 7

Seminars on Science

Online Science Professional Development at the American Museum of Natural History[1]

Robert V. Steiner, Maritza Macdonald, Rosamond Kinzler, and Myles Gordon

In 1998 the American Museum of Natural History (AMNH) began to explore the ways in which it might take advantage of technology to put its scientific resources (a scientific staff of over 200, collections of 32 million artifacts and specimens, and a library of over 350,000 volumes) to use in supporting the professional development of science teachers nationwide. The museum's scientific staff and extensive resources were leveraged to create Seminars on Science, a set of online courses in the life, earth, and physical sciences. Now in its eighth year of operation and with the support of The Atlantic Philanthropies, Seminars on Science is providing teachers with an opportunity to deepen their content knowledge, to interact with working scientists and master science educators, and to gain valuable resources for their classrooms.

There are currently nine courses in the Seminars on Science catalog; course titles include Genetics, Genomics, Genethics (molecular biology); The Diversity of Fishes (classification, anatomy, and morphology); Space, Time and Motion (physical science); In the Field with Spiders (classification, anatomy, and morphology); Earth: Inside and Out (dynamic earth systems); Sharks and Rays (ecology, classification, and evolution); astrobiology and cosmic evolution (physical science); The Link Between Dinosaurs and Birds (evolution and classification); and The Ocean System (integrated science). A tenth course, for instructors in Seminars on Science, is titled Teaching Science Online.

In this chapter we provide a brief description of the Seminars on Science program, including its underlying vision, strategy, and plan, as well as theoretical perspectives from a variety of fields.

THE STRATEGY FOR EDUCATIONAL IMPROVEMENT

Seminars on Science is based on the idea that teachers can deepen their understanding of science, as well as of scientific inquiry, when treated as adult learners, through connection to research scientists and scientific and educational resources, as they grapple with challenging contemporary scientific research within a networked community of teachers.

The program's concept of "teacher quality" involves knowledge and appreciation of one or more scientific disciplines and their interrelatedness, an understanding of the process of scientific inquiry (including the centrality of questions), an awareness of resources (including digital resources) for the classroom, a dedication to their own inquiry and continued professional development, heightened confidence in the uses of instructional technology, and a fundamental sense of wonder and passion for science that will inspire their students.

Rather than mandate any of these outcomes or embed them in specific curricula, Seminars on Science provides teachers with tools, resources, and experiences that can facilitate and inform classroom change. It is the participating teachers who ultimately determine the extent to which their potential is realized in practice.

The parts of the educational system this model addresses include (1) the current shortage of well-prepared science educators ready to meet the "highly qualified" requirements of NCLB legislation; (2) the rapidity of scientific change, which requires educators to be informed about emerging issues and applications such as genetic engineering, local water quality concerns, and habitat destruction; (3) the need for educator competency in the use of educational technologies; (4) the isolation of teachers from one another; and (5) the lack of ready and equitable access to scientists and scientific resources for educators and students.

Throughout the last eight years, the offerings of Seminars on Science have been shaped and informed by current research on teacher-education change, as well as on adult and student learning.[2] Course design was informed by the desire to expand opportunities for teacher learning, to foster heightened understanding of educational technology, to provide scaffolded support for science learning using visualizations and models; and to increase opportunities for learners to receive feedback and to engage in reflection on their own learning process. In selecting the required teaching skills for our course rubrics we drew upon a range of materials—in particular, the certification requirements for science teachers from the National Board of Professional Teaching Standards and the National Science Education Standards.[3]

The program has recently benefited from its work with Teachers for a New Era (TNE), a national initiative to improve the quality of preservice and induction-level teaching. Among TNE's principles and concerns are the ways in which teacher-preparation practices promote content knowledge among prospective teachers, engage faculty in the disciplines of the arts and sciences, model pedagogical content knowledge, and document their impact on student learning. Researching the use of Seminars on Science within this teacher preparation context is of compelling interest to many of the TNE institutions and the AMNH.

DESIGN PRINCIPLES, THE COURSE MODEL, AND ASPECTS OF IMPLEMENTATION

In addition to research concerned with teacher development in the area of science teaching, we have also looked to the research literature and our own experience learning and teaching in museums. Some of this research focuses on science-rich settings.[4] It has been essential to the design of face-to-face professional development at the AMNH and has influenced instructional-design decisions in the online courses. The resulting course model is represented in figure 1 and includes the following central components:

- Courses focus on an area of contemporary scientific interest and are correlated to the National Science Education Standards. Each course provides a model of inquiry-based exploration for teachers. The emphasis is on exploration of authentic science, with a focus on questions, practical application, and, where appropriate, social policy, as well as on the dynamic nature of scientific knowledge.
- The courses are developed by a team that includes AMNH scientists (principal authors of the weekly essays), educators, professional developers, and educational technologists, writers, and graphic designers.
- The development process begins with the team developing a course of weekly modules and then continues in a cycle of course rollout, evaluation, and revision.[5] Courses typically undergo two cycles of revision over the course of 9 to 18 months (depending upon the frequency of the offering) and undergo further updates as needed on an ongoing basis. The ini-

tial course rollout usually takes place on a pilot basis, with a group of 20 to 30 participants, the same typical range of our other course enrollments.

- Courses are six weeks in length, organized into weekly modules with content from diverse media, required assignments, and participation in asynchronous discussion forums. The number of enrollments in a course section ranges from a minimum of 13 to a maximum of 30.
- The weekly modules are typically framed around one essential question, such as "What is Energy?" "How has the Atmosphere evolved?" or "What threatens the Diversity of Fish?" as well as desired outcomes. The appreciation of participants for object-based teaching is enhanced through their own reading of essays, viewing of images and videos (for instance, a perspective from one of the participating scientists or a laboratory tour), experiencing interactive simulations, and exploring related websites.
- Discussion forums provide a space for expert-novice interactions among research scientists, expert science teachers, and learners. The scientists provide content expertise, ask questions, share professional experiences, respond to postings of student work, and encourage participants in their efforts. The educator facilitates and guides discussion of both scientific content and classroom application. The combination of scientist, educator, and participants provides a rich discourse around the content.
- Participants are evaluated on the basis of a rubric that takes account of their weekly assignments, a final project (either a research paper or a lesson plan based upon the course material), and their overall contribution to the course discussion.
- Registration, the course management system, and a 24-7 help desk are provided by eCollege.
- Course resources are available to participants on a CD for their own or classroom use during and following the course.
- Participants have the option of enrolling for graduate credit offered through partnering higher-education institutions or enrolling as individuals unaffiliated with a current institutional partner (but perhaps matriculated elsewhere). Current partners include Adams State College, Adelphi University, Bank Street College, City University of New York, Hamline University, Plymouth State University, and Western Governors University.

An illustration of how the model components are used in a typical course week: In week 3 of Earth: Inside and Out, the topic is "How has the Earth's atmosphere evolved?" Within this broad question, learners read essays by AMNH scientists in order to study how rocks provide evidence for the composition of the early atmosphere and for its subsequent evolution. These essays describe how different the early atmosphere was, how the presence of tiny microbes over three billion years ago produced the oxygen that we now breathe, and how these ideas are supported through interpretation of the geologic record. The surprising connection between the evolution of life and that of the Earth, across vast scales of time, is supported by images of the beautiful banded iron formations now in the AMNH Hall of Planet Earth, captured on an explanatory video by Edmond Mathez, a curator in the museum's Department of Earth and Planetary Sciences, as well as on a website at the University of California, Berkeley, about 3.5-billion-year-old bacteria that still survive. Learners build upon their field experience of the previous week, when they "read the rocks" of their local area, using geologic maps and perhaps the resources of a local nature center to research the formation and evolution of their regional geology. Dr. Kinzler (a coauthor of the course and frequent course scientist) and Pat Raynock (a regular course instructor who is a master science teacher in Pennsylvania) interact with learners as they consider how and why "The present is the key to the past" is such an important tenet of earth science.

CONTENT, SKILLS, AND MODALITIES OF TEACHER LEARNING

Seminars on Science deepens teacher content knowledge and its application in the classroom as outlined by the National Board for Professional Teaching Standards and the literature differentiating content and pedagogical content knowledge.[6] Seminars on Science provides opportunities for teachers to learn these different perspectives by modeling them in the following ways:

- Strengthening content knowledge through essays, readings, and discussions with scientists
- Using pedagogical strategies of essential questions, evidence, and analysis; introducing tools of inquiry for each specific science discipline; using scientific visualizations; and sharing participant work through online discussions
- Using rubrics that make explicit the skills, understandings, and attitudes of scientific content and pedagogy offered and modeled in the course
- Calling for assignments that emphasize development or implementation of teaching units or research studies, defining whether and how they are appropriate in a particular context, for a specific population
- Providing feedback on a regular basis and offering specific scaffolds for improvement or revision—in much the same way that scientists are always expected to be asking new questions and charting new directions

LEARNING MODALITIES: DISTRIBUTED, BLENDED, OR HYBRID?

Seminars on Science was designed as a set of graduate-level asynchronous online courses in order to provide maximum access and flexibility for the teaching community across the country and to take advantage of the many pedagogical benefits that come with an asynchronous structure. Asynchronous interaction provides learners with an opportunity to think, to explore resources, to reflect, and to compose their contributions. At the same time, it reduces the performance pressure often experienced in traditional classroom settings and encourages a democratization of a classroom discussion often dominated by a few vocal participants.

In a few cases, Seminars on Science courses have been hybrid experiences, with online learning complemented with face-to-face activities. For example, a cohort of learners from the Tucson Unified School District met twice following the conclusion of the semester to reflect on their experiences in Space, Time and Motion and to plan the infusion of course resources into their instruction. Closer to home, the AMNH offers participants from the City University of New York a chance to visit the museum and to tour a relevant hall (such as the Hall of Planet Earth) with the course scientist and, if available, the instructor. Some of these CUNY students have also combined Seminars on Science courses with additional laboratory offerings to meet course requirements. The program has also experimented on a limited basis with virtual chat tools, providing a few live chat sessions with Charles Liu, one of the course scientists, during the offering of Space, Time and Motion in 2004. Other tools, which include blogs, telephony, PDAs, and instant messaging, may well be incorporated into the course model as it evolves over time.

While the courses were designed to be, and remain, primarily online experiences for most participants, they do require participants to engage in a set of experiences that involve them directly in the process of scientific inquiry, including both online and field-based experiences. Thus, teachers may find themselves consulting genetic databases, collecting rock specimens in their locale, gathering spiders, investigating DNA replication through an interactive simulation, or cutting up a fish purchased from a local fishmonger to get a firsthand lesson in anatomy and morphology.

As the AMNH pursues opportunities for adopting and adapting Seminars on Science into both preservice education and in-service professional development, we anticipate greater emphasis on blended combinations of online and face-to-face experiences. We are actively working with both current and potential partners in higher education to conduct research on the use of

Seminars on Science courses and modules in such settings. We recognize that such hybrid offerings will require an appreciation of the curricular, instructional, and institutional contexts in which learning takes place, along with possible modifications to the Seminars on Science model.

THE TECHNOLOGY INFRASTRUCTURE

Seminars on Science partnered initially (2000–03) with Classroom Connect to provide a learning management system. We then switched to a technology partner that could provide a more robust platform, one that would enable the AMNH to exercise more control and to collaborate more effectively with a range of institutional partners. After a year of study and discussion, eCollege was selected as the technology platform because of its demonstrated history of partnership facilitation, its end-to-end platform support (including a 24-7 help desk), its cost-effectiveness, and its scalability to at least several thousand annual participants.

The eCollege platform contains much of the same functionality as other leading systems:

- a learning management system to handle course enrollments, course tracking and progress, learner-performance monitoring and assessment, individual-learner and aggregated reporting, course evaluations, and learner data management
- a dynamic course delivery system to provide a fully AMNH-branded solution with templated dynamic page generation and user-specific course access, a system that supports all content formats and plug-in formats, such as QuickTimeVR, Flash, and Shockwave
- a course development system with editor tools for systematically assembling media assets into well-formed units as well as for assembling units into well-formed courses; a system for developing surveys, quizzes, and assessments; and a course export system for archiving

Situated within the AMNH Education Department, Seminars on Science is a collaborative program between the department's National Center for Science Literacy, Education and Technology (NCSLET) and its Professional Development Group. NCSLET includes a cadre of educators and educational technologists that create websites for teachers, students, and the general public, extending the AMNH's reach beyond its physical walls. NCSLET has been the primary locus of course development. It maintains a program website at (http://learn.amnh.org) that includes information and registration access for potential participants as well as course access for current participants.

While broadband access is not required, it can be helpful. The CD-ROM of resources that is provided to each course participant also contains all the rich media from the course and serves as an alternative to Web access when network traffic causes delays. While originally intended to deal with slow modems and access issues, the inclusion of CDs has been adapted as a standard course feature, useful as a resource for teacher learning or classroom use.

PARTICIPANT COMMITMENT

Seminars on Science courses last six weeks, remaining open to participants for an additional week to allow for the submission of the final project. Because they are rigorous, semester-equivalent graduate courses, a substantial time commitment from participants is required. Over 60 percent of Seminars on Science learners report spending more than seven hours per week working on course-related material, and approximately 35 percent report spending more than ten hours.[7]

Weekly course assignments include a wide range of activities, such as collecting rocks and spiders, investigating kitchens for genetically modified foods, or sampling temperatures in a data-set visualization to discover hydrothermal vents, as well as one or more questions to be addressed in the discussion forum.

The course model requires that all learners submit a final project that reflects their deepened content knowledge and represents a synthesis of course content and resources. The overwhelming majority opt to do a curriculum plan that consists of at least one week of lessons. A survey of previous learners indicates that over 80 percent reported that they planned to use their project in their classroom.[8]

Despite the considerable challenges of a semester-equivalent graduate course compressed into a six-week time frame, the program had a course completion rate of 95 percent for the summer 2005 semester, with slightly lower rates during the fall and winter semesters, when, presumably, commitment to professional development tends to be limited by classroom needs and other responsibilities.

FACULTY PREPARATION AND SUPPORT

Faculty preparation and support is essential to the success of Seminars on Science. In the early offerings, museum staff met daily to review the interaction in the discussion forums, to discuss responses, and to coach and mentor faculty. After more than 70 course offerings, we now have more experience, a more experienced faculty, a process for preparation and support, and a faculty training course. Central to the entire process and the model is the curriculum manager, a master teacher/professional developer with classroom science education experience in a range of grade levels and in multiple disciplines. In addition, she or he has participated actively in scientific research programs and has extensive experience facilitating discussions online. The curriculum manager's responsibilities are to oversee faculty preparation and development and to monitor all courses as they are in motion. The curriculum manager also teaches the instructor-development course Teaching Science Online.

The instructor-development process typically begins with a course participant expressing an interest in teaching (instructors are required to first serve as participants in the course they wish to teach). Course faculty and the curriculum manager evaluate the individual's depth of knowledge about the scientific content as well as her or his ability to communicate and interact with others in an online environment. Upon completion of the course, the potential instructor then begins Teaching Science Online, the online faculty development course. This three-week course covers general issues of online pedagogy, science instruction, and specific aspects related to Seminars on Science, such as how to use the various tools to set up and moderate online discussions. The next step is to serve as a teaching assistant during an active course. An experienced educator mentors the person as he or she learns to use course tools and moderate discussions. If the person's work is satisfactory, they are presented with the opportunity to instruct their own section during the next offering. During this session the new instructor is in frequent e-mail and phone contact with the curriculum manager to assess progress and ensure a successful course offering.

Scientists also receive preparation and support. The project director who leads the Seminars on Science—which includes multiple layers of course design, partnership development, promotion, external funding, evaluation, and other components—and the curriculum manager meet with new course scientists to provide them with an overview of the program. Together they discuss strategies for responding to questions posed in the discussion forum, for sharing their research experiences, and for deepening an online conversation—for example, by posing additional questions to the teachers, asking teachers to investigate a particular website, or sharing their views on relevant science policy. New scientists are monitored closely both for the quality and the frequency of their postings and receive feedback, typically from the curriculum manager, as needed and appropriate.

Although detailed studies of the time required to serve as course scientists and course instructors have not been conducted, anecdotal information suggests that the typical course scientist spends approximately 4 to 10 hours per week in the discussion forum, while course instructors typically spend 10 to 15 hours per week in discussion and assessment activities.

Additionally, the curriculum manager monitors courses in progress by reading discussion posts and evaluating grading of assignments. Weekly conversations are held with course faculty to talk about discussion and assessment strategies as well as issues related to student performance. The curriculum manager assesses faculty performance on the basis of course observations and through learner evaluations that are completed at the end of each semester. In addition, periodic independent evaluations by Inverness Research Associates assess overall success of the courses and the faculty.

PROGRAM RESEARCH AND EVALUATION

The first phase of Seminars on Science (1998–2002) focused on the design of a course model and course development. We summarize here some of the key findings from Phase I, the central thrusts of which were testing the validity of the course model and studying the design, development, and implementation process. These findings focus on Seminars on Science as a professional development program and online initiative. A complete report, including perspectives on Seminars on Science as a project initiated by an informal science institution, is also available.[9]

These findings are based upon research and evaluation efforts conducted by our colleagues, drawing from the experience of 536 learners in more than 35 states who participated in Seminars on Science courses between May 2000 and July 2002. Approximately 70 percent were science teachers. Approximately 35 percent of all teachers responding taught in elementary schools, with the balance in middle school or high school. Inverness Research found the typical course participant in Phase I to be "an established veteran teacher with an interest in science and with the initiative to seek out personal learning opportunities."

Key findings related to professional development show that

- The courses are effective at providing teachers with authentic learning experiences. Among the findings were that 84 percent of participants reported that they gained valuable scientific knowledge and that 83 percent increased their understanding of how different kinds of scientists do their work.

- The courses demonstrate that scientifically rigorous courses can be made to be both engaging and accessible for K–12 teachers. Evaluation indicated that 80 percent preferred Seminars on Science to other professional development programs, including locally available, face-to-face programs.
- Seminars on Science courses not only add to teachers' science content knowledge but also provide teachers with resources and activities they can use for their teaching. Eighty-three percent of the respondents reported that they acquired valuable new teaching resources, and many indicated that, in various ways, they were already incorporating their Seminars on Science experience into their current teaching.

In addition, the evaluators report:

- Teachers tell us that the courses strengthen their personal relationship with the discipline.

On the end-of-course survey participants report that

- The course(s) added to their own personal knowledge (91%) and provided a bank of resources they can draw on for their own learning (83%).
- The course-taking experience gave them deeper insight into the work of scientists (76%).
- The experience rekindled their passion for science and the work of science (74%)
- They are motivated to learn more about the course topics on their own (72%) and to take more science (67%).
- Their work in the class has made them more of a science expert from the point of view of colleagues (35%).

The courses enable teachers to bring more to their instructional relationship with students. In addition to sharing newfound or rekindled enthusiasm for science with students, teachers bring back to their students

- new kinds of media and materials (77%) and other new resources (71%) they can use in science.
- new content (72%) and learning experiences that can serve as a good model for the kind of work they ask students to do (73%).

Perhaps most importantly, almost three in five of the teacher-participants (60%) say that their experience in the course(s) gave them an opportunity to show students that they too are learners, and almost half say that student confidence in their teaching has increased (45%).

The teachers are also using course resources to connect their students to the discipline. Although the courses are designed primarily as adult learning opportunities teachers say that they are taking what they learned back to the classroom.

- Seven in ten (71%) have used what they learned as background to create a lesson or unit for their students.
- Six in ten (60%) have made some of the resources available to their students.
- Five in ten have explored course resources and materials with their students (48%) or had students do some of the same investigations that they did (45%).

Hence, the evaluation found that these courses provide a foundation for teachers to model inquiry for their students by being given an opportunity to inquire themselves, in the company of their peers, at a more sophisticated and adult level. As a result, teachers can internalize not only what is known in the natural world but how it is known; the inextricable intertwining of theory and observation; the role of technology in elucidating the structures and processes of the natural world; and both the conceptual and practical challenges of hypothesis-testing, data collection, analysis, and interpretation.[10]

Access and innovation have been the key issues in online education for Phase I of Seminars on Science. As we move forward into Phase II, which will continue through 2006, the important questions include

1. How does one structure the syllabus for an online science course in a manner that is inquiry-based and engaging and that takes advantage of the vast resources of the museum?
2. What functionalities need to be built into the user interface and navigation? What support systems are needed for instructors and learners?
3. What lessons are to be learned with respect to course communications, pedagogical strategies, and the use of media?
4. How do we leverage the vast human and material resources of the AMNH for maximal effect online?

We learned several things from the course development process. Prototyping of the courses was essential, with many revisions and adjustments along the way. In addition, the decision to rely upon an existing course management system, rather than creating one, seems appropriate in retrospect, because it allowed us to focus on both content development and pedagogy. (However, the original platform used during Phase I, while sufficient in the early stages of our work, has now been replaced by one that seems better suited to our needs.) We also learned that scientists enjoy the flexibility and innovative opportunities associated with teaching online. Finally, we believe that the program has created innovative opportunities for taking advantage of the museum's scientific expertise and extensive collections through the development of imagery, video, and interactive simulations.

The analysis of Phase I of Seminars on Science documents numerous examples of the impact of the program in the classrooms in which participants teach. We excerpt one sample here:

> One 5th/6th grade teacher took two courses . . . because they "fit so well with what I wanted to do in class with my students. I felt it would give me the background to do some new things in class, to get information from experts and to learn about resources I could use in class." The teacher used the courses as background and as a knowledge base for her teaching; implemented the lesson plans she had done for course projects; created online activities for students; and utilized the course CDs as resources in her classroom.

The Phase I evaluation documents additional examples of classroom applications.

During Phase II of the program (2002–06), Inverness Research will determine the extent to which the project achieves the following outcomes:

- Providing valuable learning opportunities for teachers to learn science, both through standalone Seminars on Science courses and in combination with other experiences
- Continuing to provide teachers with access to authentic science and to draw upon the vast scientific expertise and resources of the museum
- Increasing the capacity of the program to serve larger numbers of learners
- Gathering lessons for the field, particularly as a model that uses technology to leverage the assets of science-rich institutions in the service of teacher professional development

In evaluating this phase of the program, Inverness Research Associates will continue to evaluate new courses. They will also continue to evaluate information through a variety of survey instruments and will document case studies of the pilot partnerships, particularly those with higher-education institutions, and will focus on issues of collaboration across institutions, as well as on learner perspectives of the program. This work is ongoing and is expected to be published sometime in 2006.

INTEGRATION WITH THE LARGER EDUCATIONAL COMMUNITY

A primary goal of our current efforts is to integrate the Seminars on Science program into the larger educational community. This goal is connected with a broader philosophical and social agenda, namely using online professional development to address issues of educational access and equity.

In our first outreach and marketing efforts, the program reached a self-selected audience of experienced teachers who were looking for something to further their personal knowledge, keep them engaged, and nourish them intellectually. We then worked with Inverness Research Associates to identify potential partnerships within the higher-education, K–12, and informal science institution sectors that could ultimately broaden the reach of the program. As a result, we developed new partnerships in different parts of the country.

Working closely with educators at the City University of New York, we submitted Seminars on Science to a process of course review by science education faculty and administrators. The most rewarding stages of the program have been recognition from and being awarding credit by a large public institution. As the primary institution preparing teachers for the New York City schools, CUNY has access to a large pool of teachers at various stages of development, education, and certification. Through our partnerships with CUNY and other institutions, we are now seeking to augment preservice education and in-service professional development for a wide range of teachers at different stages in their professional lives and with different levels of prior knowledge, by using an array of face-to-face and online modalities.

THE FUTURE: SCALE AND SUSTAINABILITY

As we indicated earlier, the first phase of Seminars on Science focused on the design of a course model and course development. The evaluation of Phase I established the feasibility of the goal and the effectiveness of the model, highlighting successes while also suggesting improvements for the future. The current phase of the program focuses on understanding the opportunities for situating Seminars on Science within the larger framework in which professional development takes place in the United States and on the development of a plan for sustainability. The American Museum of Natural History is now actively engaged in scaling up Seminars on Science in order to expand its impact on science professional development and to provide a stable financial foundation for the future operation and development of the program. Our efforts are focused on increasing both "impact" (degree of transformation) and "reach" (number of individuals and organizations influenced).

From the outset of this work, the AMNH has viewed itself primarily as a content provider. The initial question that drove the development of Seminars on Science was whether the AMNH, using networked learning technologies, could marshal its authentic scientific resources—including its researchers, collections, and exhibitions—to help address the national shortage of science teachers with an adequate level of content knowledge. While we had strong convictions about teaching, learning, and professional development, we recognized that the museum was neither a school district nor an institution of higher education. We lacked statutory responsibility for defining classroom pedagogy, accreditation as a teacher preparation institution, and even a built-in constituency of potential course participants. The museum had "real" science, but to achieve scale in all of its dimensions would require partnership, which has been and continues to be a defining characteristic of our work.

Seminars on Science has steadily grown since the rollout of its first courses in 2000. The program has more than doubled its annual enrollments during the past two years, with approximately 520 annual enrollments during the 2004–05 academic year. The enrollment growth is particularly notable given the program's decision to more than double course fees (from $200 to $445), beginning in fall 2004, in order to place the program on a more solid financial footing. The drive toward higher enrollments—and the partnerships that can help generate those enrollments—arises from the need to achieve greater economies of scale and to generate revenues to support program operation. While seeking greater enrollments and as funding permits, we will continue to refine the existing courses, develop new ones, incorporate new and emerging technologies, and document, evaluate, and disseminate our work.

The first phase of Seminars on Science (1998–2002) focused on the design of a course model and course development. The evaluation of Phase I established the feasibility of the goal and the effectiveness of the model, highlighting successes while also suggesting improvements for the future. The second phase of the program (2002–06) focuses on understanding the opportunities for situating Seminars on Science within the larger framework in which professional development takes place in the United States and on the development of a plan for sustainability.

Our initial efforts to partner with institutions of higher education, school districts, regional intermediaries and informal science institutions suggested that while Seminars on Science was generally well received across the board, the courses connected particularly well with higher education, as indicated by their high enrollments and retention rates. For many of these partnering colleges and universities, Seminars on Science provides a robust array of online science resources not otherwise available. At the same time, through these partnerships, both the museum and the higher-education institutions were able to tap into new markets and to develop a new, if modest, revenue stream by offering graduate credit to learners who were not affiliated with the college or university and who were often hundreds or thousands of miles away. These partnerships—formalized through memoranda of understanding—have enhanced the visibility of the program, added enrollments to the program and, in the case of the City University of New York, allowed us to begin experimenting with the creation of hybrid models. Our plan is to continue to build these partnerships with individual institutions. In collaboration with institutions involved in initiatives such as Teachers for a New Era, we will also learn more about the integration of the Seminars on Science courses and online learning in general into institutions of higher education and teacher preparation programs, and the impact of these programs on student learning in the classroom. While this work with higher-education colleagues has been productive to date, we are confident that the courses can also be integrated into district or statewide professional development efforts. We hope to realize these opportunities in the future, perhaps in conjunction with one or more of our higher-education partners.

Although these partnerships are essential to the program's growth and impact, we must not lose sight of the fact that about 80 percent of current program enrollments are individuals who are not matriculated at one of our higher-education partners. Although approximately 50 percent apply for graduate credit from one of the partner institutions as nonmatriculated students, most of our enrollments are K–12 teachers from across the United States, including a large number of middle- and high school teachers in the Northeast, where familiarity with the museum is likely to be strongest. According to a 2004 Seminars on Science marketing survey, these individual teachers are taking the courses to meet recertification requirements, to achieve salary increments, or out of personal interest.

In order to increase individual enrollments, Seminars on Science has created an array of marketing and promotion strategies, drawing upon outside expertise as needed. The primary marketing channels include the Seminars on Science website; the homepage of the American Museum of Natural History; a marketing relationship with the National Science Teachers Association (including print, Web, and a listserv); AMNH listservs (including former course participants and educators interested in the museum); direct mail; print advertisements in science education, technology, and professional development publications; state science-education publications; and direct marketing using search-engine technology. The program also offers incentives and discounts to program participants who enroll in additional courses or recommend the program to their friends and colleagues. The cost-effectiveness of these various efforts has been monitored (typically through promotion-specific URLs and by querying registrants) and the results are used to refine the allocation of limited marketing funds.

The costs of the program to the learner compare favorably with other semester-equivalent graduate courses—whether offered online or in a traditional format—particularly considering the high level of instructional and technical support. Graduate credit is available at considerably lower rates than the $1,400 typical of a three-credit online graduate course in education. However, in order to avoid significant increases in course fees in the future, it will be important to continue to grow enrollments, thereby keeping the relatively fixed administrative costs moderate on a per-learner basis. Program expenses include both fixed administrative costs (staffing includes a project director, a senior project manager, a curriculum manager, and an outreach coordinator) and the enrollment-dependent costs of instructional and technology support.

To date, funding for the program has been provided largely by grants, primarily from the generous and long-term support of The Atlantic Philanthropies. As that funding draws to a close in mid-2006, we are working to ensure that adequate funding can be generated to support anticipated program costs, including administrative, instructional, marketing, technology licensing, per-student technology, evaluation, and new-course-development expenses. Potential funding sources under the current course model include course fees, a share of graduate credit fees through contractual arrangements with our partners, grants, and museum funds. We are also considering ways in which we might increase available revenues, building on our experience but extending beyond the current model. For example, we have begun to explore expanding the model (with hybrid offerings, certificate programs, recertification programs), adapting the courses for new audiences (nonteacher adult learners, students in virtual high schools), and licensing the course model and course assets. While it is a significant challenge, we are optimistic about our ability to sustain the effort.

In terms of impact (degree of transformation) and reach (number of individuals or institutions affected), Seminars on Science is a scalable model. The potential impact of the program on individual learners, through open enrollment, and on institutions, by embedding Seminars on Science courses in in-service and preservice programs, is significant. There is potential expansion of the number of learners, limited presently by the availability of instructors (and of course scientists currently affiliated with the museum) and the capacity of the course management system. Within the current model, we are aiming for a steady state of 1,000–1,500 learners per year. Extensions of the current model and new partnerships could take us well beyond those numbers.

For Seminars on Science, the challenges of impact, reach, and sustainability go hand in hand with the remarkable opportunities they present for promoting effective teacher professional development and improving the learning and teaching of science.

CHAPTER 8

Embedded Professional Development

Learning through Enacting Innovation[1]

Sasha A. Barab, Craig Jackson, and Elizabeth Piekarsky

In the last decade we have seen a number of exciting developments in computer science with respect to innovative technologies, in the research community with respect to insights into teaching and learning, and in the commercial gaming industry with respect to spaces that support deep engagement. Whereas schools are sometimes struggling to achieve even mandatory participation (research has revealed a steady decline in the academic motivations of individual students from grades 3 through 9, the entertainment industry is proving wildly (and sometimes problematically) capable at capturing the attention and passion of kids. While having exciting implications for K–12 schools, these new developments in computers and entertainment have yet to significantly impact curriculum development and the pedagogical toolkits of most teachers. In fact, using these new technologies, pedagogies, and playspaces for learning in schools can require substantial shifts in teachers' thinking about curriculum, and about conceptual and philosophical change, the development of new skills, and access to different curricular tools for use in their classrooms.

The question that guides this chapter is how to best support teachers in making these shifts. In answering this question, we will share our experience in supporting teachers in using the Quest Atlantis Project as part of their classroom offerings. As a platform for teaching and learning, Quest Atlantis (QA) brings with it a host of challenges and opportunities. QA uses immersive technologies, draws upon the genre of computer and video games in informing its design, requires deep levels of student inquiry, and often challenges or modifies teachers' usual roles as facilitators of learning.

Quest Atlantis is an NSF-funded learning and teaching project that uses a 3D multiuser environment to immerse children ages 9 to12 in educational tasks. Currently, Quest Atlantis has over 4,500 registered users from five continents who participate in formal school environments, as well as in some afterschool settings.

While our work is situated in the context of the Quest Atlantis Project, the professional development (or PD) framework underlying this work has implications for thinking about PD more generally. Smylie and Conyers argued that PD models cannot be imposed, but instead should be situated in, and respond to, the everyday teaching needs of teachers.[2] A broader question arises: How can we situate professional development meaningfully in the sociotechnical contexts of teachers, honoring their day-to-day efforts and leveraging the complex meaning of the actual teaching experience, while also providing the stimulus for serious pedagogical and curricular innovation?

In our embedded professional development (EPD) framework, we leverage the informal activities of teachers—as they are implementing curriculum in their classrooms—as points through which to stimulate change. The authors view PD as a process involving the implementation of innovative curricula and, simultaneously, reflection on the underlying frameworks and implications in terms of student learning. In this way, we are advancing an embedded framework for professional development that respects the work of teachers and their ability to reflect upon, evaluate, and adapt to complex classroom conditions, while at the same time engaging them in progressively more innovative forms of curriculum.

AN EMBEDDED FORM OF PROFESSIONAL DEVELOPMENT

We work to embed PD in rich implementation experiences through which teachers individually and collaboratively reflect and evolve their teaching practices. Professional development in this model is situated and authentic, a part of daily practice. We recognize that professional development is a constant process for good teachers. It takes place informally as teachers reflect on what went well in their lessons. While traditional PD models may not encompass these informal practices, they are no less legitimate in their effects on the classroom.

In the case of implementing Quest Atlantis, development often involves reconciling our designed structures with teachers' own usual practices, as

FIGURE 1   Embedded Professional Development Components

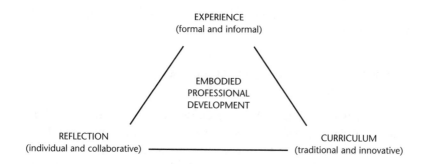

they reflect on how Quest Atlantis compares to other forms of curriculum and what they can do to improve and customize the experience. Often, teachers discuss their Quest Atlantis experiences with other teachers or with the research/design team. These discussions can take place through face-to-face dialogue in school hallways or the teacher lounge, through text-based interactions over e-mail or in project bulletin boards, or even through individually and collaboratively examining videos of teacher practice and examples of student work. As the implementation of QA presents challenges and structures for reflection, these less formal processes are reinforced, reified, and legitimized.

Our embedded form of professional development (or EPD) has elements of formal and informal experience, of innovative and more traditional curriculum, and of individual and collaborative reflection (see figure 1). In this chapter we will provide an overview of each of the separate components of our framework for supporting PD. However, while these components are presented sequentially for clarification purposes, in practice the three relate and transact in ways that give meaning to the other elements. While the reader might view our characterization of an embedded form of professional development as a simple reaction to more formal models, we do not view things as this simplistic.

In our work as designers and educators, we have had to juggle tensions continually. We think of tensions not as problematic dichotomies that need to be overcome, but as complex dynamics that can serve as catalysts for "messy," real-world decisions and negations that actually fuel innovation.[3] This has meant understanding the value of multiple perspectives and determining ways to ensure that our model provides for adaptive enactment. We will provide richer insight into these tensions, their theoretical roots, and how we have worked to juggle them in practice. However, to appreciate the framework being advanced it is necessary to first understand the context within which our work takes place. This is the curriculum around which our teachers are engaging in PD.

THE CONTEXT IN WHICH OUR PROFESSIONAL DEVELOPMENT IS EMBEDDED

Our curricular work begins with the premise that games are a significant medium for supporting learning.[4] We view videogames as contexts with rich narrative structures, ideologies, and embedded practices that constitute a meaningful form of play.[5] Elsewhere, we and others have discussed the play within and in relation to videogames as having "discursive richness, depth of collaborative inquiry, complexity of game play, opportunities for consequentiality, rich perception-action cycles, exploration of situated identities, and the complex forms of learning and participation that can occur during game play."[6]

At one level, curriculum developers and even instructional designers can only marvel at the diverse ways in which these games support complex learning, thinking, and social practices. However, using most videogames in a classroom context would be inappropriate given their tendency toward transgressive narratives and lack of connection to academic content and standards, as well as the fact that most games were designed primarily for entertainment purposes.

Still, it is our belief that videogames and their compelling structures—embedded scaffolds, unfolding missions, nested goals—can be effectively leveraged to establish a new kind of curriculum. At the same time, bringing videogame structures into the classroom is not without problems. It requires teachers and students to become comfortable with novel technologies, learner-directed activities, failure as a natural part of game play, multiuser collaborations and ownership, hidden rule sets, competitive activities, and nonmandated or unexpected student activity. Further, supporting this type of game play inquiry, and ensuring that students learn from the experience, may require that teachers take a much more facilitative than directive role. It is with an appreciation of the potential benefits and challenges of using the videogame medium to support academic learning that we designed the Quest Atlantis environment.

Building on strategies from online role-playing games, Quest Atlantis combines features used in commercial gaming environments with lessons from

FIGURE 2   A Screenshot of Quest Atlantis

This screen shows a scene from a village on the left and the homepage for a Quester on the right.

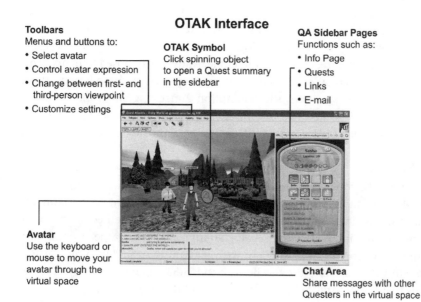

Toolbars
Menus and buttons to:
• Select avatar
• Control avatar expression
• Change between first- and third-person viewpoint
• Customize settings

OTAK Interface

OTAK Symbol
Click spinning object to open a Quest summary in the sidebar

QA Sidebar Pages
Functions such as:
• Info Page
• Quests
• Links
• E-mail

Avatar
Use the keyboard or mouse to move your avatar through the virtual space

Chat Area
Share messages with other Questers in the virtual space

educational research on learning and motivation.[7] Using the virtual environment (see figure 2), players can travel to virtual places and perform educational activities (known as Quests), talk with other users and mentors, and build virtual personae. The core elements of Quest Atlantis are

1. a 3D multiuser virtual environment,
2. learning Quests and unit plans,
3. a storyline, presented through an introductory video as well as novellas and a comic book, that involves a mythical Council and a set of social commitments, and
4. a globally distributed community of participants.[8]

As discussed further below, an important characteristic of Quest Atlantis is that the teacher and her students can participate in Quest Atlantis at different levels of breadth and depth, which can change based on their individual levels of commitment.

CORE TENSIONS IN PRACTICE

Traditional to Innovative Curriculum

As educators with an ideological agenda, we do not simply leverage existing opportunities but work to provide teachers with innovative curriculum through which novel and potentially transformative experiences occur. In this way, we have worked to develop a type of educative curriculum that supports teacher learning as well as student learning.[9] As opposed to many other forms of professional development or support, such as summer workshops or out-of-context seminars, the assumption underlying our work is that the curriculum itself will create opportunities through which teachers can reflect deeply on their practice, especially in response to the experiences of their students.

Our classroom implementations of QA have involved some teachers who were initially hesitant or even resistant to using a technology-rich "educational game" in their classrooms. In part because of student enthusiasm and demonstrated learning, some of these same teachers have begun to engage more fully the innovative, gamelike, narrative, and social aspects of our curriculum and community. As such, we refer to this as an "evolving curriculum" in that over time the teacher can individually engage in implementations that leverage more innovative aspects of the curriculum.

As an example of this progression, one author of this chapter is a teacher who has been using the Quest Atlantis context for 18 months. Beth began Quest Atlantis by showing the project video in her classroom to set up the underlying narrative and by assigning a number of Quests. While all Quests involve inquiry and are grounded in real-world problems, and while some Quests may last upward of a week, the majority can be completed within one or two class periods, working somewhat in the manner of traditional worksheets but framed in the larger QA narrative structure. Furthermore, given that Quests are directly connected to academic standards, Beth was able to fairly easily fit Quest Atlantis into her existing practice.

About three months into her use of the curriculum, Beth then tried the Taiga unit, a two- to three-week-long virtual simulation of a wildlife park that has a polluted river running through it. Here, students navigate their avatars around the virtual Taiga environment, clicking on programmed nonplayer characters who provide information related to their perspectives of the cause of the pollution.

In the simulation, if students interview the right virtual characters and complete some initial activities successfully, they become able to collect and analyze virtual water samples. Using information garnered from interviews as well as physical data, students are asked to formulate hypotheses about the source of the problem.

This simulation constitutes a fairly complex unit with both relevant and irrelevant information. In implementation, students experienced many moments in which they were frustrated and not really sure of what to do next. For Beth, it was a challenging unit, with innovative technology, inquiry-based and student-directed learning, and game structures that included academic content as well as other narrative information.

In this implementation the Taiga unit also involved some competitive play, opportunities for failure, and activities that for some were motivated by extrinsic rewards. Furthermore, student success required systems-level understandings that were not located in any specific curricular abstraction but emerged across the experience, with different students developing different conclusions. In remediating understandings, Beth had to allude to information distributed across multiple interactions and contained in numerous locations in the virtual environment. Additionally, given the inquiry focus of QA and the commitment to maintaining student ownership, Beth struggled to carry out this task in an inquiry-facilitative manner. At this point in her professional thinking, Beth's PD involved becoming more fluent with technology and developing a richer appreciation for how to support inquiry-based learning.

This curricular experience was challenging for Beth. It required a unique technology-driven form of PD, and it even forced a relatively radical change in her pedagogical approach. Although Beth was aware of problem-based learning (PBL) and inquiry learning, and even had taken some seminars on these approaches, she had never been able to fully and successfully implement this type of real-world curriculum with her students.[10] She had known that as a theory PBL was a great idea, but she lacked enough tools in the traditional text and activity books to implement a PBL-based unit. Quest Atlantis provided the background, content, and all the complexities of PBL in a virtual world that students were already personally connected to.

Beth was surprised to become a learner with her students, unraveling the mystery of the disappearing fish. Instead of being in the position of just asking right/wrong questions, she was on the same playing field with respect to the authentic question as were her students. Beth found being a facilitator and a learner with her class professionally stimulating. Her role had changed, and the students maintained leadership roles both in determining the ecological problem and providing an improvement plan for this virtual (and real-world) problem. As a result, Beth now looks for more ways to give students real-life roles with problems to solve in other curricular areas.

Beth then attempted Anytown, one of the most gamelike curricular units in the Quest Atlantis repertoire. Anytown allows students to work on descriptive writing activities through investigating a virtual town where they are eventually asked to take on the role of a reporter. In this role, students can choose different topics to develop articles around. The design is intended to allow each story to arise naturally as students interact with the 3D environment, nonplayer characters, and associated puzzles. Anytown involved students working on different activities at the same time and progressing at very different paces, with many occasions of doubt and even moments of failure, in an environment with even more distributed meanings, in which the "facts" were not told to students. Beth found herself in the uncomfortable position of having relatively little control over her students' learning—even less than in the Taiga unit, in that there were more opportunities for students to follow individually defined learning trajectories as they worked on self-chosen activities.

The Taiga situation called for Beth to leave much of the experience to her students' explorations, with possible understandings unfolding as she worked as a support and learner along with the students—a new pedagogical stance for her. In reflecting with one of our team members, Beth discussed this experience as being quite uncomfortable yet personally transformative, affecting her understanding of what the domain of teaching could include and the ways in which students can learn.

She was surprised that although all of her students were working on different tasks, the majority were on-task in terms of the work. This amazed Beth, as she said that only rarely are all the students on task, doing different things and happily helping classmates. Key to the success of this unit, from Beth's perspective, were the rich and meaningful content of the learning, "letting the kids go" to solve mysteries at their own pace, and daily class wrap-up discussions in which students could share their difficulties, get strategies from peers to overcome them, and share their successes.

Beth described the joy her students experienced while engaging in a very complex learning environment. This unit provided a structure for learning with many paths for students to take. Students thrived on creating their own path of learning in contrast to a traditional teacher-directed unit. Beth stated that because of this experience, she is much more comfortable at seeing learning and teaching as a web of opportunities for kids instead of a fixed set of sequential activities. She also has come to appreciate the value of her students having ownership and the role of advanced technologies to support deep inquiry.

The levels of curricular complexity in the Quest Atlantis context serve as scaffolds, slowly expanding teachers' zone of proximal development from more traditional lesson experiences to ones that truly integrate some of the most innovative aspects of game design and inquiry-based learning—a type of curriculum that may have proven too disconcerting to teachers when they first began collaborating with us.[11] Professional development, in our EPD framework, is not the focus of teachers' experience but an epiphenomenon that comes out of their experience with implementing innovative curricular experiences.

Our reluctance to engage in explicit telling should not be taken as ambivalent or uncritical. However, as with other models of curriculum for change, the critique is not imposed by some outside group but emerges out of the implementation experience.[12] Accordingly, participating teachers have not simply been funneled into taking up the ideologies and methodologies embedded in the Quest Atlantis experience. They have been key players in critiquing and supporting the technological, narrative, and social structures of our design. When teachers have championed Quest Atlantis, we believe they have done so out of the promise and experienced value of Quest Atlantis as a motivating and evolving curriculum.

Formal to Informal Activities

Over the last decade there have been many calls for a new pedagogy, one that highlights active learners engaged in meaningful inquiry on authentic problems that matter to them.[13] Few teachers would deny that it is valuable for learners to be actively involved in the learning process, or that inquiry is an important component to deep learning, or that lessons should involve issues and contexts that are relevant to students. However, as teachers continue their own education, these features are often notably missing from their own formal PD. Commenting rather critically, Miles stated:

> A good deal of what passes for "professional development" in schools is a joke—one we'd laugh at if we weren't trying to keep from crying. It's everything that a learning environment shouldn't be: radically under-resourced, brief, not sustained, designed for "one size fits all," imposed rather than owned, lacking any intellectual coherence, treated as a special add-on event rather than as part of a natural process, and trapped in the constraints of the bureaucratic system we have come to call "school."[14]

While we might view Miles's critique as rather severe, in working with teachers we have found that this statement resonates all too often with their own experiences. In general, PD occurs through formal training and involves some external change agent who focuses on "educating" the teachers, a process that frequently involves sharing the latest insights and the expectation that teachers will later implement these ideas in their classrooms. Even with an exceptional "PD trainer," the content of the experience is not usually owned by the teachers, does not build or leverage their rich situated experience, and does not directly relate to their particular classroom.[15] In contrast, we and others are arguing for models that situate PD around teachers' experiences, such that it does not occur as an "add-on" activity, but becomes seamlessly integrated into their everyday teaching practices.[16] As we have discussed, our commitment is to simultaneously providing teachers with rich curricular content that meets their existing classroom needs and affording them opportunities to innovate their teaching by implementing progressively more challenging curricular experiences.

Clearly, such a model is an explicit shift from a formal to a more informal framework of PD. However, such a unidirectional shift does not truly capture our thinking or experience. For example, all new Quest Atlantis teachers begin participation with a one-day workshop. During this workshop, we embed them in the curriculum—deconstructing the experience so that they appreciate the technological challenges, the pedagogical commitments and assumptions underlying true inquiry, and the opportunities involved in using a playspace such as Quest Atlantis to support learning.

In addition to ensuring that teachers know the basics of using Quest Atlantis, we ask teachers to reflect on their local school climate and develop a list of professional goals and student learning outcomes that they expect to achieve through their implementation of Quest Atlantis in their classroom. In support of this critical reflection, we use a number of the protocols to support deep inquiry (see appendix A for an example).[17]

Following this initial full-day workshop, in some cases we then meet for a half-day at least once a month. During this period, we break up into groups of three or four and collaboratively examine student learning with a focus on improving instruction. Each group of participants is expected to have an overall professional development goal for their collaboration, to which discussions become framed. For example, the goal of the group may be to increase their understanding and use of inquiry-based pedagogy, technology in their classes, metacognitive strategies among students, gender differences, student engagement, deep content learning, or the usefulness of playspaces for learning. During the first couple of meetings, groups are expected to use either the Tuning Protocol (see appendix A) or the Consultancy Dilemma

Protocol (see appendix B). Whereas the former usually involves examining examples of student work, with the goal of improving instruction to meet a particular outcome, the latter protocol is appropriate for critically examining a particular problem or dilemma.

As the groups become more effective at meeting their particular goals, the next stage can involve reviewing relevant articles and, where appropriate, celebrating successes. We also use monthly meetings to do less formal check-ins and technology tune-ups, or to provide a space for teachers to talk more generally with colleagues about teaching and learning.

We support both formal and informal activities, with an emphasis on supporting teachers in implementing curriculum and in meeting goals that matter to them. For example, Beth's experience has included some of the information reflection activities discussed above, in addition to more formal workshop or group discussion experiences. Ultimately, we designed these activities to push teachers to try innovative technologies and practices while at the same time asking them to push back on us as educational researchers and designers. Central to all these activities is helping teachers to become reflective practitioners, while working individually and while working with their peers.[18]

This characterization has much in common with *lesson study groups*.[19] In this model, teachers come together to develop a common lesson, use video to capture their own classroom implementation of the lesson, critically examine the experience, and finally integrate what they are learning into future iterations of the lesson. We have built on this idea, having university educators as part of the dialogue and using online technologies to capture the implementation and support discussion among teachers who are located in different places and who examine the work at different times.

As we have worked to situate these activities in more online settings we have learned much about the role of trust and the challenges of mixing formal and informal models. In fact, while the idea of anyplace, anytime PD is attractive in theory, our experience is that teachers also like bounded structures. Having formal frameworks wraps constraints around informal participation, so that in some cases teachers may get credits or simply formal acknowledgment for completing a particular PD trajectory. For example, we give credits if they complete an agreed-upon number of reflective sequences and curricular implementations that represent a unit of PD.

In the next section we discuss our commitment to supporting reflection and some of the technical structures that we have developed to support collaborative reflections, highlighting the challenges and opportunities of achieving this online.

Individual to Collaborative Reflection

The importance of critical reflection has long been recognized, with the work of Donald Schön making a significant contribution to better clarifying the meaning and value of reflection and the advancement of the notion of a *reflective practitioner*.[20] In Schön's work, the reflective practitioner is someone who is able to respond to problematic contexts through reflection, effectively solving the particular problem while at the same time learning from the experience. He distinguishes between reflection-*in*-practice and reflection-*on*-practice, suggesting that both types are important. Reflection-*in*-practice involves taking time in the moment of the activity ("thinking on our feet") to gauge one's performance and assess how the activity is progressing. Schön describes it as follows:

> The practitioner allows himself to experience surprise, puzzlement, or confusion in a situation which he finds uncertain or unique. He reflects on the phenomenon before him, and on the prior understandings which have been implicit in his behaviour. He carries out an experiment which serves to generate both a new understanding of the phenomenon and a change in the situation.[21]

Reflection-in-practice involves transacting with our experiences, connecting with our feelings, and attending to our theories in use. It entails building new understandings to inform our actions within the situation that is unfolding. The more common PD model of reflection-*on*-practice involves taking a step back and examining a particular experience after the fact, again connecting with our feelings and attending to our theories in use for making sense of the experience.

The notion of testing theories, or as John Dewey might have put it, "leading ideas," is central.[22] It allows us to understand experience more deeply and critically. For Dewey, inquiry is a process that allows one to transform an indeterminate situation into one that is determinate. There are clear steps or patterns to inquiry. One begins with a doubt that motivates reflection. One may then proceed through a problem statement, then to some sort of hypothesis formation, and then to action that will resolve the original discomfort or disequilibrium. In the best scenario, the end state of the inquirer is not the same as the beginning state; the actions that lead to restoration of functioning also change the understanding and practice of the inquirer as he or she transacts with the environment of the inquiry. Meaningful reflection and, as described by Dewey, learning and development more generally occur through the cycle of disequilibrium and restoration of equilibrium that entails translating theory into action.[23]

This process, called *praxis,* is not a unidirectional process but a transactive one involving inquiry, and through which theory and practice mutually inform one another. In this way, theory can come from action, just as action can come from theory. The reflective practitioner is continually developing theory-in-action and through this process undergoes a form of professional development. In our work we care less about labels for theories and much more about supporting teachers in developing informal theories that have practical significance to their work. Teachers know and use these theories not because they want to use the current term that is popular in education circles, but because of the theories' embedded significance to their everyday practice.

We have already discussed how we facilitate this reflection through informal and formal activities. In this last section, we wish to briefly touch on the importance of supporting both individual and collaborative reflection—the latter being a critical component in allowing new ideas and perspectives (theories) to enter the reflective process of participating teachers.

We have found that our inquiry-based curriculum necessarily provides the teacher with numerous opportunities for reflection-in-practice in that the activities are frequently student-led, with the teacher devoting much time to supporting inquiry rather than providing lectures or checking to see if students have the one correct answer. Teachers work side by side with students to help them examine the implications of different responses with respect to the particular task.

The tasks in Quest Atlantis are usually just above student ability, requiring much facilitation from teachers, who ask probing questions, work to help their students more deeply engage the core issues, and even provide just-in-time lectures when appropriate. In supporting reflection-on-practice, we encourage teachers to participate in a listserv with other teachers and to consider taking on more of the breadth (varying types of participation) and depth (game-like, collaborative, learner-centered curriculum) of the overall Quest Atlantis design—a trajectory frequently motivated by their students' expressed interest. We also discuss the use of protocols and use these to facilitate groups in which teachers examine one another's work. Over the last couple of years the first author has also developed other sociotechnical structures that teachers can use to individually and collaboratively reflect on their work.

One example of a project that has been used by a number of Quest Atlantis teachers and which is part of our PD framework is our work on the Inquiry Learning Forum project.[24] This example illustrates the multifaceted network of our EPD, in which we draw on various resources that constitute the professional development of an individual teacher.

For the Inquiry Learning Forum (ILF), we designed and evaluated the salient features of an electronic knowledge network to support a Web-based community of in-service and preservice mathematics and science teachers sharing, improving, and creating inquiry-based pedagogical practices (see http://ilf.crlt.indiana.edu/). Founded on our previous research and consistent with our pedagogical commitment, we designed the ILF around a "visiting the classroom" metaphor, with the belief that teachers need to be full participants in and owners of their virtual spaces.

The ILF consists of a variety of Web-based structures all related to encouraging online collaboration. While there are discussion forums and other relevant resources, the essence of the website is its video examples of inquiry. When a teacher selects a specific classroom lesson, he or she can view seven to eight video segments of the implemented lesson. Additionally, he or she can view an overview of the lesson, reflective commentary from the teachers, descriptions of activities, lesson plans, student examples, and connections with both state and national standards. (See figure 3 for a screenshot of Beth's classroom as hosted in the ILF.)

As teachers build the cases of their lesson implementation, they are asked to reflect on individual segments, a process that requires teachers to question their actions and assign meaning to pedagogical decisions and at the same time to reflect on the value of the pedagogical decision for supporting learning. For example, on one of Beth's classroom reflections she posted, "Justin [student teacher] and I modeled how to write a script with one sample before the entire class. This proved to be a helpful exercise as we asked for their [the students'] input and criticism of our process."

When examining the larger lesson, one begins to appreciate how this overlaps with the cognitive apprenticeship approach advocated by Collins, Brown, and Newman for supporting student learning of cognitive tasks.[25] In this approach, the teacher first *models*, then *coaches* and *scaffolds*, with the goal being to gradually *fade out* teacher intervention so that the student can engage in the behavior without the support of the teacher. During this process, the teacher explicates the thinking underlying her actions; thereby modeling for students in a form of *cognitive apprenticeship*. This approach could be taught didactically in a PD workshop; in Beth's case, it becomes embedded in her practice as she works with her student teacher to explore effective ways to support her students in the inquiry process.

At one level, Beth's reflecting on her classroom is an independent activity; however, teachers also share and comment on their teaching experiences with other teachers by using the ILF or through discussion groups. Making

FIGURE 3 Screenshot of Beth's Classroom as Hosted on the ILF

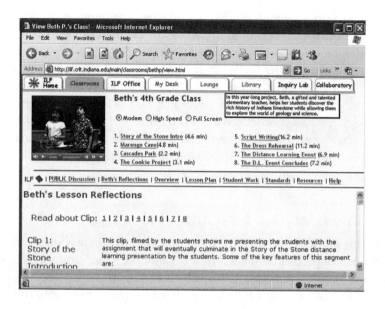

use of collaborative dialogue and critique, teachers can develop particular insights through the eyes of other colleagues.

Video clips and reflections are placed on the ILF website so that other teachers can learn from and discuss the implementation process. Also provided are lesson-based bulletin boards where teachers can come together and critique each other's practice, establishing a critical community of inquiry around which PD occurs. In this way, other teachers can also participate in the PD that the practicing teachers are experiencing—from a distance and at their own pace. For example, commenting on Beth's lesson implementation one teacher stated, "The cookie clip was also one of my favorites because it allowed students to control the room and the questions. This project has inspired me to do big projects in the classroom without fear of the students being involved." By taking what all too often takes place behind a closed door and moving it into a public space that stimulates critique, Beth is taking a type of risk that we view as an essential part of collaborative reflection and PD more generally. Having an available, captured experience in an online forum where teachers can meaningfully reflect on a common artifact provides a rich set of resources for stimulating collaborative PD.

We have found that an essential component of supporting critical reflection is that we create bounded groups in which small numbers of teachers who have developed some level of trust and have overlapping goals can come together and critique each other's practice. In order to support deeper critique in online collaboration, we have found that it is first necessary to have face-to-face opportunities for teachers to meet each other and build some level of trust.[26] We might bring together a group of Quest Atlantis teachers who already have a history or who have met face to face, and then use the online resources and connections as an extension to these existing relations. More generally, the online resources and interactions available through the Inquiry Learning Forum become not just the means of supporting PD but tools to further strengthen burgeoning relations.

CONCLUSIONS: PARTING THOUGHTS

Underlying our framework for PD is the belief that knowing is an action distributed across people, tools and resources, and the situations in which one acts. At their core, knowing and learning involve participation in meaningful activities and not acquisition of abstracted content.[27] Extending this line of reasoning to PD, our focus is on supporting meaningful participation with the teachers, stimulating them to continually grow their practice and to critically reflect on this evolution both individually and with their peers.

In this chapter, we shared our experience with supporting professional development, highlighting the core conceptual biases and tensions (drawing on formal and informal experiences, using traditional and innovative curriculum, and supporting individual and collaborative reflection) that have guided this work and that have emerged into a framework for our EPD. With this innovation, we have been supporting teachers in using a multiuser playspace to support both academic and personal development. While still early in its evolution, this framework has been quite successful for guiding those teachers with whom we collaborate. Over time, we have witnessed increased use of the more innovative aspects of our curriculum, suggesting a growing confidence in our teachers' ability to implement technology-rich, inquiry-based pedagogy.

It is also our finding that teachers have evolved their broader educational perspectives, and our observations further indicate a widening of their instructional palettes with respect to supporting children in inquiry-based learning. Furthermore, we are witnessing these teachers taking on more leadership roles, supporting other teachers as they also begin to implement more inquiry-based curricula in their classrooms. Finally, we are hearing from our teachers a renewed interest in their own teaching, as they are challenged along with their students.

This framework offers both formal and informal forms of professional development, as well as activities and supports that occur both online and face to face. It involves teachers taking risks in their own teaching, talking with other teachers, and listening to their students. Indeed, for many teachers, the possibility of offering their students an engaging context for learning may be more of a catalyst for participation than the need to achieve a legitimization of their professional development. However, given the innovative nature of the Quest Atlantis context—inquiry-focused, problem-based, experiential, and technology-rich—teachers using QA are often forced to evolve their own thinking and practice, especially as they use more gamelike aspects of the environment. QA is an example of a catalyst curriculum that stimulates teacher change, as it is difficult to use Quest Atlantis in traditional ways for extended periods of time.

We hope that over time we will further formalize this framework, while continuing to ensure that it supports teacher ownership and validates authentic practice. As we attempt to balance the tensions, pushing too much in the direction of the informal structures may limit the usefulness of the framework. Making it too formal or abstract, however, challenges the likelihood of acceptance and ongoing usage by teachers who already have busy schedules. We have tried to advance a middle ground: one that honors teachers and makes them our priority, while at the same time exposing them to new opportunities through which their practice can evolve.

The direction and pace of this evolution transacts with the evolution of the curriculum itself. It is driven largely by teachers' interests and the engagement of their students. Where we do have clear commitments and agendas, we introduce these as embedded in our curriculum, with professional development being an outcome of, or at the very least transactive with, successful curricular implementation. In this way, we use the Quest Atlantis curriculum to support a rich form of praxis that situates teachers' professional development in activities that are of direct value to them.

APPENDIX A
TUNING PROTOCOL

Adapted from protocols developed by the National School Reform Faculty (http://www.NSRFharmony.org)

This protocol is for examining teacher lessons in order to improve the lesson plan with respect to particular goals, at the same time building collegiality among participants. Optimal group size is from five to eight participants. Each group should have an overall professional development goal for their collaboration, toward which discussions will be framed.

1. *Introduction (2 minutes):* First is an overview of the process. Here, the facilitator, who has previously met with the presenter, states the goals and reviews the process for the group. The time frame is also reviewed. It is the facilitator's job to ensure that the group observes the allocated time for each step of the process.

2. *Presentation (10 minutes):* Next is an overview of the context of the work. The presenter should introduce the focusing question that the group is to respond to. At this time he or she may also discuss how this work relates to the larger professional development goal of the group. During this time it is important that the participants simply listen—this is not a dialogue.

3. *Clarifying Questions (5 minutes):* Participants ask clarifying questions to understand facts only. Participants should refrain from making judgments or suggestions. The presenter participates in the conversation, responding to posed questions to help clarify the facts.

4. *Examination of Project Work (10 minutes):* Participants look closely at the work. The presenter provides the group with enough data for participants to offer critical feedback. This usually consists of a copy of the lesson plan, examples of student work, and evaluation strategies. Participants should focus on presenter's focusing question, writing down thoughts on a note pad as they examine material.

5. *Reflection on Warm and Cool Feedback (2 minutes):* This is final pause time in which participants reflect on what they have read, with respect to the focusing question.

6. *Warm and Cool Feedback (10 minutes):* Participants share feedback with one another while presenter is silent. Participants simply discuss what they see, sharing their opinions in dialogue with each other. Begin with warm and move on to cool, then cycle back and forth.

7. *Reflection (5 minutes):* Presenter reflects on feedback and responds to comments and questions with participants silent. This is not a time to be

defensive, and the presenter doesn't have to respond to every comment, only those that he or she thought were useful.

8. *Debriefing (5–10 minutes):* Conclude with a facilitator-led discussion of the tuning experience. This is a time for the group to debrief about the process. While there might be some conversation about the content of discussion, it is more focused on the process.

APPENDIX B
CONSULTANCY DILEMMA PROTOCOL

Purpose: A Consultancy is a structured process for helping an individual or a team think more expansively about a particular, concrete dilemma.

Time: Approximately 50 minutes

Roles: Presenter (whose work is being discussed), Facilitator (who meets with presenter and frames Consultancy), Critical Friends (who offer critique)

Process:

1. The presenter gives an overview of the dilemma with which he or she is struggling and frames a question for the Consultancy group to consider. The framing of this question, as well as the quality of the presenter's reflection on the dilemma being discussed, are key features of this protocol. If the presenter has brought student work, educator work, or other artifacts, there is a pause here to silently examine the work or documents. The focus of the group's conversation is on the dilemma. (5–10 minutes)

2. The Consultancy group asks clarifying questions of the presenter—that is, questions that have brief, factual answers. (5 minutes)

3. The group asks probing questions of the presenter. These questions should be worded so that they help the presenter clarify and expand his or her thinking about the dilemma presented to the group. The goal is for the presenter to learn more about the question he or she framed or to do some analysis of the dilemma presented. The presenter may respond to the group's questions, but there is no discussion by the Consultancy group of the presenter's responses. At the end of the ten minutes, the facilitator asks the presenter to restate his or her question for the group. (10 minutes)

4. The group talks with each other about the dilemma presented. (15 minutes) Possible questions to frame the discussion:

   • What did we hear?
   • What didn't we hear that we think might be relevant?

- What assumptions seem to be operating?
- What questions does the dilemma raise for us?
- What do we think about the dilemma?
- What might we do or try if faced with a similar dilemma? What have we done in similar situations?

Members of the group may suggest solutions to the dilemma. Most often, however, they work to define the issues more thoroughly and objectively. The presenter doesn't speak during this discussion, but instead listens and takes notes.

5. The presenter reflects on what he or she heard and on what he or she is now thinking, sharing with the group anything that particularly resonated for him or her during any part of the Consultancy. (5 minutes)
6. The facilitator leads a brief conversation about the group's observation of the Consultancy process. (5 minutes)

CHAPTER 9

Online Teacher Professional Development[1]

A Learning Architecture

Thomas M. Duffy, Jamie R. Kirkley, Rodrigo del Valle,
Larissa V. Malopinsky, Carolyn M. Scholten, Gary R. Neely,
Alyssa Wise, and Ju-Yu Chang

In this chapter, we describe our efforts to build an online professional development environment that is theoretically, pedagogically, and practically consistent with what we know about effective support for teacher professional development. The system that resulted, the Learning to Teach with Technology Studio (LTTS), consists of 60 courses delivered through our own Web-based learning management system. Since the program began, we have enrolled approximately 600 students, approximately 70 percent of whom are practicing K–12 teachers, 23 percent of whom are preservice teachers, and 7 percent of whom are college faculty and school administrators. Because we built our own learning management system, we have been able to engage in an iterative design process based on feedback from our learners as well as on our own reflection on our mentoring process and the student learning activity. Our initial work focused on the design of inquiry-based lessons and the integration of technology as a tool for inquiry. All but a handful of courses teach these skills in the core content areas and thus, while our focus is on inquiry learning and technology integration, pedagogical content knowledge is a part of most courses.

Although we began with a specific focus, the LTTS learning architecture and management system applies to almost any problem-centered learning context. We have since developed course suites on algebraic reasoning, classroom management in a learner-centered environment, and professional development for national park employees.

We begin the discussion of LTTS by providing the research and theoretical base that guided our design process. Perhaps most importantly, we link that research and theory to practice by clearly describing the design commitments that arise from it, along with the specific design principles that define the LTTS learning architecture. Finally, we describe our evaluation of LTTS and discuss the implications. We conclude this introduction by providing an image of the LTTS learning environment from the perspective of a new student.

Because learners can begin an LTTS course at any time and move at their own pace, a teacher comes to the LTTS website when she has the time and the need for professional development. She searches a catalogue with over 60 courses, all of which are described in terms of the curriculum problem they address. She chooses the one that best meets her needs, then she enrolls and has 12 weeks to complete about 30 hours of work. Because this is self-paced, she is not constrained by a fixed syllabus schedule or the need to meet the schedules of other students. Rather than learn with a class of students, she will work one on one with a mentor who will provide feedback on her work as well as encouragement and guidance when needed.

She begins the course by reading a curriculum problem and an approach to addressing that problem. For example, one course addresses the difficulty of assigning Internet projects in which students can learn to critically evaluate resources. It proposes using WebQuests as a strategy for addressing that problem.[2] The teacher sees five to seven tasks serving as proximal goals to focus her on building a lesson plan consistent with the problem statement and the principles for inquiry-based instruction. A rich variety of online resources are available (more than 40 per course), so she can find resources that are consistent with her level of understanding and most appropriate for the grade level and content she teaches.

Each task requires her to submit work on her lesson plan and provide a rationale that reflects the concepts integral to the course. The mentor evaluates and discusses the work and rationale to ensure that the teacher understands the concepts she is applying and that the application addresses her classroom needs in a way that will engage students and support their learning. The learner can log into the course whenever and as often as she wants, just as long as the course is completed within 12 weeks. At the end, she completes a reflective self-assessment of her work relative to the learning goals, and the mentor provides feedback on both that reflection and the final project submission. The mentor uses a rubric designed to evaluate inquiry-based lessons to evaluate the final work in the course. Once the mentor provides feedback on tasks or the overall project, the LTTS learner has the option to revise work and resubmit it as needed. On average, learners take advantage of this opportunity, resubmitting tasks an average of 1.5 times. The theoretical framework and the research on professional development that provided the foundation for this design effort are described below.

THEORETICAL FRAMEWORK

In designing LTTS, we needed to integrate our theoretical position on learning with the research on pedagogy as well as what we know about the practical issues in providing professional development. Our theoretical view is reflected in the constructivist framework, with a focus on the situated and social nature of learning.[3] Addressing the theoretical foundations of our constructivist view, Savery and Duffy describe three principles:

1. *Understanding comes from our interactions with the environment.* We cannot talk about what is learned separately from the learning activity itself.
2. *Cognitive conflict or puzzlement is the stimulus for learning and is a major factor in determining the organization and nature of what is learned.*
3. *Knowledge evolves through social negotiation and through the evaluation of the viability of individual understandings.* All constructions are not equally viable; it is not a matter of *anything goes.* The social environment is primary in providing alternative views and additional information against which learners can test the viability of their understanding.[4]

Thus, learning is a self-regulatory process of struggling with "the conflict between existing personal models of the world and discrepant new insights" in order to construct new models of understanding.[5] That understanding must be accommodated by society if it is to be viable; an individual's identity (expert, novice, or mad) is developed in relation to "relevant" communities of which she is a part. Thus, a teacher's identity as a professional evolves in large part based on her relationship with members of the teaching community of practice (CoP) with whom she interacts. It is within this CoP that one tests ideas and receives feedback. It is also where more central members provide mentoring to more peripheral participants.[6]

Cognitive apprenticeship emerges out of situated learning theory as an application to educational contexts.[7] With cognitive apprenticeship, the emphasis is on learning that is authentic not only to cognitive tasks but to the environment, community, and context in which it is used. An important part of the cognitive apprenticeship framework is the role of a more knowledgeable mentor. A mentor is one who establishes an engaged and trusting relationship for the purpose of professional development and guidance. Mentors provide opportunities for their mentees to develop competence through cycles of observation, practice, and assessment.[8]

PEDAGOGICAL RESEARCH

This theoretical perspective is consistent with the research findings on the pedagogy of professional development. For example, Desimone, Porter, Garet, Suk Yoon, and Birman, in a three-year longitudinal study, focused on professional development experiences that were associated with teachers adopting a more project-centered teaching strategy. They identified the frequency, time, and characteristics of any professional development that a teacher engaged in over the three-year period and examined the relationship of those characteristics to the teacher's reports of change in practice as validated through classroom observation.[9] Three characteristics associated with a greater use of project-based learning were identified: consistency of the professional development with the teacher's goals and curriculum standards; active learning; and collaboration through teacher networks, mentoring, and study groups.[10]

Kennedy's review of research on professional development practices, like reviews by Richardson and Placier and by Sykes and Bird, identified a fourth characteristic of effective professional development: a focus on content knowledge.[11] A more extensive analysis of the literature by Darling-Hammond suggests that it is not just learning the content domain, but understanding the content domain in the context of teaching—in other words, pedagogical content knowledge—that is most strongly associated with teaching effectiveness.[12] In fact, Shulman notes that teachers need to have not only an understanding of their subject area but also the ability to transform the subject matter in a way that promotes student understanding.[13] In sum, the pedagogical research indicates that professional development must be relevant to the teacher's classroom context and actively involve the teacher in project- or problem-based inquiry in which both pedagogical content knowledge and teaching knowledge are learned. Also, as Blumenfeld et al. argue, this learning must occur over sufficient time to allow for cycles of experimentation and reflection.[14]

While the research literature clearly identifies the critical attributes of professional development, they are seldom realized in the programs offered. What dominates professional development is short, one-shot programs lasting less than eight hours. Parsad, Lewis, and Farris, in a national survey of teachers, report that while 80 percent of teachers participated in some professional development over the course of a year, a majority (57%) reported that it was a program lasting less than eight hours.[15] While 74 percent of teachers reported participating in technology integration professional development, 61 percent reported that the program was one day or less. Similarly, 72 percent participated in professional development on new methods of teaching, but 59 percent were in a program of eight hours or less.[16]

As Richardson and Placier and others note, perhaps the most consistent data on professional development is that these short programs are not that effective.[17] For example, in Parsad et al.'s (2001) survey, technology integration and new methods of teaching were two areas in which teachers felt least prepared: only 27 percent felt well prepared to integrate technology, and only 45 percent felt well prepared to implement new teaching methods.[18]

PRACTICAL CONSIDERATIONS

There are several reasons why one-shot professional development programs dominate, and all the reasons center on practical issues of time and financing. First, sustained participation by a teacher requires an almost Herculean commitment. Professional development, while supporting teaching, sits on top of teaching as another commitment in an already very busy schedule.[19] Second, face-to-face meeting increases travel requirements and the need to coordinate schedules, compounding the time commitment. Third, the need for travel and time out of class greatly increases the expense in administering the program. Thus, many of the "model" programs reported in the literature can only be sustained through major research funding. Finally, many of these programs are based on the framework and skills of a particular individual, and short meetings are what can be managed most easily.

It is for these practical reasons that we, like many educators, have turned to the Internet as a vehicle for delivering professional development. Of course, the growth of online instruction does not necessarily indicate the quality of the instruction. As Duffy and Kirkley note, many view online learning as a threat to education, one that lowers the quality of instruction. However, as they also note, many others view online learning as a highly promising educational opportunity in which the affordances and constraints of the medium not only lead to ease of access and affordability, but also encourage the adoption of more learner-centered teaching practices.[20] These differing perspectives reflect the fact that in online learning, as with traditional face-to-face learning, the instructional quality and level of learner engagement vary widely. Thus, we emphasize that the value of online learning is in meeting the practical needs of cost and access, not in any inherent pedagogical advantage or disadvantage. The pedagogical advantage of any course, online or face-to-face, lies in the quality of the learning experience and architecture. This means modeling and supporting learners in engaging in learner-centered practices.

LTTS LEARNING ARCHITECTURE

Based on the theoretical, pedagogical, and practical issues discussed in the previous section, we identified four design commitments that guided our work in building LTTS. The teacher professional development online learning environment must be

- Relevant to the teacher
- Easy for teachers to access
- Theoretically and pedagogically sound
- Scalable and sustainable (cost-effective)

In describing these design commitments and the underlying principles, we have been willing to sacrifice conceptual elegance in order to be clear as to what we consider essential in our design. Thus, it would be far more elegant to include a commitment to relevance as part of the commitment to theoretical and pedagogical soundness. It reduces the number of commitments and, of course, any learner-centered theoretical framework would include relevance as a fundamental characteristic. However, we call out relevance as a separate design commitment because, in spite of its centrality to theory and in spite of the fact that it is such an obvious requirement, it goes unrealized in many professional development programs. Too often the focus is on learning the new, most important thing with an assumption that its application in the teacher's classroom will be obvious. Or, if there is an application, too often it is a general application that everyone can talk about. But what is at issue is supporting teachers in applying these concepts to their particular classroom; it is the situated interpretation of the concepts that is central to developing a rich understanding. Because this is so fundamental, yet so often missed in spite of the "learner-centered" mantra commonly heard today, we feel it is essential to call it out as a specific design commitment.

While there may be disagreement over the level of description, certainly few would disagree with these four design commitments. We expect they would apply to the design of almost any learning environment. Most importantly, however, the commitments must be interpreted for specific contexts. Thus, the instantiation of these commitments in the design of LTTS as an online professional learning environment is what is critical for this discussion. What follows are 12 design principles that flesh out these commitments as we implemented them in LTTS. As with the design commitments, we have chosen not to try and synthesize several principles to create overarching principles. Our goal is to be explicit in identifying what we consider to be the important principles to which a designer should be attending.[21]

Commitment 1: Ensure That the Materials and the Learning Experiences Are Relevant to the Learner

Relevance is not just a characteristic of the materials used for learning, though of course that is central. Effective design must help the teacher draw linkages between the learning resources and concepts and her classroom, both through the framing of the activity and the support provided to her in moving from theory to practice. There are three design principles that support the relevance of LTTS professional development for teachers.

1. *Situate learning in teaching problems.* The focus is on classroom issues that teachers encounter, often stemming from the curriculum and standards they have to use in teaching. LTTS courses are problem centered: Each course begins with a teaching problem and all learning is centered on addressing that problem.
2. *Provide choices to ensure that a teacher can find the problem relevant to her needs.* In teacher professional development, one size does not fit all. Not all curricular problems are relevant to all teachers. Rather, needs arise from the teaching context. LTTS provides a catalogue of over 60 courses, permitting a teacher to select the course that meets her current needs and goals.
3. *Design the learning activities so they lead to an outcome that can be applied in the classroom.* There is no reason that teacher professional development should not be immediately applicable to the classroom. The ability to apply professional learning is critical. The outcomes of LTTS courses are specific products, such as lesson plans or projects that can be used immediately in the classroom. However, the emphasis is not just on developing these projects for one's own classroom but also on demonstrating under-

standing of the concepts related to inquiry-based approaches to teaching and learning.

Commitment 2: Create a Theoretically and Pedagogically Sound
Learning Environment to Support and Scaffold Teacher Inquiry,
Engagement, and Reflection

As noted earlier, our team committed itself to creating a constructivist learning environment that supports situated learning. Additionally, we examined the professional development literature to identify variables that impact the success of professional development experiences. Based on the theory and research, we committed to creating a problem-centered environment in which the learner is guided through reflective cycles of inquiry. Following are the design principles emerging from this commitment.

4. *Use problem-centered learning as an approach to support teachers' ongoing cycles of inquiry and reflection.* The core pedagogical strategy in LTTS is one of problem-centered learning. Each course begins with a teaching problem (e.g., the challenges of teaching mathematical graphing concepts), and the course centers on using a specific strategy for addressing that problem (e.g., making concepts visible using graphing calculators).

5. *Provide a scaffolded work environment that supports learning, development, and reflection processes.* While problem-centered learning provides many advantages, Hedberg argues that many learners find managing their own learning process and resources to be difficult.[22] Our experience suggests that the limited immersion of distance learners in the learning context creates a need for more scaffolding and structure of the learning process. With LTTS, we sought to design an inquiry environment where scaffolding is used strategically for three purposes. First, the scaffolding supports teachers as they attempt to apply both content and pedagogical principles to the design of their lesson. Second, the scaffolding provides proximal goals to sustain motivation as teachers work through the course. Third, teachers are scaffolded in reflecting on the work and their understanding as they move through an LTTS course.

Two strategies employed in LTTS scaffold learners: (1) Subtasks guide the problem-solving activity and (2) a mentor supports the learner's understanding and reflective processes. The LTTS architecture provides support and guidance for the problem-solving through a series of five to seven tasks, with each task representing a step toward addressing the problem and creating a solution (such as a lesson plan or project; see figure 1). With each task, the learner is provided with a specific aspect of the project

FIGURE 1   WebQuest Task Showing LTTS Problem-Centered Design

TE401

Supporting Internet Exploration with WebQuests:

How do I design a WebQuest to meet my curriculum goals?

Author: Carey Smith

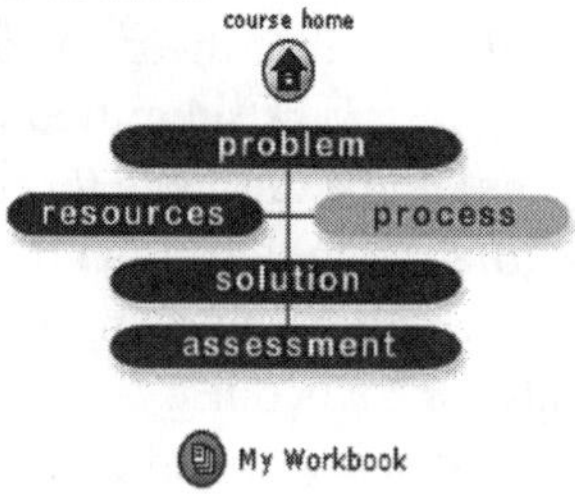

course home

ACTIVITIES

① Explore WebQuests and establish goals for your WebQuest.

② Choose a topic and define a task for your WebQuest.

You are here ③ Create the Introduction for your WebQuest.

④ Identify resources for your WebQuest.

⑤ Develop the task and process sections for your WebQuest.

⑥ Design the evaluation and conclusion sections for your WebQuest.

⑦ Consider additional issues critical to implementation of your WebQuest.

Activity 3: Create the Introduction for your WebQuest.

Having identified your goals, selected a topic, and defined the student task, you can begin creating each section of your WebQuest. In this activity, you will build the Introduction section for your WebQuest.

Task and Guidance

The Introduction section provides an overview of the topic, the goals, and the task for the learners. Most importantly, the Introduction section must make the topic exciting for students from the very beginning. You should take your students' backgrounds and interests into consideration when developing the introduction. How will you capture the students' interests through your Introduction? In addition to sparking students' interest, the introduction should set the context for the Quest by foreshadowing major concepts and principles. The Introduction should build on prior knowledge by explicitly mentioning important concepts or principles that will be critical for students to understand in order to accomplish the task. Consider the following as you develop the introduction:

to develop (such as a list of possible WebQuest topics), guidance on how to approach the task (for instance, examine curriculum goals, standards), and useful resources from the full pool of resources for the course. Given this general strategy, it is the learner's responsibility to apply the core concepts and strategies to create an inquiry lesson for their classroom.

Only through mentoring can we support teachers in linking theory to their classroom practice. LTTS provides a cognitive apprenticeship environment in which the mentor provides alternative perspectives while giving feedback on the teachers' work, always focusing on understanding in the context of the learner's own classroom. While we have experimented with supplementing the human mentoring with an agent, no automated system can provide the necessary personalized linkage to the learner's particular classroom context. Because LTTS mentors are former teachers with expertise relevant to the modules, they can provide the dialogue needed to probe understanding and to promote deeper understanding of the concepts and strategies, offer alternative perspectives on the linkage to the learner's classroom, and help motivate the learner.

6. *Support the teacher in linking conceptual understanding and practical application.* Too often, problem- or project-centered learning focuses on producing the "product" without enough emphasis on understanding the concepts underlying the design of the product.[23] In LTTS, most work submitted by the learner includes both a lesson plan component and a rationale for the strategy reflected in that plan. Additionally, learners complete an end-of-course self-assessment in which they review their product and answer a series of reflective questions designed specifically for that course.

7. *Provide a rich array of resources to support the learners' individual needs.* LTTS provides a rich array of learning resources (an average of 44 per course), permitting the teacher to find resources that are most appropriate to her particular classroom context and interests and to compare approaches represented in those resources. The courses are designed to be a work environment for the learner. There are no assigned or required readings. In order to provide structure, some readings are recommended, but it is always the responsibility of the learner to identify resources relevant to her context. The mentor supports that process.

Commitment 3: Provide Professional Learning Opportunities That Offer Ease of Access and Flexibility

In teacher professional development, the bulk of accessibility issues rest with the commitment the teacher must make to the schedule and time requirements. Teacher professional development should be available as a teacher needs it and has time for it. Three design principles support ease of access and flexibility:

8. *Provide short, focused courses addressing specific issues.* We seek to walk the middle ground between full-semester courses and online resource environments.[24] Thus, LTTS courses are designed to engage the teacher in sustained work but are centered on a single curriculum issue. Courses are designed as one-credit courses requiring about 30 hours of work.

9. *Allow students to work at their own pace.* The Web environment has been heralded as permitting "anytime, anyplace" learning. But what is most critical to teachers is "any pace" learning. Teachers need the flexibility not just to decide whether to work in the morning or evening, but to be able to take a week off when there are particular demands at school, or perhaps to compress work during a period of free time. Self-pacing

is where the real freedom of the Internet rests. Teachers have up to 12 weeks to complete an LTTS course and may move at any pace they wish. Of course, self-pacing means that there is not a cohort involved in a course—again, teachers work in collaboration with the mentor.

10. *Provide just-in-time access.* LTTS provides the freedom to register for the course and begin work at any time, 24-7. If professional development is to meet the needs of the teacher and the constraints she works under, then she must be able to access teacher professional development when the need and opportunity arise—not when someone decides to offer the program.

Commitment 4: Design a Model of Online Professional Learning That Is Scalable and Sustainable

Too many excellent professional development programs are dependent on grant money to sustain even their current level of effort; thus they end when the grant money ends. In our design commitment to scalable and sustainable environments, the focus is on cost-efficiency. Two of our design principles address the two most costly factors in the design and delivery of instruction: mentoring and materials development.

11. *Scaffold the mentoring.* A major design goal is to develop strategies that will increase efficiency in mentoring (currently 3.5 hours per learner) without sacrificing the quality of the interactions. We have done this through two primary development efforts: tools to aid mentors in tracking and interacting with learners, and a conversational agent that can complement the work of the human mentor.

We interviewed several online course instructors and found that the majority of their time was spent on logistical issues that required a substantial amount of time (tracking progress of learners, sending e-mails to encourage completion of tasks, understanding where each learner is in her understanding of key concepts). Thus, in an iterative design process, we developed a series of tools to support those logistical requirements. For example, a mentor can see a complete record for all students being mentored. With each row in a display representing a learner, the mentor can see the time a learner has left in the course, the date activities were submitted and if feedback has been provided, and the last time the learner logged in. Additionally, from that record, the mentor can see the work submitted by the learner, prepare and send feedback, review the course and prior work, send messages that include some pre-specified content, and take notes on the learner and course. This tool and related tools have greatly reduced the time mentors spend on management issues.

We also developed a conversational agent to supplement the work of the mentor in providing information, guidance, and perhaps even motivation.[25] The agent takes the form of a woman who appears on the screen and talks to the learner. The text and movement of the agent are preprogrammed, so several agent files are available. A particular file is programmed to become active in response to specific actions of the learner as tracked through their mouse clicks in the course. Hence, when the software detects the student entering the course for the first time, the agent can welcome the student to the course and provide an orientation. It can also be used to caution a learner if, for example, she is attempting to submit work but has not consulted any of the resources. We are currently developing a test of the benefit of the agent in providing a mini-lecture on learner-centered concepts as they apply to each of the tasks in the course. The agent is being programmed to give the task-specific minilecture when the student first goes to that task. After the agent has been activated and its presentation has been completed, it closes and a small icon remains in the upper corner of the screen. Thus, students can always revisit the advice. Again, the goal is to provide support for routine tasks that then frees the mentor to spend time on discussion, questioning, and providing feedback on the more complex issues of learning.

12. *Provide external resources as primary content.* A rich array of resources is necessary for each course in order for the course to serve a wide range of learners and for the resources to be relevant to the individual contexts of those learners. It would simply be too expensive to write all of the content materials for a catalogue of 60 courses, each of which serves a wide range of learners. Thus we have focused on writing a learning support structure for each course and then identified resources available on the Web to support student learning. Software is used to monitor the links to those resources to make sure they remain active.

EVALUATION OF LTTS

LTTS has been operational since January 2002. The total enrollment has been about 600 learners; however, we have data from only about 300. Learners pay an enrollment fee for which they get a certificate of completion to count toward continuing education units. In this larger sample, most (59%) paid the course enrollment fees themselves; the remainder had their fees prepaid by their district through an arrangement with LTTS. Learners may pay tuition in addition to an enrollment fee to receive graduate credit; 40.7 percent took the course for graduate credit.

The data on learner background and end-of-course evaluation reported in this chapter are based on a subset of 107 enrollments for which we have complete data. Within this sample, 84 percent of the enrollments led to course completion, a rate we are pleased with given the self-paced nature of the courses. Other data on online professional development suggest completion rates of 40 percent to 70 percent.[26] The 90 enrollments leading to course completion represented 73 individual learners, with 10 learners taking between two and four courses each.

Who Enrolled in the LTTS Courses?

Demographics on our learners were obtained from registration data that they completed voluntarily before enrolling in a course. While the bulk of enrollments were from the United States, our learners are from eight countries, including countries in South America, Africa, the Middle East, and Central Asia. The majority of the learners (70%) were teachers seeking in-service professional development, and a reasonable proportion (23%) were preservice students. The majority of the learners (49.3%) were between 26 and 35 years old, and among the in-service learners, 44 percent had between 6 and 15 years of teaching experience. However, a wide range of ages and years of teaching experience were represented. The learners were distributed across levels of schools, with 31 percent, 26 percent, and 44 percent teaching in elementary, middle, and high schools respectively.

We asked learners an open-ended question as to why they took the LTTS course. Two main reasons accounted for over 50 percent of the responses: relevance to their needs (26.8%) and flexibility (29.1%). The responses were consistent for both preservice and in-service teachers.[27] The responses also suggest that our design commitments of relevance and access were important to the learners. Postcourse evaluations discussed later in this section indicate the degree to which learners perceived LTTS as successful in meeting those commitments.

Did Our Learners Learn?

As part of the end-of-course evaluation, we asked learners to use a five-point scale to rate their agreement with the statement "I learned a lot in this course." We also asked an open-ended question as to what they learned. The mean rating was 4.19; 87.8 percent of the learners indicated that they agreed or strongly agreed that they "learned a lot." An analysis of the data indicated that this was true, regardless of their experience with technology or learner-centered teaching.[28] There were 107 responses to the open-ended question of what they learned, with 44.3 percent of the responses referencing a pedagogically related aspect of teaching, such as integrating technology as a tool for inquiry, inquiry approaches to teaching, or authentic assessments. The remaining responses could not be evaluated in terms of the relation to pedagogy because they referred to very specific learning and the pedagogical base was not clear—for instance, learning about online learning.

Of course, the stronger assessment of learning is in the actual performance of the learners—the lesson plan they developed and the rationale they provided for that lesson. The difficulty of grading or comparing this work is that there are many different courses a teacher may take, and within a course the work is tailored to the teacher's classroom. However, we have developed a rubric that can be applied in evaluating any inquiry-based lesson and hence across courses and classroom contexts. It consists of twelve criteria under seven categories, each rated on a four-point scale (see table 1). In one application of the rubric, two raters, after training, were able to score lesson plans with 89 percent agreement.[29] In future work, we plan to use this rubric for looking at pre-/postcomparisons and for comparing different approaches to achieving similar professional development goals.

Did the LTTS Course Impact Teaching Practices?

We conducted a follow-up survey of in-service teachers who had completed a course six months to one year earlier in order to see if they used the lesson or project they developed in the LTTS course in their classroom.[30] We also asked these teachers if the LTTS course impacted their teaching more generally. Of the 51 teachers solicited, only 20 responded. These 20 teachers tended to be older (50% were 45 years or older) and had more teaching experience (50% had taught for 16 or more years). Most of the teachers (75%) reported that LTTS impacted how they teach, with most reporting that they were using more inquiry-based or learner-centered approaches in their teaching. For example, one of the teachers, Jamie, told us, "I now use inquiry and research daily. . . . I now encourage children to dig deeper." Another teacher, Ruth, commented, "The LTTS experience has impacted how I do my lesson plans. I'm more aware of my students and their needs."

Half of the respondents said the lesson they developed in their LTTS course was used in the classroom. All of these teachers indicated satisfaction with the lesson and with the level of student engagement, but several indicated that the lesson took more time than they anticipated, while others indicated a need to modify the lesson prior to teaching. The reasons cited by those not using the lesson in their classroom were far-ranging, including maternity

TABLE 1   Rubric Used to Evaluate Inquiry-Based Lesson Plans

1. *Learner-Centered*
   - The lesson encourages students to be involved in critical thinking decisions.
   - The lesson supports student choice by providing open-ended sections related to pacing, selection of topic, or end design of the end product.

2. *Inquiry-Based*
   - The lesson requires students to address a *semi*-structured question, exploration, issue, or problem.
   - The problem is meaningful to the student and grounded in life and work beyond the school.
   - The lesson provides steps for helping students identify relationships between different topics or subject areas.
   - The lesson helps students develop habits of mind of asking questions about evidence, viewpoint, pattern and connection, supposition, and why things matter.

3. *Engaging*
   - The lesson provides opportunities for *all students* to be actively engaged in constructing, connecting, and applying their knowledge.
   - The lesson requires a high level of interaction, communication, or collaboration with others.

4. *Consistent with Goals/Objectives*
   - The lesson goals are consistent with an inquiry-based/problem-solving outcome.

5. *Appropriate Assessment Strategy*
   - To what extent are nontraditional (individualized; based on work task) assessment strategies described?

6. *Role of the Teacher*
   - To what extent does the lesson describe how the teacher supports student inquiry?

7. *Use of Technology*
   - To what extent is technology used as a tool to support student inquiry?

leave, being at the wrong time of year for the lesson, and not having the necessary technological support or skills.

We also have data on expected transfer to the classroom from our end-of-course evaluations. We asked learners to indicate their degree of agreement with these statements: (1) I will use the product from the course in my classroom; (2) I will be able to apply the approach to other activities in my class; and (3) I expect the LTTS learning to impact my teaching. Based on the analysis of the 107 enrollments, the mean rating across these three items was 4.31, where 5 indicated strong agreement.[31] Clearly, there was a strong expectation that the learning would be applied. As with rating the degree of learning, these results were consistent, regardless of reported previous experience with technology and with learner-centered teaching practices.

How Did Learners Learn?

Within any learning environment, it is not possible to know all the details of how learners approach learning. However, we examined the click stream data of a contiguous sample of 59 LTTS learners to look at their online learning strategies.[32] Click stream data are records of the time and the location of every mouse click a learner makes. From that data, we can infer what objects in the course the learners went to and how long they stayed with those objects.

We examined eight variables, reflecting both the learners' overall approach to the course and their specific learning strategies within the course. The overall approach was defined in terms of the overall length of time online, average time between sessions, calendar time to complete the course, and total number of sessions. The learning strategy within the course was defined by the proportion of time spent with the resources, the portion of resources used, the portion of time spent on feedback from the mentor, and the extent to which the learner moved linearly through the tasks.

Using cluster analysis, we identified three types of learners: (1) mastery-oriented, (2) task-focused, and (3) minimalist in effort. The mastery-oriented and task-focused groups constituted 59.3 percent and 22 percent of the sample, respectively. Both these groups took what can be interpreted as an active and serious approach to their online work. They spent a large proportion of their time (about 25%) on the learning resources and looked at a high proportion (almost 50%) of those resources. Further, they tended to explore the course rather than progress through it linearly. What distinguishes these two groups from one another is the amount and distribution of time spent online. The task-focused group tended to spend less overall time on the course and to concentrate that time in a narrower window of calendar time. Hence, while engaging in effective learning activities as judged by the within-course actions, they viewed the course as a task to be completed, and they worked efficiently at the task.

The minimalist group spent the least amount of time online, and their click stream data did not suggest a learning orientation. The little time they did spend was distributed over more than two months on average. They moved linearly through the course and spent less than 10 percent of their time on the resources, looking at only 16 percent of them. Bonk describes one of the "myths" of online learning to be the perception that "online courses are easy," and indeed, distance-education practitioners often discuss learners

TABLE 2   Importance of Design Features as a Function of Teaching Experience

Mean rating (and standard deviation) on a 5-point scale (5 = very important) of course components as a function of teaching experience.

Teaching Experience	Resources Valuable	Mentor Helpful	Activities Relevant	Self-Pacing Important
High (6+ years) (N = 33)	4.21 (0.78)	4.48 (0.71)	4.33 (0.79)	4.76 (0.50)
Low (1–5 years) (N = 27)	4.15 (0.77)	4.44 (0.70)	4.30 (0.82)	4.63 (0.84)
None (N = 13)	4.00 (1.22)	4.23 (1.09)	3.69 (1.25)	4.00 (1.29)
All (N = 73)	4.15 (0.86)	4.42 (0.78)	4.21 (0.88)	4.58 (0.85)

who expect the experience to be not very demanding.[33] This may characterize the expectations of our minimalist group.

In sum, the analysis of online learning behavior suggests that the vast majority of the learners (81.3%) took the learning task seriously, making use of the course resources and spending a considerable amount of time online.

How Did Learners Value the LTTS Course Design Features?

Were the instantiations of the LTTS course design principles valued by the learners? Were they perceived as helpful to learning? We asked learners to rate their degree of agreement with a statement of the importance of each of four key design features: (1) the value of the resources provided in the course, (2) the helpfulness of the mentor, (3) the relevance of the activities (guided problem-solving), and (4) the importance of self-pacing. The mean ratings by our sample of 73 learners as a function of teaching experience are shown in table 2. Those with no teaching experience included both preservice students and other non-school-related professionals.

As can be seen in table 2, all four design features had mean ratings of over 4 points on a 5-point scale, except for the rating of the activities by those learners with no teaching experience. Additionally, the data show a clear and consistent trend for those with more teaching experience to rate the components of the courses higher. Because of the negative skew of the ratings, we used a square transformation of the scores to conduct a series of one-way ANOVAs of the ratings, with teaching experience as the independent variable. The results indicated that the effect of teaching experience was only significant for self-pacing ($F = 3.94$, $df = 2.70$, $p < .03$) with the "no teaching experience" group having lower ratings of the value of the self-paced component.

Earlier we argued that learners who are at a distance, like teachers in the schools, need greater flexibility in their learning environment. While learners on a campus value flexibility, they are still in a schooling environment with regular classes and a semester system. We would expect them to value self-pacing, but not as much as those teachers in the schools. The ratings certainly are consistent with our expectation.

We also pursued learner judgments of the design of the course through three open-ended questions asking what teachers felt helped their learning most, what they liked most about the course, what they liked least, and what changes they would recommend for the course design. We received 110 responses to the question of what was most helpful, but two primary features accounted for 77 percent of the responses: (1) mentoring (44%) and (2) course resources (33%). The only other characteristic to be referenced in at least 10 percent of the responses was the structure of the course (10.9%). Hence, when learners were able to freely state what they valued most about this learning architecture, the LTTS mentoring within a cognitive apprenticeship model found strong support, as did the option of having a rich set of online resources. We must emphasize that resources were reported as most helpful to learning. This is interesting given that there are a wide variety of resources, only a portion of these resources are relevant to a given learner, and none of the resources are assigned.

We received 127 responses to the question of what the learner liked most. Two primary features accounted for over 50 percent of the responses: (1) self-pacing (33.1%) and (2) mentoring (20.5%). Other characteristics that were most liked, accounting for at least 10 percent of the responses, were (1) a final product that can be used (11%) and (2) the resources (10.2%).

We received 100 responses describing what learners liked least and what changes should be made to the course (learners reported more than one characteristic). The dominant response to what they liked least was "nothing"—16 percent of the learners actively stated that there was nothing they did not like about the course. Of actual characteristics mentioned, only two involved 10 percent or more of the responses: (1) lack of interaction with other learners (10%) and (2) the amount of time and effort required for the credit offered (10%).

The lack of interaction was something that we anticipated might be a significant criticism of our courses. While we have one-on-one interaction with the mentor, there are no other learners available to discuss concepts and teaching issues in the course. To assess the importance of peers, we asked learners if they would prefer working with other learners; only 27 percent of the learners indicated that they preferred or strongly preferred to work with other learners. However, 51.23 percent indicated that they preferred *not* having a peer group. These ratings, along with the open-ended responses, suggest that although peer interaction can be important, it is not an overriding issue for the learners, at least in the context of this type of online professional learning experience. Indeed, learners rated the importance of self-pacing very highly, and self-pacing is generally inconsistent with a cohort environment. The LTTS courses are advertised as self-paced, and to some degree learners are self-selecting. However, their preference for self-pacing persisted even after taking the LTTS course, suggesting that they did find self-pacing effective. This conclusion is reinforced by the low dropout rate of only 16 percent.

REFLECTIONS ON LTTS AND ONLINE TEACHER PROFESSIONAL DEVELOPMENT

Earlier we argued that based on the literature and our theoretical framework, four design commitments are critical to the effectiveness of professional development:

1. Ensure that the materials and the learning experiences are relevant to the learner.
2. Create a theoretically and pedagogically sound learning environment to support and scaffold teacher inquiry, engagement, and reflection.
3. Provide professional learning opportunities that offer ease of access and flexibility.
4. Design a model of online professional learning that is scalable and sustainable.

Each of these commitments was instantiated in the LTTS architecture through 12 principles. While much of the evaluation of LTTS is limited to learner self-report, the findings are extremely positive. In a survey of a small sample of teachers who had returned to their classroom, half reported using the lesson they developed in LTTS, and 75 percent reported that the learning experience affected their teaching practice. The click stream data suggest most learners were invested in the course, making extensive use of the resources and exploring the course. In the course evaluations, most learners reported a high level of learning and satisfaction at the end of the course. Indeed, 16 percent wrote that they would not change anything in the design of LTTS. In sum, the careful attention to principles that instantiate these four design commitments seems to have led to an effective professional development environment.

In closing this chapter, we would like to reflect on two issues related to the development of LTTS: (1) the role of community and (2) the commitment to sustainability. In designing LTTS, we faced a tension between our theoretical beliefs about the importance of a peer-based collaborative learning environment—a community—and the practical need of allowing teachers the flexibility to move at their own pace. We saw the "class" of learners as providing a community that would offer mutual support in the development of understanding and in motivating learning. Most importantly, we saw the classroom community as serving to validate or challenge thinking about teaching—that is, contributing to the development of each member's identity as a teacher. However, practical needs clearly made group learning impossible. Thus, we turned to one-on-one mentoring, in which a knowledgeable peer was committed to coaching the learner in linking conceptual understanding to his or her application in the classroom and to sharing experiences as they might relate to the learner's classroom.

In discussions with colleagues, we often heard strong criticisms of LTTS because there were not peer groups in a class. As we probed the reasoning for this, there seemed to be a basic assumption that having a peer group was important, and that the mentor (who was a more knowledgeable peer) was not an adequate alternative. Colleagues perceived that the group's being in the same class environment generally created a camaraderie and fostered the sharing of stories, both of which our colleagues viewed as essential to learning. But the reasons for this are not clear to us. We can certainly see the potential value of a peer group, but we can also see the peer group as potentially distracting and leading to superficial discussions—offering high social satisfaction but a low level of learning. This gets to the core of the issue: Is learning with a group critical to effective professional development?

We have given considerable attention to this issue, especially since we held a similar view in the initial design stages. In the early phases of LTTS, we tried to create collaborative linkages between learners in different courses and between learners at different places in the same course. However, the feedback was decidedly negative. Learners were task-focused, the mentor was supporting them in that task, and that task was relevant to their classroom. They viewed any collaborative activity as distracting or beyond the task.

This experience has led us to question our initial thinking about the role of a classroom of peers. In fact, Barab and Duffy questioned whether a group of learners coming together temporarily for a particular event, such as a short-term class, should even be considered a community.[34] As they note, a community has a history and has future goals. Perhaps most importantly, a community continues as people move in and out and as members move from peripheral participation to more central participation. These character- istics of community, not just the simple presence of people from the same profession, are central to identity development. Indeed, the classroom peer group may more reasonably be considered a community of practice in which the practice is being a student. While this peer group may have some impact on the teacher's identity, the communities of practice that are truly critical to identity as a teacher are more centrally based, in the teacher's state, district, and school, and, in particular, in those people with whom she has ongoing interactions.

We acknowledge that teachers often do not have a strong local commu- nity of practice. They work behind closed doors and seldom have the time, or perhaps the inclination, to share teaching practices. However, simply cre- ating a classroom group is not, in our mind, creating a community of prac- tice. The shortcomings of the community of practice call for support action at the local level. Schlager and his colleagues, after much effort to support a national and even world community of practice through the online envi- ronment Tapped In, seem to have come to a similar view.[35] The work with Tapped In has now progressed to the use of the online environment as a dis- trict tool to support teachers in sharing their practices.[36]

Aside from questions of community, it is not clear to us that the classroom peer group is always or even typically a positive factor in learning or motiva- tion when compared to our mentoring model. This is particularly true in pro- fessional development, in which the goal is to learn concepts and to apply the concepts to each learner's individual context. Working in a peer group can easily result in thinking at too general a level, one that encompasses all of the teachers' contexts but consequently provides a more shallow under- standing. In the peer setting, teachers can talk about the application to their individual contexts, but it will take considerable discussion for other learn- ers to situate themselves in that context. In essence, the peer group can easily become a distraction from a teacher's thinking about the concepts in relation to her own course.

Quite frankly, we are surprised at this evolution of our thinking. However, it does lead us to realize that the theoretical work on classroom peer groups (or collaborative learning in general) needs to be articulated in considerably more detail.[37] Also requiring greater articulation is the linkage between the conceptual framework of communities of practice and classroom learning environments.[38] Indeed, we think one of the major issues in collaborative learning is to ensure relevance of the interactive experience—both from the perspective of the teacher in the class and as indexed by the learning that occurs. In our own work, we are interested in looking at the effectiveness of a consultative model of peer learning. As in the LTTS model, there would be a strong theory-practice linkage, with each teacher studying the course in reference to her own classroom. Multiple learners would each be involved in their own theory-to-practice learning within the given course context. However, the learners would have responsibility to consult one another, providing critical input. This would not be collaborative, and thus there would be no need to come to agreement. The teacher developing the project would decide whether the consultation is useful or not. This model is similar to the Learning Circles model and in our mind is more in keeping with how communities of practice actually function.[39] Of course, from our perspective, the benchmark for effectiveness would be the mentor-based model of LTTS.

We turn now to the issues of sustainability. LTTS was a research project supported by the U.S. Department of Education. One of our key goals was to assure sustainability. We think we have built a sustainable and scalable environment. We have our own learning management platform (written in Perl) and use our own Apache server; hence we can easily modify the environment and capitalize on lessons learned. We have spent considerable effort in building tools to support mentors, and we think that the use of the conversational agent makes virtual mentoring more effective and efficient. Of course, the success of a consultative peer-learning model as described above would create even greater efficiencies, though the human mentor would still play a significant role.

These successes notwithstanding, we failed to attend to one critical aspect of sustainability: marketing. As good researchers, we focused on the quality of the learning experience and assumed that if we built the "right" system, the learners would come. Not so. Enrollments at the moment cannot sustain LTTS in the long run, and we are a year past the end of the grant money. So there is no pocket of funding to support a major marketing effort. We have made attempts at marketing and finding a person to join the staff as a marketer, but it is difficult to find someone locally who has the knowledge of both teacher professional development and business marketing. Furthermore, we simply do not have the funds at this point to support any materials development for marketing. We feel this failure to plan for marketing is a very important lesson to share. Our field should be making a difference, and certainly the environments we build should make a difference. However, the work most often ends when the funding ends, and we are seldom able to institutionalize our major projects. It is not only maintaining the project that is important, but maintaining a research platform from which we can study the design concepts instantiated in that project. As a consequence, even the concepts frequently fail to have staying power once the project ends. While there are many reasons for this, we feel an early partnership to support marketing and institutionalization should be a critical component of any major project.

In closing, we emphasize that LTTS design is focused on professional development environments. While the design commitments would be the same, we would expect different principles would instantiate the commitments for a regular school environment. For example, our strategy of mentoring would likely not work in a regular school, since the teacher in the school is not a more knowledgeable peer. Similarly, our analysis of the role of communities of practice and classroom communities reflects a focus on professional development. In the regular school there is continuity with peers, and there is a history, and there are future goals that are part of the schooling process. That is, the school is a community of practice of which a particular class is simply representative of one of the practices within that community. Furthermore, the peers and the goals typically extend beyond the school to the community life, and thus the school and the role of peers in identity development also need to be understood in terms of the larger community.

CHAPTER 10

Teachers' Domain Professional Development[1]

Ted Sicker

WGBH Educational Foundation has developed a set of online professional development courses for K–12 teachers as part of its larger Teachers' Domain digital library initiative. WGBH's team offers a range of educational media skills, including video, interactive, online, and print, along with expertise in curriculum and professional development. We work in collaboration with professional development experts and academics to produce each course. A centerpiece of the WGBH approach is to embed rich media drawn from our productions into the courses to enhance adult learning, and we expect that teachers who learn using rich media are more likely to transfer this experience to their classroom practice—that is, they learn with the media they'll later use in their teaching.

The Teachers' Domain Professional Development (TDPD) courses are an outgrowth of two major streams of work that we have pursued over the past decade:

- *Teachers' Domain (TD):* Teachers' Domain is a media-rich digital library for classroom use. It contains collections of video segments, interactives, images, audio segments, and documents, drawn primarily from WGBH public television productions. Video segments are typically three to five minutes in length, often reedited and renarrated to match K–12 curricular needs. Some of the materials in TD come from partner organizations, and some are newly produced for the service. Each media resource is supported by a resource page, which presents a background essay that provides the teacher (or upper-level student) with context for understanding the content of the resource, discussion questions, and correlations to state and national standards. Lesson plans use many of the resources, modeling best practices and use of rich media in the classroom. Funding for this project has come primarily from the National Science Foundation as part of its National Science Digital Library initiative, allowing us to develop collections in life, physical, and earth and space sciences, as well as engineering. Additional funding from the Institute for Museum and Library Services and the Open Society Institute allowed us to develop a smaller civil rights history collection. Teachers' Domain has been available online for free since late 2002 at www.teachersdomain.org.

- *Professional Development Video Libraries and Workshops:* With funding from Annenberg/CPB, the NSF, and other sources, WGBH has produced videotape libraries and workshops documenting best practices in science, math, social studies, reading, and foreign language. Unscripted "fly-on-the wall" videos capture teachers from across the country, bringing to life elements of standards-based teaching practices as well as other specific teaching strategies and methodologies. We also developed supporting print and, later, online guides to use in face-to-face or self-paced professional development sessions or in more formal courses.

COURSE MODEL

In 2002, WGBH received funding from a philanthropist to create a series of online professional development courses in science. His intent in giving us the funds was to create a professional development experience, first in elementary science and, later, in middle- and high school science, that would bring teachers up to competency levels in content knowledge and methodology skills. His vision was to excite teachers about science through the power of rich media from public television, so they in turn could do the same with their students. As of September 2005, courses are complete in life science for all three levels, and in physical science at elementary and middle levels. High school physical science will be ready for the market by the end of 2005. The courses are structured in both eight-session, 45-contact-hour versions and two-session, 15-contact-hour modular versions. As with all our educational projects, WGBH has worked with outside content developers and advisors to generate the course curricula. In-house staff members oversee all editorial aspects of the courses—conceptualization, organization, voice, tone, and final polishing—and develop and run the production and distribution infrastructure.

STRATEGY FOR EDUCATIONAL IMPROVEMENT

Teachers' Domain Professional Development courses aim to improve the knowledge and skills of individual participants. The elementary and middle school courses are primarily content-oriented: The goal is for participants to increase their own content knowledge so they can better teach the content and skills appropriate for their student population. At the same time, we expose participants to a range of explicit methodologies and metacognitive strategies that they can apply to their own teaching practice. From research and focus groups, we know that many K–6 teachers are generalists and may have inadequate training in science; or, if they have studied science more extensively, they may still be teaching outside their area of expertise. In the high school courses, we do not attempt to teach higher-level subject-matter content, but instead allow participants to use self-reflection and inquiry-based learning to examine the content they teach and come to understand new ways to teach it. We encourage participants in all of the courses to consider new approaches and make modest, practical changes to the lessons they teach. We implicitly encourage participants to use the sort of rich media they've experienced in their learning—if not the same digital library resources—with their own students.

BALANCE OF CONTENT AND SKILLS

As mentioned in the previous section, elementary and middle-school courses are built by assessing the most critical areas of subject-matter knowledge for teaching science at those levels. Content developer and advisor input, along with the Science Content Standards (chapter 6) of the National Science Education Standards and national and state credentialing guidelines, inform the course content. We then develop content by drawing from a range of sources, including rich media and readings, and present it in an activity sequence that also incorporates hands-on activities.

As the team produces the course, we create opportunities for participants to reflect on their own experiences as learners both in and out of the course. Our goal here is for participants to gain insight into their own thought processes about the content and then to apply their insights to examining and understanding student thinking. We include several video examples of student interactions and responses for participants to reflect on and compare to their own experiences with students. We also include several "lab" activities where participants work with a small group of their own students to explore student thinking.

Course sessions highlight a range of instructional practices, including "surfacing" and building on prior knowledge, using effective questioning, making predictions and reconciling prediction and observation, using models, setting up "fair" experiments, using evidence to defend a position, and integrating technology. Activities are structured so participants can experience these practices as well as view them in action through classroom video examples. Underlying all course content is inquiry-based, constructivist learning and a self-conscious exploration of the metacognitive strategies employed.

Course activities help participants develop formative assessment skills, since effective learning depends upon assessment of the learner's status at the beginning of the process and at specific points along the way. The results of formative assessment can help teachers shape and reshape lessons in progress. One irony, given the publishing infrastructure of the online course environment, is that while a facilitator can refocus attention or suggest modifications in assigned work, the course itself is static, unable to change in response to the individual participant's progress with the material.

Classroom management is not a specific focus of the courses, but in reflections and group discussion, participants can consider how they might apply what they have read or observed in video examples to their own situation.

The multifaceted activities in the course address principles of universal design for learning. The content is presented in a range of ways—video, interactive, hands-on exploration, and reading—giving participants numerous ways to acquire knowledge. They can reflect on and express their understanding in multiple ways as well, such as in discussions, in more formal written assignments, in projects, and in their classroom applications. The approach of the course models what we hope participants will go on to use in their classrooms to address the needs of diverse learners.

PRIMARY METHODS OF TEACHER LEARNING AND DISTRIBUTED LEARNING MODEL

The structure of the TDPD courses is based on the assumption that adults, like children, acquire knowledge by building upon what they already know and constructing it in their own way. Accordingly, each course session follows a five-part learning model based upon the BSCS 5E instructional model (engage, explore, explain, elaborate, evaluate).

1. *Invitation*
    - creates interest in a particular content topic;
    - gives learners a clear view of the purpose of the lesson; and

- uncovers each learner's prior knowledge so that he or she is aware of existing understanding.

2. *Exploration*
   - provides learners with a common base of information on particular aspects of the topic through hands-on activities, Teachers' Domain resources, and readings;
   - involves learners actively in the learning process; and
   - models one or more metacognitive strategies for learning and understanding that learners will encounter throughout the session.

3. *Explanation*
   - provides opportunities for learners to offer and discuss their own explanations of what they explored;
   - provides learners with feedback on their explanations through comments from the course facilitator and other participants or through resources or readings that offer a scientifically valid way of explaining the content; and
   - enhances scientific vocabulary for effective communication.

4. *Application*
   - provides learners with the opportunity to apply what they've learned earlier in the session to a new instance or to their own experiences; and
   - provides learners with the opportunity to see how people other than themselves have applied what they've learned to a related situation.

5. *Putting It into Practice*
   - reviews the metacognitive strategies and content from the session; and
   - provides opportunities for learners to apply metacognitive strategies to their teaching experiences.

Each session of a TDPD course includes a similar set of learning activities as it progresses through the five-part structure outlined above. Participants work through the session page by page. Each page provides one or more of the following:

- instructions for reflection
- TD resources of all five media types
- articles, short essays, and book excerpts in PDF format
- journal writing opportunities
- hands-on activities
- discussion board prompts
- writing portfolio assignments

In some instances, custom features, such as online polling or click-to-reveal hints and answers, add additional opportunity for phased interaction with the content.

The courses are designed for an entirely online, asynchronous, facilitated experience, requiring about one week per session, but an individual or a group can also use them as self-paced, nonfacilitated study. In these scenarios, participants can print out their assignments to submit to appropriate organizations for credit. Except in a pilot run, WGBH has not offered the courses directly, but instead licenses them to a presenting institution, such as an intermediate service agency, a school district, a public television organization, or a university. The presenting institution determines the schedule for completing tasks and the criteria for evaluating performance.

Discussions take place in the Forum. Each session includes a discussion about the session's topic and related teaching and learning issues. Prompts peppered throughout the session encourage participants to add to the discussion and to respond to and build on each other's ideas. In the eight-session versions of the course, there is an ongoing discussion concerning the final assignment. The course facilitator or designated contact can post assignment schedules and other pertinent information on an announcements board. Participants can discuss information or ideas, questions, problems, or general thoughts on teaching and learning in a free-form "Passing Notes" board.

The Portfolio is where participants can save and submit written work and discuss it online (in blog format) with the facilitator. Each session includes approximately two portfolio assignments, short essays in which participants synthesize and apply what they have learned in the session. Often, one assignment is content-oriented while the other is about methodology or lesson ideas. The Portfolio also can include a "Compare Your Answers" feature, where participants can write a response to a question and then compare their response to a sample answer provided by the course developers.

An eight-session course includes a final curriculum design project in which participants develop a set of activities on science topics for students at their level, adapt a lesson they currently teach, or, if more ambitious, design a new lesson based on their experiences with content and methodology in this course.

A facilitator's guide gives guidelines for running the Forum discussions and for evaluating written assignments. In the future, we hope to develop rubrics for assignments and discussions that facilitators or accreditors can use to evaluate participant performance.

Approaches to presenting materials in the courses were developed by our academic advisors and are based upon the literature for professional development and on how people learn, including the works of Loucks-Horsley, Bransford et al., and Black et al.

An outline of our philosophy includes these points:

1. Start by surfacing learners' prior knowledge before drawing them into learning new subject matter.
2. Use metacognitive strategies that help them monitor their own learning, including

   • Self-assessing prior knowledge
   • Making, investigating, and analyzing predictions (comparing their predictions with the results to see where they differ, seeking an explanation, making a new prediction)
   • Writing descriptions or making drawings, charts, or concept maps (checking to make sure that they have completed all the required labeling or annotation for the drawing or description; whether their language or diagram communicates what they want to get across in adequate detail; whether a peer can understand what they've recorded)
   • Using feedback to monitor their level of understanding (using questions, comments, or comparative answers from peer discussion, the facilitator, or the course itself in Compare Your Answers to find the impetus to think more clearly about their understanding of a subject)
   • Finding, using, and analyzing evidence to back up an opinion or a hypothesis (checking whether they have backed up a statement or idea with evidence; deciding whether the evidence makes sense; considering whether they could have come to a different conclusion based on the same evidence or if there is another plausible explanation)
3. Provide feedback on their thinking whenever possible.
4. Give learners a sufficient bank of knowledge to allow them to use it effectively.
5. Challenge learners to increase their level of knowledge, since people learn most when they're "at the edge of confusion."
6. Provide opportunities for learners to explain concepts in their own words, since people learn effectively when they need to teach a concept or present it to others.
7. Use assessment approaches that help learners develop metacognitive strategies for self-assessment, in addition to providing content-based responses for those who evaluate them.

TYPE OF INFRASTRUCTURE

TDPD courses use WGBH-developed infrastructure, which allows instructional materials to integrate seamlessly with the Teachers' Domain digital library. A sign-on brings participants or facilitators into Teachers' Domain, where a link to "My Courses" brings them to the list of courses in which they are enrolled. At present, the licensing institution informs TD staff of user enrollment; then the TD staff sets up account privileges. Participants and facilitators (as well as "lurkers" such as evaluators) gain differing levels of access to the course environment, such as the ability to post to certain discussion boards, to view or comment on Portfolio assignments, and to track which assignments have been submitted or commented on (and by whom). To get the most out of the course, participants should have a broadband connection and a recent computer with a standard browser and plug-ins (Flash and QuickTime), because of the embedded video and interactive materials. Otherwise, no special software environment is required.

At present, uploads to the course environment are text-only, which imposes some limits on the kinds of materials that participants can share in discussions or submit as assignments. For instance, while several sessions include diagramming or concept-mapping activities, the current environment does not provide a way to upload any electronic representation of these materials. Should funding become available, we will improve this aspect of the service.

We explored using an off-the-shelf learning management system such as Blackboard or WebCT, but found the structure of these products did not allow us to fully integrate content, access to rich-media resources, discussions, and Portfolio features. We experimented with porting one course to Blackboard in a potential licensing situation, but the resulting course environment, though providing essentially the same material and activity sequence, was very disjointed. Unfortunately, the trial did not yield much data about how the learning management system affected student or facilitator involvement.

COURSE IMPLEMENTATION

Participants are expected to devote about six to eight hours of work per session, spread over one or two weeks. Participation includes working through all activities presented in the session and, in some cases, completing supplementary readings that may add additional time. We encourage a merger of theory and practice, but we do not expect participants to try out a new teaching strategy or content concept as part of an actual classroom lesson while working through a session. A participant may not be covering that content or may not even be in the classroom while taking the course; if they are in fact teaching the topic, they may find it difficult to integrate new instructional materials or methods midstream. Very consciously, we include several lab activities participants can try out with one student, a small group, or student surrogates, so that they can then report back on the results of these activities in discussions.

At present, high-quality enactment is left up to each licensing institution to develop and monitor, although if further evaluation were to be funded, the potential evaluator has proposed ways to ensure fidelity of facilitation through trainings and monitoring of implementation.

RESEARCH AND EVALUATION

In 2003, WGBH engaged Deborah Muscella of muscella.com to formatively evaluate a pilot version of the first TDPD course, Teaching Elementary Life Science. The first four sessions of the course were pilot-tested with 16 teachers in April and May 2003. The last four sessions were tested in October and November 2003. At the time, a key research objective, in addition to determining course quality and impact, was to examine whether the course would be effective for both a more standard, facilitated delivery and a less formal, self-facilitated study-group approach.

The evaluation had five goals:

- Determine if the course enhanced teachers' knowledge of life science;
- Discover if teachers perceive themselves as using inquiry teaching or enhancing their practice of inquiry teaching through their participation in the online course;
- Profile the backgrounds of course participants in science;
- Compare the participation of teachers in a course facilitated by an instructor and a nonfacilitated course; and
- Assess teachers' perceptions and experiences in participating in the online course.

To address these questions, Deborah Muscella developed the evaluation protocols shown in table 1.

What follows is a summary of the results from the pilot study, arranged topically:

TABLE 1 Evaluation Protocols for the Course "Teaching Elementary Life Science"

	Spring 2003	Fall 2003
Teachers' Knowledge of Life Science	Pretest Responses to course assignments	Pretest Responses to course assignments
Teachers' Perceptions of Their Using Inquiry Teaching	Pretest Telephone interview	Pretest Telephone interview
Teachers' Background in Science	Pre-course questionnaire	N/A
Participation of Facilitated and Nonfacilitated Course Participants	Analysis of online conversations Telephone interviews	Analysis of online conversations Telephone interviews
Teachers' Reported Experiences in Participating in the Online Course	Telephone interviews E-mail between individual teachers and staff	Telephone interviews E-mail between individual teachers and staff

The curriculum

- Teachers felt the entire curriculum package, including videos, readings, resources, and Web links, was a powerful tool for learning.
- Complex concepts such as DNA and cell mitosis and meiosis were understandable because video or other media illustrated concepts presented in the readings.
- The media sparked curiosity. After watching a video, teachers read the background essay on its resource page to delve more deeply into the particular concept portrayed or to clarify their thinking.
- Kindergarten teachers were challenged by the material, since it wasn't readily apparent how to implement the content in their classroom, but they persisted because of the compelling nature of the course design.

Teachers' knowledge and attitudes about life science

- Intellectually challenging content stimulated teachers' learning.
- Despite highly challenging content, teachers felt the course design allowed them to rise to the challenge.
- Teachers who expressed some discomfort with their own knowledge of science showed the most change between their pre- and post-tests.
- Several teachers reported instances of changing their attitude about the science content.

Influence on teaching

- Being learners of life-science content and watching inquiry learning in practice allowed teachers to consider their own teaching without having to immediately change their practice.
- The plot study (an ongoing, hands-on activity in which teachers returned each session to observe a specific aspect of a chosen plot of land) validated the power of observation and the appeal of using such an approach with students.
- The video clips of inquiry classrooms modeled exemplary practice without judgment and enabled teachers to confront real or imagined deficits in their own teaching practice.

Forum discussions

- After the initial spring sessions, teachers reported that the online forums were not focused enough. WGBH then developed more focused prompts for each discussion instance. As a result, teachers participated more often and produced more substantial posts.
- Some teachers found the requirements for online discussions time-consuming; however, even these teachers found reading the responses of their colleagues helpful in their own learning.

This initial formative evaluation informed further course development, in which we followed the basic approach established for the original pilot course. While no additional formal user evaluation has taken place, early marketing of the courses showed that while intermediate service agencies were eager to offer the courses, the teachers they served were often reluctant to sign up for the full eight-session, 45-contact hour experience. Accordingly, we have developed an alternate version of the four courses completed prior to spring 2005, in which the material is segmented into two-session, 15-contact-hour courses. These are being offered to the market in fall 2005. While sequential, these modular versions do not depend upon each other, although we recommend that a participant be familiar with the content presented in an earlier course before taking a later one in the series. The newer courses will also be offered in both versions.

FUTURE PLANS FOR EVALUATION

Looking ahead, WGBH is exploring grant opportunities to work with EDC/CCT to evaluate the impact of Teachers' Domain Professional Development courses and resources on teacher content knowledge, teachers' ability to use rich media, and ultimately the impact of the resources on student achievement. Another focus would be to examine how the intensiveness of professional development impacts teacher and student outcomes. Using graduated levels of exposure to professional development course modules, the evaluation would determine how intensive the professional development experience needs to be to show evidence of impact. If funded, EDC/CCT will use an experimental design, randomly assigning teachers to a control group or one of four treatment groups, taking one shorter course module, two modules, three modules, or four modules.

Depending on whether the courses are offered in a facilitated or self-paced manner, EDC/CCT has proposed two approaches to deal with issues of fidelity. In the facilitated approach, they will develop measures of fidelity for the professional development modules and examine the extent to which professional development facilitators are implementing these activities with fidelity. In the second, they will use nonfacilitated versions of the courses, where participants will follow a self-paced model, having access to Forum discussions but no requirements to participate in them. EDC/CCT also will develop indices of fidelity for teacher participation in the Teachers' Domain courses and field-test these measures with a small separate sample of teachers.

Control teachers will be asked to carry out their instructional activities as they would normally. They will participate in the project during a two-year period for which they are serving as the control. Treatment group teachers will implement module 1 in the first semester of the first academic year; module 2 in the second semester of the first academic year; module 3 in the first semester of the second academic year; and module 4 in the final semester. Treatment group teachers will be asked to respond to instrumentation at various times over the two years, even if they are no longer participating in a Teachers' Domain module.

Data will be collected and appropriate instrumentation developed in three primary areas: teacher content knowledge, teachers' use of rich-media resources, and student achievement. We also will obtain general demographic information on the teachers and measure the fidelity of the professional development experience.

To measure changes in teachers' content knowledge over time, EDC/CCT will use two forms of assessment. First, they will draw on praxis-like items to assess teacher content knowledge. They will also develop scenarios to place the teacher in the type of authentic situation that they might face in the classroom. Teachers will be asked to diagnose a student's understanding or misconceptions on a particular problem; to cite evidence, in response to a sequence of probes, for their determination; to specify questions that they might ask to help the student address the misunderstandings, and to define strategies to help remediate the problems. Scoring rubrics will be designed and parallel forms of the scenarios will be constructed for each content domain.

To examine whether teachers' use of rich media changes over time, EDC/CCT will collect data through teacher surveys and logs of how and how often teachers use media-rich resources. They will construct a brief instrument that asks teachers to record incidents that relate to the use of media resources and will ask them to note how often they access the Internet, the Teachers' Domain website, their use of other Web-based resources, and the frequency with which they use various technologies to enhance their instructional activities. EDC/CCT will ask if the materials are used as a core part of the class or in a more supplementary way. They will also monitor whether teachers are using the resources as add-ons to their existing lessons, for diagnostic purposes, for remediation activities, or for other reasons. They will ask if the materials are being used in whole-class settings, in small groups, or among individual students. WGBH will make available navigational data, providing information based on users' registration, about the number of assets each teacher accesses, the number and kinds of videos and other files they download, and other data relevant to their rich-media use.

Student achievement will be measured in a pre-/post- format by using released items from NAEP assessments across differing levels of difficulty. Using the NAEP items also will enable EDC/CCT to compare the performance of the students in the study with that of a nationally normed sample. In addition to the standardized achievement tests that provide indications of impact on student learning, they also will determine the extent to which there is impact on student perceptions of how their teachers' classroom practice is changing. They will administer a brief questionnaire to middle- and high school students about their teachers' teaching and their teachers' use of rich media. To account for achievement differences among students and classes they will examine the standardized assessment measures used in each district in the study. To the extent possible, they will standardize across the different tests to create a proxy measure for previous student achievement, which they will use as a covariant to control for the potential differences in achievement or ability level across classes.

SCALABILITY, COST-EFFECTIVENESS, AND SUSTAINABILITY

WGBH's marketing strategy for the Teachers' Domain courses features a licensing model through which organizations across the country are authorized to deliver the courses in ways that best fit their unique needs. Through licensing, an organization has maximum flexibility to determine its own course timing (including start and end dates) and participant mix. Because courses can be delivered on a local or regional basis, staff developers have the opportunity to gather participants during or after the course for other related professional development activities.

Our pricing structure provides quantity discounts for licensing multiple courses to encourage wide distribution and repeat orders. The fee for each type of distributor is based upon the general breadth of educational population served (for example, specific pricing for an individual school differs from pricing to a district). Each distributor is free to set its own prices to the participant, allowing it to meet the organization's particular goals, whether they are mission-oriented or financial.

WGBH expects that licensing fees eventually will cover the costs of operating and marketing the entire Teachers' Domain service. Where possible, local organizations offering the service, including other public television stations, will host proxy servers to reduce direct bandwidth costs. The business plan does not assume that revenues will cover the development of new courses or of new support resources; WGBH will continue to seek grant funding for such activity.

Processes Supporting the Regional Evolution of Effective Professional Development

Milwaukee's Initiation of a Professional Support Portal

Ilona E. Holland, Chris Dede, and Kathy Onarheim

THE PROBLEM: EDUCATIONAL WOES LINKED TO INADEQUATE PROFESSIONAL DEVELOPMENT

The evolution of the Milwaukee Public Schools' Professional Support Portal (PSP) began at the turn of the millennium. In 2000, the Milwaukee Public Schools (MPS) system was the 27th largest school district in the country, serving over 103,000 students in 165 locations. It was also one of the nation's poorest; over 75 percent of students received free or reduced-price lunch. As table 1 indicates, like other urban districts Milwaukee has a diverse and socially challenging demographic to educate.

Data from the 2001–02 school year showed that the majority of the population was African American, with a rich diversity of Latino, Asian, Native American, and other nonwhite populations. Additionally, a sizeable population had a learning disability or limited English proficiency. The achievement of this student population was low. Depending on the calculation formula used, graduation rates for 2002–03 ranged from 60.7 percent to 36 percent, indicating a great loss of human potential.[1]

TABLE 1   Milwaukee Public Schools Enrollment Data for 2001–02, in Percentages

African American	58.9
Latino	16.5
White	15.9
Asian	5.1
Native American	1.0
Other nonwhite	2.3
Students with disabilities	15
Students with limited English proficiency	7.5
Students receiving free or reduced-price lunch	>75

Low student achievement was not the only problem facing the district: Teachers were leaving at a high rate. In 1993–94, Milwaukee hired 173 new teachers (3% of the teaching workforce) to replace those who had retired or left for other reasons. By 2001–02, Milwaukee was hiring approximately 1,000 new teachers a year, with 10 percent of the teaching force resigning annually. In particular, new teachers (those with one to five years in the field) were leaving the district in droves; the district's data collection measures are incoherent, but an approximate estimate is that by 2005, 37 percent of the new teachers who entered the district in 2000 had already left. With baby boomers nearing retirement age, the district anticipated its retirement rate would increase steadily, exacerbating the problem of finding, inducting, and retaining new teachers. Furthermore, as more and more teachers were new hires, traditional face-to-face professional support programs, such as experienced teachers mentoring new teachers, were no longer scalable or sustainable.

The problem of low student achievement was partially due to these difficulties in teacher retention, as well as to related issues of teacher quality. A constant stream of new teachers inexperienced in working with the MPS student population—many still learning the fundamentals of their profession—was undermining the quality of instruction. As is typical in many urban districts, policies developed in collective bargaining with the teachers union meant that inexperienced teachers new to the district were frequently placed in the most difficult teaching situations, further worsening both the teacher-retention rate and student achievement. Resources allocated to manage this situation through the conventional professional development methods MPS had traditionally used were clearly inadequate and could not stretch any further.

Teacher improvement, with an emphasis on new-teacher induction and retention, was a crisis that demanded immediate attention. By lowering the rate at which teachers were leaving the district, MPS estimated it could save a considerable amount of the money expended on the recruitment and induction of new teachers—as well as increase student achievement through providing a more experienced and consistent teaching force. More-effective professional development was also seen as a mechanism to improve the quality of teaching overall in the district, thus reducing student dropouts and raising educational outcomes. All these factors provided political and financial incentives to expend resources in evolving a new approach to professional development that would increase teacher induction, retention, and quality.

PART OF THE SOLUTION: A PROFESSIONAL SUPPORT PORTAL

Strategy for Educational Improvement

School failure, like school success, is a process, not an event. In 2001, the conditions within the district were right for the germination of seeds of change. The district superintendent was a forward-thinking one flanked by district leaders and staff who had vision, know-how, connections, and creative ideas. Attempts to move the district from a troubled status to one of smooth, successful operations began with the involvement of all stakeholders, including schools, teachers, families, the community, business leaders, the state, and external experts. A National Technology Advisory board was assembled to provide expert guidance and direction in the application and scaling of technology as a part of improving teaching and learning; one of the authors cochaired this advisory board with John Morgridge from Cisco.

Business and community leaders, as well as local institutions of higher education, were brought together to form the Milwaukee Partnership Academy, a new citywide organization whose mission was to identify and enable opportunities for collaborations and support in changing the way MPS worked. Funding from the Joyce Foundation enabled experts from Harvard and EDC to work with MPS across distance. Through broadband telecommunications, Internet-based videoconferencing, and virtual collaboration tools, these experts were able to address issues of professional development, leadership, evaluation, and portal design and implementation.[2] Under the guidance of the district's chief information officer, technology teams charged with improving professional development through computing and telecommunications were created, composed of experienced teachers and technology-fluent staff.

Together the stakeholders began to revise the view of the future for MPS and how the district might eventually achieve its goals. The concept emerged of developing a Web-based professional support portal that would promote teachers' flexible thinking and collaborations while ensuring opportunities for access to information, experts, and colleagues. Central to the idea of this portal was building on the district's existing successes in professional development by creating a virtual umbrella under which current strengths and new externally guided insights could merge.

Assumptions and Goals Underlying the Portal Design

The portal project is driven by the assumption that enhanced teacher quality would lead to improved student academic achievement. This assumption is based on several premises: The first premise is that if teachers feel connected with each other, the community, and the district through collaborative processes centered on building skills for educational improvement, their motivation for quality instruction will increase, and they will feel less isolated and more empowered to attain expert teaching. A second premise underlying portal development is that if teachers are actively supported in developing their own definition of quality instruction, they will strive harder toward achieving that ideal. A third premise is that if all students are to develop twenty-first-century skills for a global knowledge-based economy, then their teachers must also attain (1) personal efficiency in learning skills (thinking and problem-solving, information and communication skills, and interpersonal and self-direction skills); (2) competence in using information and communication technologies (ICT); and (3) proficiency in using assessment and feedback mechanisms that feature personal reflection as well as expert and peer evaluation.[3] Portal developers believe that if all these conditions are met, teacher induction and retention rates will improve and overall quality of instruction will rise.

The portal design recognizes that teachers need a safe and supportive environment in which they can apply new knowledge to real-life contexts and everyday problems. This strategy requires diverse representations of knowledge integrated with a wide array of learning tools and administrative applications and presented within the context of broad communities of practice and learning. Also, unlike more traditional professional development programs, the vision for the portal project's success includes the entire Milwaukee community. Student achievement is not seen as the teacher's job and the child's challenge, but rather everyone's opportunity to contribute to mutual growth, learning, and success. Although the particular problem of teacher retention and induction served as the immediate impetus for the portal's initiation, learning within the community is the beacon toward which the portal has been continually guided.

Such an ambitious approach to professional development requires a convenient and flexible mechanism to support teachers' growth as inquirers, learners, collaborators, coaches, communicators, and networkers, as well a design that supports and encourages adult learners' needs for professional respect and autonomy. To be effective, teachers also need just-in-time information of all kinds (such as lesson plans, forms, case studies, and articles on pedagogy), access to centralized online administrative systems (such as an electronic grade book), and mechanisms for collegial support (such as online discussion groups or mentors) available at any time of day.

From the perspective of other stakeholders, parents need a flexible and convenient vehicle for communicating with schools and teachers about their children's progress, as well as for learning about an array of topics such as the district's academic expectations, homework reports, reading lists, specific academic content, lunch offerings, and sports schedules. Building principals need a means of sharing their vision for academic success and a coherent, centralized building-oriented delivery system. The district central office needs a centralized venue for standard procedures and forms to ensure their timely distribution, access, and completion, as well as an easily accessible format for support services scalable for cost-effectiveness.

Overall, if children are to become better learners and higher achievers, everyone in the district and the community needs to be able to work more efficiently and effectively. A portal provides a solution for encouraging and sustaining this complex amalgamation of services.

THE CURRENT STATE OF THE MPS PROFESSIONAL SUPPORT PORTAL

What Is a Portal?

On the surface, a portal looks like a website, but it differs from a website in three fundamental ways. First, a portal permits each user to personalize the presentation and organization of information that appears on the screen. In essence, an end user can determine the priority of information being shown at any time. For example, teachers may want their homepages to welcome them with lesson plans designated for that day. An administrator, on the other hand, may want his or her personal calendar to appear first.

Second, a portal offers the functionality of supporting online collaboration. A portal incorporates space where multiple users can post shared documents, leave comments for each other on an asynchronous bulletin board, or have synchronous chats. Thus, a portal enables types of virtual collaboration that complement face-to-face activities.

Third, a portal can offer a smorgasbord of tools and applications, all accessible through a single login and overarching interface, enabling the user to move among them without interruption. In contrast, websites do not provide any of these affordances. To achieve the vision and goals described earlier, developing a portal was essential, even though no prior examples in districts existed to provide a model for this design.

MPS Portal Infrastructure

The MPS portal is supported by a commercial platform created by Plumtree. Plumtree provides commercial portal solutions to connect disparate work groups, IT systems, and administrative processes (see http://www.plumtree.com). This application of the portal solution is relatively easy to use and provides a variety of customized work spaces, called portlets, through the "My Page" design strategy, as shown in figure 1. Specific resources are linked to community discussions as well as to collaborative tools for creation, implementation, problem-solving, and analysis of effectiveness.

The information structure is designed from the user's point of view rather than from the organization's perspective. Therefore, the portal is constructed in tiers for its users. Customizable portlets can be nested and linked to meet individual professional needs. Figure 2 exemplifies specific user-customizable portlets created around the daily operational tasks of a school librarian.

Through the portal's My Pages feature, as shown in figure 2, a librarian is no longer isolated from others who have the same responsibilities but can interact professionally across distance to access information on a just-in-time basis, to build collaborations, to participate in projects, and to receive and offer professional support.

The community structures reflect a variety of working groups. Communities are created by classifying 1,039 job codes into six categories: teachers, new teachers, school administrators, district administrators, support personnel (degreed, certified, or licensed staff who do not have direct student assignments), and support staff (such as clerical, facilities, and food service workers). Each work group has its own community designed around needs and functions. Work-group communities are created with specific standard defaults as a foundation (for instance, a collaboration page that has announcements, shared documents, a calendar, and collective discussions) and are encouraged to grow based on specific needs that participants identify.

FIGURE 1   My Pages Customizable Portlets

The information structure is designed from the user's point of view rather than from the organization's perspective. Therefore, the portal is constructed in tiers for its users. Customizable portlets can be nested and linked to meet individual professional needs.

FIGURE 2   A Librarian's My Pages

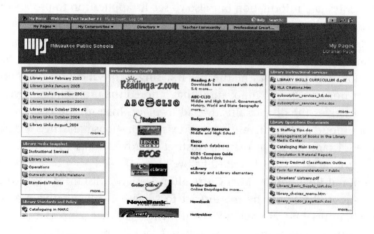

Finally, the Knowledge Directory (shown in figure 3) offers users visible and accessible connections and alignments to specific resources—strategies for assessment, related communities, relevant information, additional portlets that can be accessed or added to My Pages, and contacts or experts in the content areas being explored. The Knowledge Directory is a repository

FIGURE 3   Knowledge Directory: Searchable, Dynamic Repository of Resources

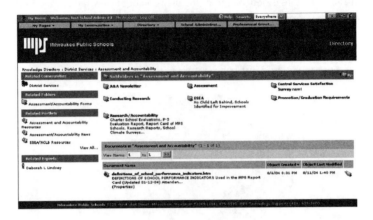

of interconnected content and resources. Through the Knowledge Directory, the portal emphasizes not only easy access to professional development services but a connectivity among resources that interweaves presentational material and human expertise. The Knowledge Directory helps the user not only to assimilate information but also to see its application to professional practice and knowledge building.

By design, the MPS Professional Support Portal supports a wide variety of technology initiatives from both within and outside the district. Since its conception, the portal has neither been a single consolidation of internal resources nor an external innovation that ignored the professional development initiatives the district already had in place. Instead, the portal epitomizes a unique and creative fusion of existing in-house and new external resources. Examples of preexisting district-approved tools that were integrated into the portal are described below.

The portal incorporates MPS Curriculum Design Assistant (CDA), which is an in-house tool used by the district to "create a collaborative environment where teachers are able to post/find lessons that support their day-to-day work in classrooms. This Web-based tool (http://mpscda.milwaukee.k12.wi.us) is continuously accessible. When used in the creation mode, the CDA guides its users through lesson design options that are research proven, searchable and standards-based."[4]

Tapped In is also available through the portal. Tapped In (http://Tapped In.org/Tapped_In/web/about.jsp) is an external, Web-based, real-time virtual learning environment designed to enable community and continuous professional development with anytime, anywhere access. Educators can extend their professional growth beyond courses or workshops with Tapped In online tools that enable them to work with and learn with colleagues and experts. Powerful communication mechanisms such as synchronous and asynchronous discussions—coupled with support tools such as white boards, sticky notes, and Web-page viewers—allow educators to build and sustain communities of practice.

Finally, Teachscape, a commercial professional development venture (http://ts2.teachscape.com/html/ts/public/), provides examples through video case studies of standards-based lessons taught in urban elementary school classrooms. These videos showcase exemplary teaching, highlight sophisticated pedagogies, and facilitate personal and collective reflection.

Method for Teacher Learning

Although the portal provides access to numerous tools, its primary mechanism of teacher professional development is based on the model of learning communities as put forth by Bielaczyc and Collins.[5] Learning can occur in isolation, but the MPS PSP is designed to encourage collaboration and learning from and with others. The portal embraces the notion that school is a community of learners in which everyone—including teachers, principals, parents, and students—participates in both teaching and learning. In its current initial phase, the portal's emphasis is squarely on teacher professional development and retention. However, the portal project team intends to guide further design through development strategies based on support that encourages distributed and collaborative learning not only among participants within a particular building or district, but also among participants in the greater community and beyond.

The portal supports the tenets of strong learning communities by enabling (1) interaction with those with diverse expertise, (2) a focus on a shared objective of continually advancing collective knowledge and skills, (3) an emphasis on learning how to learn, and (4) mechanisms for sharing what is learned.[6] The Milwaukee PSP is consistent with what Bielaczyc and Collins note about classroom learning communities: "In a learning communities approach there is also the notion of a community identity. By working toward common goals and developing a collective awareness of the expertise available among the members of the community, a sense of 'who we are' develops. In the absence of a learning culture that builds a collective understanding and views its members as learning resources, most classrooms fail to develop a strong sense of community identity."[7] The portal is designed to scale these insights about community learning from the classroom level to the district level.

As teachers change their perceptions of themselves from "answer-filled experts" to "accomplished novices"[8] and begin the process of learning anew, they develop skills that can enable lifelong learning for themselves as well as for their students, while at the same time building a culture of professionalism and collegiality. In order to facilitate this type of knowledge building and to establish a basis of collaborative groups who would inform the development of the portal, Milwaukee developed a cadre system for new teachers, hosted on Tapped In. In 2002 and 2003, through the use of Title IID funds and state competitive grants, respectively, 150 new teachers were given laptops with 24-7 tech support and full connectivity. In exchange for the computers, the teachers agreed to participate in online communities, use the portal as it was being developed, and provide feedback for needs assessments and formative evaluations to inform the further development of the project.

Each cadre is a group of new teachers with two leaders, who are experienced teachers. Cadre sizes range from 11 to 26 teachers. The groups are each composed of a mix of members from the novice to the expert, from the inexperienced to the seasoned, from the "lurker" to the active participant. The cadres are closed communities that others cannot join without consent of the facilitator, and online and face-to-face meetings are attended by members only. These sessions provide a safe place to take risks, expose misconceptions, find people who play similar roles, admit ignorance, share experiences, offer resources, and build knowledge. The cadres not only serve as a vehicle to encourage buy-in for other aspects of the portal project, such as the knowledge directory, but also provide psychosocial support for new teachers, in hopes of increasing induction and retention.

HOW IS THE PORTAL UNIQUE?

Boundaries

A notable difference between the portal and other professional development initiatives is that its boundaries are different. Most professional development efforts have a defined beginning and a clear ending point. A course starts one week and ends a certain number of weeks later. A program is available during certain months of the year only. In contrast, the portal does not expire or conclude; its services and community supports are available every day of the year, any time of day. Participants are provided the autonomy to use as much or as little of the site as they wish. They can engage in "legitimate peripheral participation" or can make this their central means of learning and collaborating. Individual teachers can decide what to do and when to do it, and each person may or may not choose to tell others about his or her work.[9] The portal is based on the assumption that if teachers are treated more professionally they will find greater enthusiasm and motivation in their work. Most other professional development initiatives do not support such an unbounded experience.

The boundaries for professional development content are also different for the portal than for more conventional approaches. Content is not limited to core subject matter, pedagogical strategies, and assessment practices but includes information needed for day-to-day administrative and management skills. Part of the service of the portal is that it offers a mechanism for standardizing and simplifying the delivery of information to all MPS teachers, yet at the same time fostering an individual's leadership and sense of community.

Milwaukee was and still is a decentralized school district. Therefore, much decision-making occurs at the building level. Consequently, numerous forms, standard procedures, applications, and documents were produced, stored, and accessed in a multitude of locations. Keeping track of and gaining access to these applications, forms, and procedures presented a challenge to everyone. New teachers, in particular, were overwhelmed and fearful that they might miss important dates, fail to submit required forms, misuse applications, or be remiss in completing expected administrative tasks. These pressures were exacerbated by different buildings having different expectations, and by the central office constantly announcing new policies and procedures. The portal provides the district with a means to preserve the culture of local autonomy while at the same time offering a uniform method for delivering information and professional development in an accessible, consistent way across all schools.

Reciprocity

The portal is neither a course nor a program but a professional resource that supports teaching and learning by supporting authentic learning communities. These communities contribute to the portal's growth and development while at the same time tapping into its rich assets and networks. The greater the contributions by its participants, the more the portal can grow and the more responsive it can be. Thus, the portal is built on an important reciprocal relationship with its end users, a relationship that the district must foster to succeed in its goals.

Content is developed and posted by fellow learners (teachers, staff, specialists, administrators, experts, and, in the future, parents). Knowledge accrues and is refined over time. The portal supports the provision of core content, lesson plans, examples of pedagogy, assessment practices, case studies, courses for professional development, management tools, library resources, central services, synchronous and asynchronous discussions, informal chats, and online presentations. Online communication skills are developed through both online and face-to-face training sessions. Classroom management and pedagogical skills are modeled through video case studies, are discussed in cadres, and are the topics of online events, all available through the same portal mechanisms. All resources and information are archived to encourage both collective memory and the ability to sense and respond to shifts in participants' purposes and needs.

Challenges

Content is not prescriptive, but rather responsive in nature. Professional needs expressed by participants drive both the content posted on the portal project and the workshops offered in support of the portal. The challenge is to remain abreast of the needs of the community and to provide relevant information and training to enable professional growth and understanding. This task is daunting, and it is one of the issues that has slowed the evolution of the portal. The core issue is the proverbial chicken-and-egg conundrum: Without users there will be no content, and without content there will be no users. Since the portal is very young, the content on the portal is limited and is constantly being developed and posted. Consequently the odds are that when individuals visit the portal, they may not find what they need. If users do not find the portal to be useful, they will stop visiting the portal and providing feedback on what they need. This can result in a lack of awareness of newly developed portal content, a lack of interest in the portal, and a consequent diminishment in content development itself. If there is no call for content, there is no incentive to create it.

Finally, although the district had been focused on enabling and encouraging teachers, staff, and administrators to post content, an additional challenge will ultimately become the removal of outdated and inaccurate content. Removal of content is not typically the responsibility of participants involved in professional development, but a communitywide portal requires community cooperation and the shared responsibility to keep it up to date and accurate. Sometimes, deciding what to remove can be as challenging as knowing what to create.

Bottom-Up Development

Although the original incentive for the portal took root in the district central office, circumstances altered the portal's developmental course. Within the first year of its inception, the superintendent left and, with him, many of the core gifted staff. As is often the case, new leadership brought new priorities. Consequently, the seedling was moved "outdoors." Fortunately, however, the stakeholders' portal project team and the technology team stood ready to tend to it. The decisionmaking center shifted, and the portal became a grassroots initiative informed by outside experts, businesspeople, higher-education faculty, parents, teachers, and administrators. This shift further solidified the vision of building a true community of learners and set the tone for deeper collaborations. Portal development became the result of extensive stakeholder interactions with the portal project team.

Paradigm Shift

Ultimately, the success of the portal relies on a major paradigm shift in school district culture and the total integration of all district departments. Few professional development projects require such extensive involvement and commitment. As Sheehan and Jafari have noted:

> Portals present unique strategic challenges in the academic environment. Their conceptualization and design requires the input of campus constituents who seldom interact and whose interests are often opposite. The implementation of a portal requires a coordination of applications and databases controlled by different campus units at a level that may never before have been attempted at the institution. Building a portal is as much about constructing intra-campus bridges as it is about user interfaces and content. Richard Katz (2000) sums it up concisely: "A portal strategy is difficult and perilous because many on campus are weary and suspicious of another new enterprise-wide information technology initiative, and because portals, by definition, require across-the-institution agreements on approach and design that are hard to achieve in loosely coupled organizations like academic institutions."[10]

The challenging observations put forth by Sheehan and Jafari were fully realized in Milwaukee. Many district staff could not see the purpose for recasting information that already existed in drawers, on shelves, and in peoples' memories and making this material available on the portal. Why did HR suddenly have to work closely with content developers? Why should teachers become content developers when their class responsibilities already consumed all their time? Why should the math department talk with the special education division? Dede has noted that "the fundamental barriers to employing new technologies effectively for learning are not technical or economic, but psychological, organizational, political, and cultural."[11] Having to position a paradigm shift while simultaneously building online communities and developing portal content is an incredible challenge that most professional development initiatives do not have to face. However, this very integration of services, and the construction of bridges between "silos," is itself a crucial element for district improvement.

GOALS FOR THE PORTAL

Fundamentally, the portal is designed to achieve four basic outcomes. The first is to address the immediately pressing problem of teacher retention. The goal is to *reduce teacher attrition* by leveraging resources to provide effective induction services and to better support new and experienced teachers through online mentoring, access to information, and opportunities for distributed knowledge building.

The second goal is to *support the development of a community of learners* that eventually extends beyond the limits of school building personnel. This would result in venues within the portal for exchanges with a variety of external stakeholders—such as parents, business leaders, and educational experts—in order to increase collective understanding and to extend students' learning beyond classroom settings and hours.

The third goal is to *change districtwide educational practice and culture* so that all information would be centralized and staff could work more efficiently, effectively, and coherently to support knowledge building and contribute to improved student performance. This goal includes the challenge of scaling the portal to serve approximately 7,000 teachers. The pervasive and overarching fourth goal is to *increase student achievement.*

These goals are not readily attainable. They will take time, they will necessitate major shifts in the ways people work and think, and they will require "negotiated accommodation."[12] Before these goals can be realized, the portal must be embraced and adopted by the various constituencies within the Milwaukee Public School District. This initiative is currently in the midst of that adoption process.

In discussing the needs of teachers, Dede stated that "A major challenge in professional development is helping teachers 'unlearn' the beliefs, values, assumptions, and cultures underlying schools' standard operating practices."[13] Altering deeply ingrained and strongly reinforced rituals of schooling within an entire district takes a great deal of effort, coordination, patience, planning, and support. This does not occur in one magical moment, but it can take place gradually yet systematically through fostering professional communities.

EVALUATION OF THE PORTAL PROCESS

Over the course of the last three years, evaluation efforts have focused on formative assessments. Most of the evaluations have been small in scale (with approximately 30 to 40 respondents) and have been directed at gathering reactions to specific portal features, identifying participant needs, or getting feedback on the perceived value of workshops, training sessions, or online events. These evaluations generally took the form of online and face-to-face surveys, online tasks with e-mailed return comments, and guided discussions across distance with the Harvard evaluator via videoconferences.

Although the portal was officially unveiled in August 2004, it has yet to be fully adopted. Since the goals are ambitious and require the cooperation of so many, only initial and partial forays toward full implementation have been accomplished. Therefore, it is premature to conduct summative evaluations. Formative evaluations have provided MPS with data to inform decisions and have surfaced and highlighted newly developed ideas, features, and opportunities for potential participants.

MPS has focused its more recent formative evaluations on best practices for portal adoption. Informal and formal evaluations have centered on *business processes* (including the identification of tools and training needs, informal discussions with stakeholders about potential portal usage, and formal interviews with district leaders about their perceptions of the portal), *content development* (including feedback about informational needs of new teachers and assessments of quality assurance for posted lesson plans), *community building* (including training preferences, workshop assessments, and feedback on online facilitation), and *marketing the portal* (including a districtwide awareness survey, as well as guided discussions about issues of scaling).

The portal project team has worked hard to respond and adapt to changing needs as these became apparent, while remaining responsive to guidance of several stakeholder groups as well as to the advice of outside experts. Since the findings from formative evaluation are not highly generalizable, we will highlight only those evaluations that had the greatest observable impact on the portal's progress, were more unusual, or involved the greatest number of individuals.

Business Processes

By 2004, the portal project still was not an announced priority of the district central office and the new superintendent. This was of concern because a lack of executive sponsorship was an obvious potential cause for failure of this initiative. "Someone outside the portal project team needs to be excited about the portal. . . . This sponsor should secure funding for the project, articulate a clear message about the need for the portal, and resolve organizational roadblocks that limit adoption of the system."[14] Although MPS had the support of outside stakeholder groups for the portal, this initiative was suffering from a lack of sponsorship from the district office. Without this support, critical departmental integration would languish, and many obstacles would remain unmoved.

To address this problem, face-to-face interviews with five members of senior management, including the superintendent, were conducted by the evaluator to assess perceptions of the portal and how the central office thought the portal might best be used. The interviews occurred in 2005 after the members of the administration had a chance to see the portal fully designed.

The purposes of the interviews were threefold. First, these discussions were to acquire insights into how senior management envisioned the role of the portal and its usage. Second, interviews assessed potential areas of interest about the portal upon which further communications could be built. Finally, the interviews served to share information about the portal itself with key personnel.

Findings from the interviews included the discovery that the central office was strongly motivated by the conviction that "information is knowledge, and knowledge is power." Since the portal's inception, the portal team had been stressing the portal's potential for addressing educational communities and practice. The portal's logo reflected this emphasis with the words "The Way Milwaukee Works." A disconnect was now detected: The district central office was not as much interested in how the portal would change the way MPS worked as it was in the information that would be available to MPS and the knowledge that could be built. The portal project team immediately changed their presentations to stress the importance of information and knowledge.

As a result of this shift, within a few months the superintendent had asked for a personal training session in the use of the portal and had sent a letter to all departments informing them to send forms and procedural information to the project portal team for posting, since he was taking the official MPS website off the Internet and replacing it with the portal. Of course, the interviews alone were not responsible for this shift in attitudes, but the information delivered through them provided an alternative communication approach and portal emphasis that proved to be effective.

Content Development

As was stated earlier, without content the portal was neither helpful nor engaging. In order to ensure that content would be relevant to participants, several surveys and guided discussions were conducted over distance by the evaluator. The results from these feedback mechanisms were essential in determining the initial selection of content topics in 2003, as well as subsequent efforts in 2004 to extend this content to meet the needs of a gradually growing group of participants.

For example, a frequent request from teachers was to have access to high-quality lesson plans that were relevant and clearly connected to both state standards and the MPS learning objectives. To ensure the quality of lesson plans available through the portal, the user was provided with direct access to the Curriculum Design Assistant and to the Knowledge Directory.

The CDA now guides a teacher through the steps of creating an effective lesson plan based on standards. Immediate access to standards and to resources such as Bloom's taxonomy and Gardner's multiple intelligences assists teachers in looking at their practices and communicating the connections and alignments for others to replicate.

The CDA has processes that provide a built-in quality check on the design of effective learning environments for students. Upon initial completion, a plan is submitted to an online process of peer review based on a four-point rubric. Each reviewer reads the plan and provides comments and questions, which the system then e-mails back to the primary author. Holistic scoring is used; once a consensus score is recorded, the plan is tagged as Blue Ribbon, Quality, Needs Work, or Oops. The system attaches a discussion and note area to each plan that allows teachers to communicate with one another about their work. Feedback guides the revision process, and ratings are applied. The program is utilized by teachers on the building level as well as by preservice teachers. This feature offers the opportunity for continual growth, structured expert evaluations, and professional interaction.

Currently, the CDA has approximately 3,600 plans in its database. Seventy-eight are Blue Ribbon plans; 2,300 are Quality plans; 800 are Needs Work or Oops plans); and 422 are backlogged awaiting review due to early technical problems.

Community Building

Although the portal's development was slowed by several setbacks (the portal also required a midstream shift in platform vendors), the portal project team steadfastly prepared the way for the development of a community of learners by building the cadre system. Formative evaluation was used to assess facilitator and teacher needs, gather feedback on discussion topics and on the quality of training, determine strengths and weaknesses of cadre interactions, and assess the usefulness and comprehensibility of specific online professional development events. Formative evaluation was used so frequently, in fact, that some cadre facilitators integrated the evaluation process into their meeting structures, creating their own instruments modeled on those that had been provided to them

The instrument that proved to be most useful, however, was a self-assessment tool for online facilitators. MPS struggled with the issue of how to help facilitators realize the areas in which they needed to improve. In reading transcripts of the cadre discussions, it became apparent that different facilitators needed to develop different skills. Even though the portal project team did not wish to single out any of the facilitators and make them feel inadequate or self-conscious, facilitators themselves needed various types of targeted, individualized professional development. As cadre membership had climbed to over 400, the need for effective facilitators was a constant concern.

In 2003, a group of participating new teachers were asked to identify those competencies that they thought were necessary for an effective online facilitator. Based on their responses and on a review of the literature, a list of 15 competencies for an effective facilitator was created. A self-assessment tool was developed the following year and distributed via e-mail to all facilitators.

The 15 competencies were divided into three categories: professionalism, relationship skills, and content delivery. The facilitators were each asked to rate their abilities in each competency on a three-point scale (advanced, proficient, or needs improvement). They were also asked to identify in writing one strength in each category, and one way they could grow in relation to each category.

In order to encourage honest reflection and to minimize the feeling of being judged, the cadre leaders did not turn in their written responses. Instead they brought their completed self-assessments to a face-to-face meeting facilitated via videoconference by the evaluator in April 2004. After an extensive discussion, each cadre leader submitted a completed worksheet indicating three competencies that they would like to target for improve-

TABLE 2   Competencies Listed Most Often by Cadre Leaders as Needing Improvement

Question: List three competencies below that you would like to target for improvement and strategies you would use for improving each.

Competency Needing Improvement	Percent	Number of Respondents (N = 34)
Shares information, resources, and ideas with other cadre leaders and MPS staff	44	15
Provides reminders about PSP and district events	35	12
Exhibits proficiency with Tapped In and is able to assist others	29	10
Models behavior that supports healthy and active online interaction	26	9
Posts monthly discussion questions accurately and on time	26	9

ment. Table 2 presents those competencies listed by at least 25 percent of the cadre leaders.

In addition, cadre leaders identified strategies that they thought would lead to the improvement of each of the competencies. To improve their ability to share information, facilitators frequently mentioned the need to spend more time in responding to cadre leader comments, to post more often when cadre questions arose, and to schedule time to focus on resources and research. Strategies for improving their competency at providing reminders of PSP and district events included making an effort to check the calendar more regularly, posting reminders the day before, and encouraging cadre members to share important dates. In order to become more proficient with Tapped In, facilitators acknowledged needs to ask for help from others and seek technical assistance, to spend more time practicing and exploring, and to attend more training sessions. Both the list of competencies needing improvement and many of the suggested strategies later served as the basis for planning training and online events for 2004–05.

The portal project team found that the implementation of a self-assessment was also useful in facilitating interactions with the human resources department and the teachers union. An assessment tool that was not a top-down evaluative judgment was a welcome shift in district culture, as the teachers were able to evaluate their own abilities. The tool also became a validation for decisions made, showing that decision-makers care about what teachers think. Even those teachers who were not invited to return to serve as facilitators next year left feeling appreciated and glad to have participated. The self-assessment helped clarify the skills required to be a facilitator, providing individuals who did not possess these skills, or possibly even the desire to improve them, with a graceful exit.

Finally, the instrument served as a model for other incentives within the district. In the beginning of the 2004 school year, principals decided to use this model to create a self-assessment tool to help evaluate their own efficacy. This type of repurposing leveraged the work of the evaluator, as skills and materials were being transferred to new contexts.

Marketing the Portal

In January 2005, MPS and the evaluator conducted an awareness survey of the portal. In order to demonstrate growth in portal usage over time, a baseline measure of portal awareness and usage had to be determined soon after the official launch of the portal. Although the findings were not particularly surprising, the results clearly indicated the next direction for the portal initiative.

The survey was conducted with 25 schools in the MPS district. A stratified random sample was created using four categories (elementary, middle, high, and other). Representation reflected the proportional distribution of schools within each category in the district. Administrators, teachers, and support staff ($N = 1,148$) participated in the survey. A total of 1,021 surveys were completed (a return rate of 90%). Most of the respondents were classroom teachers or support teachers (92%), and the remainder were support staff and administrators.

Participants were asked a total of 19 questions that centered on Internet usage, familiarity with the portal, participation in portal training sessions, and specifics about portal features. The findings revealed that, although 81 percent of the respondents were comfortable using the Internet and most (63%) used the Internet at least once per day, only 27 percent had ever used the portal. Of those individuals who had, most (61%) had used it only once or twice.

The majority of respondents (54%) had either never heard of the portal or had never seen it. Of those who had, almost one-third (30%) had learned of the portal through formal announcements and demonstrations. Only 19 percent had become aware of the portal through peer conversations. To make matters more challenging, of the 272 individuals who had used the portal, only 28 percent found it to be useful in doing their work and only 17 percent though it was helpful in connecting with colleagues.

These results indicate an immediate need to integrate the portal more fully into the life of MPS and market its value. As Sullivan notes, "It is probably safe to assume that the ultimate users of the portal are too busy to browse and explore the new system looking for a useful tool or interesting content."[15] Full integration and adoption requires the continuing support of district management; the delivery of content that is accurate, relevant, and compelling; the development of a community of learners who depend on the portal for information, professional growth, and knowledge building; and marketing of the portal's availability and the compelling reasons to use it. None of the portal's goals can be realized without districtwide adoption and buy-in.

Overall Use of Empirical Evidence

Although the evaluations described above provided useful information that informed the direction of the portal project, the greatest value of the evaluations was not necessarily in the data they generated. Formative data is short lived; once it is applied to confirm or change one's course, its usefulness has dissipated. Although the changes that resulted may have been significant and even permanent, another indirect value of evaluation presented itself in this project.

The constant reliance on and integration of data over the course of the last three years has led to a better general understanding of the value of data and its use in decisionmaking. This shift was documented when assessment instruments and procedures were spontaneously integrated and adopted in other settings by other constituents for other purposes. The constant evaluation efforts and their visible and positive results modeled the importance of incorporating evaluation and enabled the transfer of data-based decisionmaking to other settings within the district.

SCALING THE PORTAL, COST-EFFECTIVENESS, AND SUSTAINABILITY

The report *An Overview of Current Findings from Empirical Research on Online Teacher Professional Development* documents that investigators have conducted few empirical studies on strategies for scaling up models of online teacher professional development.[16] Yet the ability to adapt an innovation that has been successful in one local setting to be an effective usage in a wide range of contexts is vital to educational improvement. In contrast to experiences in other sectors of society, scaling up successful programs has proved very difficult in education.[17] Insights from changing operations at one fast-food location may easily transfer to every store in that franchise and perhaps to any comparable type of restaurant. However, a new type of teaching strategy that is successful with one practitioner often is difficult to generalize even to other instructors in the same school, let alone to a broad range of practitioners. In general, the more complex the innovation and the wider the range of contexts, the more likely a new practice is to fail the attempt to cross the "chasm" from its original setting to other sites where its implementation could potentially prove valuable.[18]

In the context of innovations in teaching and curriculum, Coburn defines scale as encompassing four interrelated dimensions: depth, sustainability, spread, and shift.[19] "Depth" refers to deep and consequential change in classroom practice, altering teachers' beliefs, norms of social interaction, and pedagogical principles as enacted in the curriculum. "Sustainability" involves maintaining these consequential changes over substantial periods of time, and "spread" is based on the diffusion of the innovation to large numbers of classrooms and schools. "Shift" requires districts, schools, and teachers to assume ownership of the innovation, deepening, sustaining, and spreading its impacts. A fifth possible dimension (to extend Coburn's framework) is "evolution," in which the innovation as revised by its adapters is influential in reshaping the thinking of its designers, creating a community of practice that evolves the innovation.[20]

This research on processes supporting the regional evolution of effective professional development, which led to the portal initiative, is important because a mechanism is documented that can aid with multiple obstacles to scaling. For example, Stein and Bassett note in their K–12 teacher professional development forecast that districts plan primarily to focus on internal capacity-building, "maximizing assets within the schools first and only second incorporating outside knowledge and practices."[21] Thus, resources outside of local districts must use design and delivery models that complement locally based modes of professional development—and local district cultures—in order to ensure that their offerings are adopted and integrated. The portal process, from its inception, has emphasized such an integrative approach, thus enhancing the potential generalizability and transfer of this strategy to a wide range of other educational contexts.

Our empirical studies depict a strategy that is geared to depth, sustainability, spread, shift, and evolution. In particular, the portal's philosophy emphasizing an individual and collaborative perspective on resources and responsibilities, rather than organizational views and mandates, is crucial.

This philosophy is designed to foster ownership by teachers and, over time, their evolution of its resources and communities.

Furthermore, the region surrounding Milwaukee is now engaged in initiatives to adapt the portal process and templates to other school districts, in large part through the activities of Cooperative Educational Service Agency (CESA) #1 serving southeastern Wisconsin.

CESA #1 is currently working on a 21st Century initiative, which is described as "A dynamic collaboration of district, regional, state, and national consultants, in partnership with key business partners to:

- Design and implement a 21st Century Learning Skills curriculum and instructional strategies.
- Apply technology to enable individualized learning plans for the 270,000 students.
- Develop state of the art, on-line, professional development.
- Implement a cost effective integrated data management system."

The Professional Support Portal plays a large role in this initiative as an existing technology through which all of the services included in the 21st Century initiative can eventually be linked. As the district that developed the Professional Support Portal, MPS will be able to recoup some of their investment in the creation of the infrastructure and tools through the regional use of this technology.[22]

This is an impressive example of early scaling up.

CONCLUSION

In fitting the Professional Support Portal project back into the context of the continuum of professional support initiatives as put forth by Dede, Breit, et al., the portal is different in philosophy from most professional development efforts.[23] The portal is not prescriptive, and it uses an unstructured approach to professional instruction. An explicit goal of the portal is to preserve participant and organizational autonomy.

Because the portal's approach to professional development is outside the mainstream, learning to use the portal and recognizing its strengths require additional participant accommodation. The portal requires a steeper and longer learning curve than conventional professional development models, as participants have to adjust not only to learning new content, but also to using new levels of integration, new delivery mechanisms, and new social and professional interactions. Preconceptions of learner responsibility shift from the norm, and new understandings of roles such as "teacher," "learner," "facilitator," "designer," "content provider," and "developer" must evolve.

Evolution is an essential part of the life of the portal. The implementation process is frustratingly slow at times, because of the paradigm shift required for the portal's integration. But this change in perspectives about professional development can also offer exciting opportunities for individual growth and community comprehension of new approaches to learning.

The portal is an educational experiment. Many variables that will undoubtedly influence both long-term and immediate outcomes are uncontrolled, so the course of the portal's eventual development is uncertain. The challenge for researchers is to embrace these unexpected turns of fortune and fate, seeing them not as challenges that spoil predetermined plans, but rather as opportunities for invention. Researchers must master new ways to harvest pearls of wisdom and to identify examples of best practice, models of information processing, and evidence of knowledge building. Through this openness, researchers can evolve new filters through which to view the eclipse of the familiar by the strange and the new.

CHAPTER 12

Core Tensions in the Evolution of Online Teacher Professional Development

Diane Jass Ketelhut, Erin M. McCloskey, Chris Dede,
Lisa A. Breit, and Pamela L. Whitehouse

This chapter synthesizes some ideas that emerged for us from the process of organizing, preparing research materials for, and reflecting on the outcomes of the invitational research conference about online teacher professional development (oTPD). As this journey progressed, we found ourselves dismayed by the dearth of empirical research into online teacher professional development and by the lack of teacher voice in its design, and yet impressed by the vast array of available, exemplary programs based on many different approaches and media. The perspective we present on this situation is influenced by our belief that improving student engagement and learning, teacher retention, and the effectiveness of schooling requires high-quality, sustained professional development for educators, in a combination of online and face-to-face delivery methods, that transforms current practice and policy in fundamental ways.

Through articulating what is understood and what is unknown about online teacher professional development, we seek to facilitate its various stakeholders in collaboratively developing strategies for design, implementation, and research on effective models. In this chapter, we discuss "core tensions," issues that this endeavor must face in developing a process for improvement. We present suggestions for funders, policymakers, regulators, administrators, and school leaders about ways to resolve these core tensions and to evolve online teacher professional development toward the transformative improvement of education.

CORE TENSION #1: DESIGN FOR INCREMENTAL LEARNING VERSUS DESIGN FOR TRANSFORMATION

The introduction to this volume describes the current context of school reform driving professional development efforts. This context plays an important role in one of the central tensions that emerged from conference deliberations: designing for incremental learning versus designing for transformation. Political pressures for change often promote a need for programs that produce quick and tangible results. For example, frequently a superintendent will be hired to "turn around" a failing school district within a specific time frame by rapidly raising student scores on high-stakes tests. Within this context, professional development programs typically are designed to target short-term needs through conventional educational strategies, incorporating familiar and widely available information and communication technologies. In general, these programs incrementally augment teachers' existing skills, attempting change in small steps. Such decisions make tactical sense, as professional development opportunities should prepare teachers to meet the immediate, daily challenges they encounter in their classrooms. But the political pressures of achieving changes in the short term work against strategic investments to evolve professional development models that transform teacher practice toward new approaches to learning. Transformation generates resistance from those who benefit from keeping the school system in its current form. It also takes more time and is harder to achieve and to measure.

To address the need for tangible, immediate results without eliminating the possibility of durable, deep transformation, some online teacher professional development programs are attempting to effect quick, incremental changes while also over time transforming practices and policies. The Learning to Teach with Technology Studio program (LTTS), discussed in a previous chapter, is an example of this strategy. One of the LTTS model's explicit goals is to help teachers integrate technology into their curriculum, an objective that can be accomplished quickly and measured directly. In addition, however, this project is working to transform instruction in two ways—by helping teachers infuse inquiry learning into their practice and by exposing them to an advanced pedagogical technology: an intelligent agent. Given today's pressures for rapid reform, two-pronged approaches such as this ensure that strategic transformation of teacher practices is not overlooked in the pursuit of faster, more tangible outcomes.

Transformation is fraught with difficulty because its target is constantly shifting in response to societal changes. As conventional wisdom about schooling's purpose shifts and as the nature of students and teachers alters, the aims of any transformative process similarly evolve. In order to respond flexibly to goals that are shifting over time, innovators must frequently revisit the question of what constitutes "transformation."

Transformation to Reach Today's Students

Rapid technological advances are reconstituting our temporal understanding of a "generation." Based on experiences with new interactive media, students today likely have significantly different lifestyles than their peers even five years earlier. Many children are comfortable using and working with multiple information and communication technologies, including Web browsers and search engines, multimedia applications, instant messaging, and wireless mobile devices with image and video capabilities (such as cell phones and portable game consoles)—often simultaneously. For those who have come of age using sophisticated gaming devices such as Xbox and other immersive, collaborative, entertaining experiences in their lives outside of school, the relatively simplistic interfaces and content of many learning technologies leave them uninspired. Furthermore, exposure to emerging interactive media is altering student learning strategies and styles, yet schools frequently wall off students from their strengths and interests by "unplugging" them when in classrooms.[1]

Helping teachers respond to the rapidly shifting needs and desires of an increasingly diverse student population requires more than just straightforward, content-based "take-aways" from professional development. Teachers must themselves have experiences with media comparable to those their students have outside classroom walls, so that educators understand firsthand the strengths and challenges promoted by lifestyles infused with new media. Online teacher professional development models such as the WIDE World program, presented in an earlier chapter, use guided experiences based on accommodation and assimilation to transform teacher pedagogy in order to reach the moving target of student needs.

Transformation to Prepare Students for a Future Quite Different from the Present

The needs for change discussed up to this point all revolve around contemporary concerns. More difficult, yet even more important, is designing professional development programs that tackle transformation for future needs, such as the shift in knowledge and skills graduates of U.S. education must have for the emerging, global, knowledge-based economy. The success or failure of America's educational system over the next decade will determine the future of our economy and society for generations to come.[2] Never before has the United States faced global competition of the magnitude seen today. Whole industries, such as steel and paper, that were once U.S.-owned and world-dominant are now headquartered in other countries, such as China and Sweden.[3] A recent report, *Tapping America's Potential: The Education for Innovation Initiative*, issued by the Business Roundtable, expresses "deep concern about the United States' ability to sustain its scientific and technological superiority through this decade and beyond."[4] This report fosters a sense of urgency and calls for immediate action to secure a prosperous future for our country and our children.

In this new economic environment—the New Economy—education plays a critical role in maintaining prosperity and stimulating economic growth.[5] The level of workforce skills and the periodic need to update those skills are both rising in the New Economy.[6] Nations and workers must be prepared to shift jobs and careers more frequently, to be flexible and adaptable in acquiring job skills, and to integrate and focus a changing mix of job and education skills on business processes and problems.[7] Competitive advantage for a region, state, or nation is now built on the skills of its general workforce as opposed to its geography, trade laws, research labs, and patents. And critical to that competitive advantage are the education and skills training adults acquire in primary and secondary schools.[8]

The application of information technology to the very core of business operations has caused a profound change in the needed skills and talents of New Economy workers.[9] Markets in the New Economy are rewarding those who have high educational achievement and technical skill.[10] The worker of the twenty-first century must have science and mathematics skills, creativity, fluency in information and communication technologies (ICT), and the ability to solve complex problems.[11] Clearly, the future personal economic security and well-being of American workers is tied to educational achievement.[12] Yet the rate at which high school graduates are going on to postsecondary education is falling, not rising, particularly in science and engineering. Our country is losing vital talent because our current educational system neither engages many students nor helps them succeed. Failure to address our dropout crisis will lead to dismal economic results in the years ahead.

Much of U.S. education is still based on the premise that economic processes and institutions will mirror those of the twentieth century. Thus, at present, students are prepared to be future employees of business organizations now rapidly becoming obsolete. Current trends suggest that more students will run their own businesses rather than work for others and that as adults they must constantly, quickly, and efficiently learn new skills and information to be effective entrepreneurs. To succeed in life and to keep our country strong and prosperous, all of today's students must graduate able to deal with ambiguity and capable of higher-order analysis, cross-cultural cooperation, and complex communication.

A primary challenge for U.S. education is to transform children's learning processes in and out of school and to engage student interest in gaining twenty-first-century skills and knowledge. Education must align curriculum and learning to a whole new economic model. Linking economic development, educational evolution, workforce development, and strengthened social services is essential to meeting this challenge. The use of sophisticated information technologies in every aspect of education can provide a powerful lever for this transformation.[13]

Isolated in their classrooms from the rest of society, teachers often have little idea of the skills and knowledge required for adept performance in high-technology workplaces. Economists Levy and Murnane document how

> Declining portions of the labor force are engaged in jobs that consist primarily of routine cognitive work and routine manual labor—the types of tasks that are easiest to program computers to do. Growing proportions of the nation's labor force are engaged in jobs that emphasize expert thinking or complex communication—tasks that computers cannot do.[14]

These economists go on to explain that "expert thinking [involves] effective pattern matching based on detailed knowledge; and metacognition, the set of skills used by the stumped expert to decide when to give up on one strategy and what to try next."[15] Levy and Murnane further explain that "complex communication requires the exchange of vast amounts of verbal and nonverbal information. The information flow is constantly adjusted as the communication evolves unpredictably."[16]

Effective teachers engage in expert thinking and complex communication related to instruction, so they know about highly skilled work in their own context. However, these skills as applied in a classroom setting with children are quite different than expert thinking and complex communication applied in twenty-first-century workplaces with adults. (This is why skilled workers do not necessarily transition to classroom teaching with instant effectiveness and why adept teachers may require a period of training and adjustment when shifting careers into workplace roles.) For teachers to model skills of adult thinking and communication to children at a level youngsters understand requires sophistication both about adult performance in workplace settings and about the ways children understand the world around them. Effective teachers have the latter, but need frequent access to and immersion in our economy's rapidly evolving workplace contexts to keep current with the former.

This and related issues pose huge challenges for educators' professional development.[17] No educational improvement effort to prepare our country for a "flat" world can succeed without building teachers' capacity to innovate.[18] Online teacher professional development can provide models of educational enhancement in which the medium reinforces the message, yet the content and process of current approaches—including the exemplary programs described in this volume—must evolve rapidly if our nation is to meet the emerging global challenge.

How can professional development programs today help current teachers transform their practice to meet existing needs while strategically preparing themselves for the future? To our knowledge, there is no major program with the explicit goal of metamorphosing practice for the economic challenge we describe. However, many of the models presented in this volume do offer a bridge from current practices to deeper transformations. The Milwaukee Public Schools' Professional Support Portal is an example of preparing for "tomorrow morning" in the context of the next two decades, and later in this chapter it is discussed as a case study of managing the core tensions we delineate.

CORE TENSION #2: TENSIONS AMONG STAKEHOLDERS' AGENDAS

All stakeholders in the education enterprise want schools, as key societal institutions, to become increasingly effective—to prepare young people for the responsibilities of global citizenship, moral decision-making, family life, self-actualization, economic participation, stewardship of the natural world, the ability to confront and engage with complexity, and the capacity to advance civilization. A central aim of the comprehensive school reform movement of the past decade has been to develop a culture of continuous improvement for schools. This in turn encompasses *someone's* definition of what—or who—needs to be different, a notion of what is wrong and what would be preferable, ideas about how to steer this evolution, and some sense of what would serve as evidence of improvement. Accordingly, teacher professional development may serve one or more purposes in schools—academic, administrative, political, moral, civic, or social.

Participants at the conference represented many of the key stakeholder perspectives that have influenced current models of online teacher professional development: researchers, designers, vendors, funders (government, corporate, and private), regulators, teacher educators, and district administrators—a complex and interwoven mixture representing institutions with a range of partisan concerns. When confluent, the mix of stakeholders' partisan interests can assert a positive influence on the evolution of teacher professional development by generating partnerships that contribute to the identification of needs and the development of creative approaches to design and delivery. Also, alliances among stakeholders can act powerfully to marshal learning assets that benefit teachers and their students and to open access to new audiences and sources of funding. The case study presentations at the conference recounted many such fruitful partnerships. For example, the Science Online masters program wedded the advanced science curricula and educational software resources of TERC with the institutional reach and expertise in teacher education at Lesley University. PBS TeacherLine's multimedia assets and extensive distribution capabilities through its local affiliates joined forces with the Concord Consortium's established professional development programs for K–12 teachers of mathematics.

However, based on discussions at the conference, we note that stakeholders' interests also can diverge or conflict. When stakeholders are understandably caught up in their distinct disciplinary perspectives and in concerns about the survival of their program, this affects the overall advancement of models for online teacher professional development. As illustrations:

- Education regulators set standards and issue directives to steer teachers' instructional practices toward constructivist pedagogies, while at the same time, national education policies insist on assessment of student achievement and teacher effectiveness through metrics such as high-stakes tests, which are often inadequate for measuring how students come to understand complex material and ideas through constructivist pedagogies. Online teacher professional development providers struggle to reconcile these demands as they design content, marketing, delivery, and pedagogy for their programs.
- Education funders' short budget cycles may be mismatched to the market-driven cycles of online teacher professional development programs, creating financial considerations that shape program design more forcefully than objectives for curriculum and pedagogy. Public funders, in particular, may redirect priorities and resources in response to political changes or new, possibly faddish approaches to educational improvement, well before

emerging professional development programs based on prior policy strategies have sufficient momentum to demonstrate their value or become self-sustaining.

- As discussed in more detail later in this chapter, online teacher professional development providers, in pursuit of program models that are scalable and financially sustainable, may render themselves unable to flexibly customize their offerings to support the precise instructional strategies and teacher development priorities that local districts or individual schools adopt in order to meet goals for improvement.

- School administrators, hoping to address both teacher issues (such as isolation, accountability, career development, content expertise, or instructional skills) and student performance issues may institute professional development initiatives to enact school- or district-based curriculum and pedagogical reforms. In this situation, teachers are frequently expected to devote substantial time and energy to professional development that mandates learning new technologies, collaborating with peers (face-to-face and online), designing curriculum, reformulating instructional practices, and assuming new leadership roles. Yet constraints such as lack of release or common planning time and restrictions in union contracts may make it difficult, if not impossible, for teachers to comply—or may provide insufficient incentives for teachers to take the risks necessary to actually achieve the intended transformational change.

- The way that an academic scholar frames a "researchable" problem and defines evidence of educational improvement may fail to encompass the regulatory or marketing concerns that shape the design and delivery of an online teacher professional development program. Alternatively, a model may collect evaluation data that are useful for marketing and program development, but may not articulate measurable goals or collect valid data that the researcher would consider useful for a rigorous empirical study of the program's effectiveness.

As this analysis indicates, each of the ten program models represented in this volume has been shaped by—and has influenced—stakeholder partisanship. For example, the team that presented the Quest Atlantis project developed at Indiana University described the strong theoretical orientation and focus on technological innovation that drives their teacher professional development model. Quest Atlantis was originally developed through the interest of funders and instructional software developers to explore the potential of multiplayer computer gaming technology as an embedded learning environment for children. Its design reflects the team's beliefs about situated learning. When Quest Atlantis went into the classroom, however, the embodied, unstructured way that students function in this virtual environment did not easily fit with the classroom culture and the pedagogical style of most instructors. Teachers, unfamiliar with gaming and lacking well-developed skills in instructional technology, had difficulty envisioning how to use Quest Atlantis to meet the district curriculum requirements for standards-based instruction they were responsible for enacting.

To realize the NSF's investment in Quest Atlantis, the academic team had to design teacher professional development in order to stimulate curricular and pedagogical innovation around the use of this leading-edge technology. Influenced by a model from a different NSF-funded project, the Quest Atlantis approach to professional development was based in a strong theoretical orientation toward professional learning (cognitive apprenticeship and community of practice). However, despite their belief in embedded professional development and learning communities, the team found that not many teachers continued to use Quest Atlantis voluntarily once sponsored and facilitated projects organized by university partners ended. As the case documents, a revised, more structured, and systematic online professional development effort was required to achieve the intentions of their innovations through transforming teachers' current modes of pedagogy.

To summarize how the Indiana case illustrates challenges of partisan perspectives, the development of Quest Atlantis was driven by university faculty's disciplinary perspective and theoretical orientation, the educational software developers' reach for technology innovation, and the funder's desire to develop the learning environment of the future. In spite of some promising early experiments in the classroom and enthusiasm among early-adopter teachers, the team eventually had to consider how to include teachers who were not early adopters or leaders. Building a critical mass of participants was necessary so that the program would be sufficiently scalable and sustainable to effect the widespread changes in teacher practice and knowledge at the heart of the effort. As other chapters in this volume depict, such a divergence among goals and approaches is inevitable in any teacher professional development initiative, whether online or face-to-face.

For reasons of space, some important stakeholders were not represented at the conference: community groups, students, or unions. Also, in the discussions the voices of teachers were less apparent than those of researchers and designers. From the ten papers and conference discussions, it appears that teachers typically have relatively little input in the conception and realization of the oTPD programs in which they ultimately participate. Teachers' motivations for enrolling in online professional development programs are most often

- advancement (to meet licensing, certification, or compensation requirements determined by state boards of education, local school committees, and teachers unions); and
- compliance (to fulfill district- or school-level reform priorities determined by regulators and school administrators).

At present, the major influence of teachers on online teacher professional development programs is indirect, through the collection of evaluation data from program participants. Designers in turn respond to these assessments in order to respond to teachers' needs.

As consumers rather than codevelopers of their own professional learning, teachers more often end up being subject to, rather than party to, tensions among stakeholders all up and down the education food chain—from the funder who provides the initial grant for online teacher professional development, to the hurdles of licensure defined by regulators, to the change trajectories chosen by district leaders, to the incentives (and disincentives) determined by union contracts, to the embedded epistemological and pedagogical beliefs of the instructional developer, to the drive to innovate of the programmer who builds the technological platform, to the experiences and beliefs of the facilitator, instructor, or mentor who delivers the professional development itself. Perhaps the greatest missed opportunity in the tacit exclusion of teachers from active involvement in the design of most professional development is that oTPD providers are less familiar with, or concerned about, what might be the most powerful motivator and transformational factor for their customers: teachers' intrinsic and personal goals for intellectual and professional learning.

That teachers—a large and diverse group in their own right—have partisan interests different from other stakeholders is not surprising, and this further complicates the process of negotiating shared processes and common ground among all those involved in online teacher professional development. To exacerbate the situation, what each set of stakeholders wants varies considerably depending on the educational setting in which the professional development is implemented.

CORE TENSION #3: CUSTOMIZATION VERSUS GENERALIZABILITY

The previous section on partisanship discussed several ways in which divergent interests can complicate and even undermine the cycle of teacher professional development design, delivery, and evaluation. In conference dialogues, one particular consequence of partisanship frequently recurred as a concern: the tension between offering customization of the professional development experience to a particular individual or educational setting versus ensuring its generalizability to larger contexts or audiences. Beyond manifesting the differing goals of stakeholder groups, tensions between customization and generalizability surface when one thinks about the grain size of design and delivery: How focused or how broad should a teacher professional development program's goals be, and for whom? How do these goals relate to individual, school-based, district, state, and federal expectations for participating teachers?

Understanding this tension requires articulating the systemic context surrounding any professional development endeavor. An individual teacher resides in the larger settings of her or his department, school, and district. The effect of that teacher's participation in professional development extends beyond the teacher herself to impact her relationship with uninvolved colleagues. One of the central challenges of professional development, then, is to negotiate the tension generated by shifts in an individual's practice such that the teacher's improvement is not compromised by the needs of the larger context (for instance, her department), while still allowing the nested subsystems within a school district to function coherently.

This tension becomes even more challenging to negotiate when the needs, expectations, and assumptions of the larger context (for example, a school culture that pushes strongly for a particular pedagogical orientation) diverge from the desire for change of individuals participating in a professional development program that advocates a different perspective. Conference discussion of the PBS TeacherLine and Concord Consortium's Seeing Math Secondary program highlighted this type of concern, in which evaluators recognized the potential for the program to undermine traditional perspectives about instruction in participating districts, thus possibly affecting social networks in those settings.

Most forms of professional development are crafted to meet the perceived needs of teachers as individuals in isolation, without regard for the influence of contexts within which teachers will apply their learning. This tension was articulated at the conference, as the following examples illustrate.

"Boutique" versus "General" Programs

A distinction between two types of professional development programs came to light in conference discussions. The first type, identified herein as a "boutique" program, typically develops in response to locally defined needs or from the availability of a particular kind of resource. A boutique program might target a particular audience, such as EDC's EdTech Leaders Online, which treats its clients as partners in the coconstruction of a program of professional supports according to their needs. Alternatively, a boutique program might target a narrow, focused set of learning goals or work with very particular kinds of resources. The American Museum of Natural History's (AMNH) Seminars on Science, for example, meets both these descriptions by offering courses on the scientific inquiry process taught through the exploration of their museum artifacts.

The second model, the "general" program, typically grows out of more broadly defined and widely acknowledged needs from research and policy. The TERC/Lesley University online masters program in science education, for example, is designed to reach a wide audience (K–8 teachers) and to address a whole constellation of needs (such as content knowledge, pedagogical knowledge, collaboration, and community building). The eMentoring for Student Success (eMSS) project also targets a wide range of goals, providing early-career science teachers with both an online learning community and a mentor to meet a broad spectrum of science-specific needs.

Boutique and general programs each carry distinct advantages and drawbacks, and the complementary roles of these alternative offerings in the professional development trajectory of any individual teacher, school, or district are a promising topic for further research. In terms of the cases presented in this volume, Milwaukee's Professional Support Portal program and the American Museum of Natural History program raise two questions, respectively, that highlight issues facing any customized program: How do teachers find a boutique model that may very well fit their needs, but isn't on their radar? How do the various boutique models themselves achieve sustainability without a larger audience, more funding, or connections to partners that can sustain a program after the grant money runs out? The EdTech Leaders Online model addresses this issue by working with a series of clients to develop boutique programs for each, but this is not a path most professional development programs have followed thus far.

On the flip side of the coin, in more general programs, how do teachers customize the content or personalize the experience to meet their specific objectives, so that they feel empowered to use their knowledge in a meaningful way in their local school site context? The eMSS project, for example, is grappling with questions of the extent to which their curriculum adapts to different state contexts. Findings from the Seeing Math Secondary program illustrate another potential mismatch between program and local context: with fewer than half of the participants enrolled as part of a coordinated district or school professional development plan, the program's impact on systemic change is limited by lack of contextual reinforcement for individual change.

Finally, given the array of strategies for negotiating the customization/generalizability tension, the juxtaposition of ten online teacher professional development models raises other, crucial questions: How do the goals of any single program map onto the larger web of teacher professional development offerings? Does the ecology of professional development offerings that results from all online sources match the needs of the educational system? Over the course of a career, what are the effects of these complex interactions on teachers? Is it better for teachers to pick and choose among disconnected programs that don't necessarily share the same language, goals, or theoretical foundation? Or is it better to have someone distant to the teachers create a connected, but more general program of offerings that might not address implementation issues within teachers' local context? Or is there some way of combining the two approaches to offer a coherent experience that honors individuals' diverse needs and settings? (For a more detailed examination of how these questions play out in a concrete example, see the discussion of the Milwaukee Professional Support Portal later in this chapter.)

Personal Needs versus External Mandates

As outlined above, any individual who participates in teacher professional development occupies the center of a series of concentric circles of potential accountability and local culture; she exists within a cadre and/or a department nested within a school, within a district, within a state, and within this nation. Teachers experience informal accountability via their cultural context and formal accountability through a series of metrics, which includes state curriculum standards, NCLB-required high-stakes testing programs (such as the Massachusetts Comprehensive Assessment System), and teacher certification and licensure requirements. That same teacher also works within a less formal, but pervasive professional community comprising teachers at various stages in their careers and enacting different versions of the job: preservice teachers, beginning or novice teachers, experienced teachers, seasoned veterans, midcareer entrants, mentors, coaches, subject area or student specialists (such as those in literacy or special education), curriculum developers, and technologists. While teachers have various motivations for engaging in professional development, participants generally have particular goals for their growth and learning, objectives that may or may not align with external expectations originating from other parts of the systemic relationships within which educators operate. The following examples illustrate how this tension between internal needs and external expectations affects teacher professional development.

The potential inconsistency between internal needs and external expectations can pose barriers to teachers applying newly acquired knowledge in their classrooms. For instance, local curriculum standards might hamper a science teacher's incorporation of her growing understanding of scientific inquiry. Or, district requirements for high-stakes testing preparation might thwart a department's efforts to overhaul its pedagogical approach, either by disrupting the continuity of instruction or by limiting the time available to effect these changes in sustainable ways. Alternatively, local professional culture might constrain a teacher or department from changing the fundamentals of practice by subtly or overtly undermining and discouraging those efforts.

Over the years, the WIDE World program has witnessed many examples of these local pressures in action and has documented how these forces can compel teachers to "regress to the mean," despite participants' best intentions to enact their learning from professional development as a means to improve their practice. The WIDE World model has attempted to counteract these barriers by encouraging groups of teachers from a school or district to enroll as a team, along with administrators charged with instructional leadership, as a way of building mutual support for change in the school context once the immediate support of the WIDE World course has ended.

The tension between internal needs and external expectations can also affect the opportunities teachers have to engage in online professional development. A school may understand the needs of "beginning" teachers differently than the teachers themselves do, and accordingly might require certain kinds of professional development that differ from their own choices. Or, some online professional development offerings, because of where they originate or their reliance on virtual learning, may not meet state regulations, map neatly onto institutional definitions of "credit," or match what teachers need for recertification. The eMSS induction program, for example, frequently encounters this issue because districts must be willing to allow some of their induction to happen across distance online, which is less likely in localities or states with a highly developed induction model (such as California). Another illustration is the AMNH Seminars on Science program, which negotiated these types of regulatory challenges by partnering with several higher-education institutions in order to offer graduate credit that would meet recertification requirements. As conventional teacher professional development programs move toward virtual and hybrid models, the question of regulatory strictures becomes increasingly important, since teachers may be left with inadequate choices to improve their practice if they are denied online professional development offerings. One way of addressing these regulatory concerns is to provide compelling evidence of a model's effectiveness.

CORE TENSION #4: RESEARCH VERSUS PROGRAM EVALUATION

What are the hallmarks of success for an online teacher professional development program? How does one produce sufficient evidence of effectiveness? Who defines "quality"? These questions delineate the last core tension we have space to articulate in this volume. This core tension is characterized by two important, but sometimes conflicting needs that must be negotiated by stakeholders in professional development. On the one hand, there is a need for empirical research over the long term that provides key insights, sophisticated methodologies for studying the evolution of exemplary models, and evidence of improvement in teacher learning, teacher change, and student achievement. On the other hand, equally compelling is the immediate need for program evaluations that offer evidence of learner buy-in and usability of program design; this is important given funder requirements and market pressures such as scaling up and sustainability. A key insight arising from this tension is that online teacher professional development designers, scholars, and vendors must find ways to achieve an acceptable equilibrium between the pull of market demand and the push of research needs.

The cases in this book suggest that researchers and designers have been thinking about these goals in ways that emphasize the dichotomy between the approaches, rather than their scholarly commonalities. Program evaluations tend to ask questions about *effectiveness*, while empirical research asks questions about *impact*. Effectiveness is defined by three main questions.

- *Scalability:* Can the program move from serving innovators and early adopters to the mainstream?
- *Sustainability:* Is the revenue stream sufficient to support the program without special or external resources, and without the involvement of the initial researchers and developers?[19]
- *Cost-benefit:* Do participants believe (and self-report) that the costs (time, effort, course fees) provide sufficient benefit to make involvement worth their while?

In contrast, the goals of empirical research are more often aimed at questions about teacher learning and teacher change. To our surprise, researchers seldom attempt to find linkages between improving teacher professional development and increasing student achievement, although this may change given shifts in federal research investments. Even though most stakeholders agree that attempting to find linkages between teacher learning or change and improved student achievement is critical, as discussed in chapter 1 there is a dearth of empirical findings to date in the research literature about how and to what extent the depth, durability, or nature of teacher change and teacher learning impacts student achievement.

With these issues in mind, *impact* centers on three main questions.

- *Teacher learning:* To what extent and under what circumstances do teachers use new skills, concepts, pedagogies, resources, and content knowledge from oTPD?
- *Teacher change:* To what extent and under what circumstances do teachers alter their instructional practice with students?
- *Improved student achievement:* To what extent and under what circumstances do teacher learning and teacher change improve student achievement?

In order to put this tension into a practical context, consider the case of PBS TeacherLine. The developers/researchers reported that they could sustain their courses and program evaluations through fees but would need external resources (grant money) to support empirical research that clarifies the relationship between teacher learning and student achievement. As long as program evaluation methods provide sufficient data for vendors to develop strategies for scalability and sustainability, funding for empirical research will remain dependent upon extrinsic rather than intrinsic motivation—for example, demands from clients, regulators, and other stakeholders for evidence of impact.

The PBS TeacherLine program evaluators did try an experimental evaluation technique in order to determine a causal link between teacher participation in its courses and improved student achievement. Unfortunately, no causal link was found by the researchers. It is likely that program evaluation methods do not readily lend themselves to this type of inquiry; however, sophisticated methodologies that can provide analytic power in the complex setting of field-based studies require substantial time and resources to utilize.

For online teacher professional development programs developed using grant funding to institutions of higher education, the issue of sustainability is more severe. At the end of external funding, programs often disappear because developing revenue streams and marketing programs is not a well-accepted part of the academic culture. On the other hand, while the program is in existence the scholars involved may generate useful findings on different aspects of impact. The situation of nonprofit educational research companies as vendors is similar—once the initial source of resources winds down, online teacher professional development programs tend to disappear. This seems to be a chicken-egg conundrum: Without program evaluation methods, there is no evidence to support effective design, but without empirical research, findings that support claims of teacher learning, teacher change, or improved student achievement are lacking.

A deeper examination of this apparent dichotomy reveals complementary roles: Program evaluation provides the needs analysis and design assessment necessary for funders and marketing, while research provides strategic understandings and empirical validation about whether and how learning is enhanced by online tools and multimedia. Research is particularly important because merely knowing *whether and under what conditions* a particular model works is of substantially less value than also knowing *why*. Little is known from a theoretical or conceptual perspective about many important issues: What types of design innovations would best support scaling up across multiple contexts? What kinds of measures best capture the depth and durability of teacher learning and change? What types of teacher change most influence student achievement?

The absence of answers to these questions will increasingly plague designers attempting to improve and scale their models. For example, as discussed earlier in this section, PBS TeacherLine's program evaluators could not make a causal link between their courses and improvement in student achievement. At present, their plans to expand to new markets therefore must rely solely on strong course evaluations from participants. Another case in point is the eMentoring for Student Success program. Scholarly studies found that fewer than 10 percent of the dialogues in its asynchronous discussion forums were centered on pedagogy or content knowledge—a main goal of the eMSS program. On the other hand, participant and facilitator evaluations were very positive. As in the case of TeacherLine, eMSS program leaders plan to expand the program, in the hopes that ongoing analysis will shed more light on how well (or not) the program is achieving its goals. In response to inconclusive findings about effectiveness, gathering more data from larger participant populations is an appealing strategy, because new understandings could emerge from an analysis with more statistical power. However, this does risk clients investing in a professional development model that ultimately proves to be less effective than hoped.

The development of scholarly designs that blend evaluation with research may prove fruitful in generating findings with a broader range of explanatory power. One promising approach is design-based research (DBR). Collins, Joseph, and Bielaczyc define DBR thus:

Design experiments bring together two critical pieces in order to guide us to better educational refinement: a design focus and assessment of critical design elements. Ethnography provides qualitative methods for looking carefully at how a design plays out in practice, and how social and contextual variables interact with cognitive variables. Large-scale studies provide quantitative methods for evaluating the effects of independent variables on the dependent variables. Design experiments are contextualized in educational settings, but with a focus on generalizing from those settings to guide the design process. They fill a niche in the array of experimental methods that is needed to improve educational practices.[20]

DBR has proven to be very effective in systematic analysis of complex learning environments in authentic contexts—like eMSS or TeacherLine.

DBR differs from both conventional design and traditional research in its emphasis on adapting a design to its local context, a vital attribute for scaling up an innovation successful in one place to many other venues with dissimilar characteristics.[21] In making judgments about the promise of an intervention, differentiating its design from its "conditions for success" is important. The effective use of antibiotics illustrates the concept of conditions for success: Antibiotics are a powerful "design," but worshiping the vial that holds them or rubbing pills meant to be ingested all over one's skin or taking all the pills at once are ineffective strategies for usage—only administering pills at specified intervals works as an implementation strategy. A huge challenge we face in education, and one of the reasons our field makes slower progress than venues such as medicine, is the complexity of conditions for success required in effective interventions; nothing powerful in facilitating learning is as simple as an inoculation in medicine. DBR may be a useful method for resolving some of the tension this complexity creates between investing in either traditional program evaluation and conventional empirical research about online teacher professional development: aiding design, providing insights about theory, validating effectiveness, and articulating why a model works better under some conditions than others.

NEGOTIATING THE FOUR CORE TENSIONS: ONE PROGRAM'S ONGOING APPROACH

The core tensions described in this chapter do not arise in isolation from one another. At every point in the evolution of a teacher professional development program, one or more of these tensions are at play; often they intertwine, generating the complex landscape of needs and interests through which providers must try to navigate. As an example of analyzing the interplay of these core tensions, we articulate their influence on one of the case studies in this volume, the Milwaukee Public Schools Professional Support Portal.

To recapitulate the context for this online model's development, by the late 1990s the Milwaukee Public School District (MPS) faced acute challenges regarding teacher supply, quality, and retention. Large numbers of retirements coupled with high turnover among new teachers exacerbated the district's ongoing problems with low student achievement. In 2001, a partnership of Milwaukee civic, business, and higher-education leaders joined with state education officials and district leaders to address current problems in the Milwaukee schools and to build consensus and support for change. Among other initiatives, this group, called the Milwaukee Partnership Academy, generated ambitious plans for the development of the MPS Professional Support Portal.

The Milwaukee Partnership Academy, working with development teams in the district, articulated the outcomes they hoped the portal would help achieve. These were

- reducing teacher attrition,
- developing a community of learners within—and beyond—individual schools,
- changing educational practice and culture, and ultimately
- increasing student achievement.

The concept for the portal draws on research about learning and school improvement. Its central premise is that building a stronger professional community will retain a more knowledgeable and motivated teaching force and ultimately lead to improved student academic achievement. In a decentralized district, meeting these goals presumed some significant shifts in stakeholders' roles and agency. Consequently, making the portal the "go to" source for continuous learning in the district is "bottom-up" work in progress.

Design for Incremental Learning versus Transformative Change

As discussed earlier in this chapter, most online professional development programs are designed to augment teachers' existing skills and knowledge in small steps. The new skills and knowledge that teachers acquire are intended to result in substantial changes in practice, but often these initiatives result in only small-scale, incremental change. In Milwaukee's case, continuing low levels of student achievement were evidence that whatever teachers were taking away from their involvement in conventional professional development was not having the necessary impact in the classroom. Along with teacher turnover and retention issues, worsening student achievement in the face of the ongoing pressures of federal school reform increased the urgency for both immediate action and long-term, transformative strategies for teacher professional development. In particular, the Milwaukee portal team recognized that the professional development environment they were creating could have a major transformational impact at MPS by helping to shift educators' roles across the district and by extending the "learning community" of teachers well beyond the school, engaging parents, business partners, and the community.

One of the most significant stakeholder impacts of the portal is the requirement for a different mix of collaboration and individual agency by teachers. The change strategy behind the portal recasts teachers as possessors of knowledge and creators of content, undercutting customary hierarchies in relation to administrators. The portal's design also assumes increased collaboration among teachers and takes the tacit position that the district's work will be public and accountable. For this paradigm shift to succeed, the portal's design and deployment have to support the immediate needs of teachers while fostering deep cultural change in schools and in the district.

Another critical element of the portal's design is that it is an entirely online environment. As such, it sets a high standard for all district personnel to become committed technology users, fluent with software, digital interfaces, multimedia, content development tools, and the culture of public and quasi-public online communication. Although extensive scaffolding is required to avoid presenting a daunting short-term learning curve for many educators, this technology-based platform signifies a leap toward thinking like twenty-first-century educators and portends significant shifts in instruction and learning culture down the road.

Stakeholders' Agendas

The Milwaukee portal would not have advanced had it not satisfied multiple stakeholder interests. The MPS portal was the brainchild of a visionary superintendent, who assembled a powerful coalition of civic representatives to help MPS move toward its improvement goals. When the superintendent left the district, it was this community-based coalition of multiple stakeholders—the Milwaukee Partnership Academy—that saved the portal project from languishing without their committed leader at the helm. This group of parents, business people, researchers, university faculty, parents, teachers, administrators, and outside experts stepped up in the absence of central office leadership and actively supported the district's portal project team. The involvement of multiple stakeholders transformed the portal to a bottom-up, grassroots initiative.

Merely building the portal has not been sufficient to move the district's teaching force in new directions. Teachers often perceive that professional development mandates do little to help them with "Monday morning" concerns, and top-down demands often trigger teachers' personal anxieties about manageable workload, performance expectations, and career advancement. The demands of a comprehensive reform initiative can be overwhelming for teachers, and the presumption that they need to be "improved" can seem more like an affront than a motivator. MPS's sizable investment in the portal demonstrated recognition that teachers are critical stakeholders when it comes to making change in schools. However, the portal model meant that experienced teachers would have to "unlearn" current practices and acclimate to a new way of communicating with peers, administrators, and eventually, parents. Not only were teachers expected to become content developers for the portal, they would also need to master a series of online tools and interfaces, requiring a significant advance in technology skills throughout the district.

The portal design also needed to be able to quickly address acute problems with new-teacher induction and retention. The portal team worked with teacher leaders and local university teacher education faculty to create facilitated inductee cohorts that engage novice teachers in using the portal for learning, information, and reflection, beginning with their earliest involvement with MPS.

Administrators in individual Milwaukee schools were accustomed to local school-based management. Until principals and department heads learned how they could use the portal to communicate their leadership vision, the portal scheme threatened to become a juggernaut, rolling over building-level initiatives designed to address specific needs. Central office administrators were skeptical about claims of broad cultural change. They blanched at having to create, post, and maintain online the vast number of documents generated by a large urban school bureaucracy. Through formative evaluation, however, the portal team discovered that they could engage the central office by demonstrating the portal's usefulness for generating and sharing management data, helping district leaders fulfill their responsibilities for coordination.

Customization versus Generalizability

How can one design an online professional development environment to accommodate specific, rapidly shifting, locally defined needs—yet create a product generic enough to provide consistency and cohesion for a large school district and scalability to other districts? On the one hand, the MPS portal is designed to foster leadership and a sense of community by accommodating a wide range of custom needs identified by its users. Its design assumes that individuals and diverse groupings (within departments or schools, across departments, linking school to community) will populate the portal by creating their own customized workshops, discussions, and resources. On the other hand, the portal must standardize and simplify the delivery of information in order to demonstrate value and to attract active participation, offering enough commonly viewed content and a cohesive enough message to make the portal "The Way Milwaukee Works."

The portal's design attempts to strike a balance between customization and generalizability. This online environment provides teachers and administrators with a common point of access to an *integrated* array of internal and external information, online groups to build community, and professional development resources that stress initiatives championed by the district. Yet the portal also delivers a set of tools *customizable* by users for collaboration, reflection, planning, and creating and sharing content. Rather than engineering a prescriptive, top-down approach to school change, the portal is designed to reinforce a culture of local autonomy in a highly decentralized district by supporting the needs of each school and department and even individual teachers. As part of the integration it provides, the portal also uses advanced database and Web technologies to serve as a repository of institutional memory, intended to help stem the outflow of knowledge from the district due to turnover, as well as to support more efficient and consistent induction of new teachers.

Research versus Program Evaluation

Earlier in this chapter, we noted the importance of empirical research to understand whether and how oTPD programs are effective, with regard to how teachers are learning, how practice is changing, and how teacher learning affects student learning. We also discussed the need for program evaluation data that allow providers to respond to market pressures of scalability and sustainability. Clearly, the development of effective models for online teacher professional development requires both kinds of research. We described one promising approach to addressing both kinds of needs, called design-based research.

The design-based research approach has played an important role in the development of the Milwaukee portal. The original conception of the portal was influenced by advice from partners at the Harvard Graduate School of Education and Education Development Center, who, interested in transformational change in schools, shared recent research on student learning, adult development, professional communities, and best practices. Also, the development team wisely collected data from stakeholders within the district to drive the initial design of the portal.

As the portal's basic templates and tools are mounted, portal advocates are working to attract a critical mass of participants. As the portal evolves, extensive formative evaluation is shaping an aggressive strategy to demonstrate the value of the portal and integrate it more fully into the life of the district. Until teachers, administrators, and others in the school community participate in the portal to enhance its value, MPS will not know whether the significant investment the district has made in it will result in the desired outcomes of a more stable and capable teacher force and improved student achievement.

Will the portal, which depends on a high degree of ownership by its users, be sustainable in MPS over time? And will the portal model be scalable for effective use in other educational settings? Well-designed empirical research, independent of formative investigations about the portal, is necessary to gauge the strengths and weaknesses of the model over time. Meanwhile, the portal's developers hope that, by emphasizing individual and collaborative perspectives on resources and responsibility rather than organizational views and mandates, they have created a model both flexible enough to accommodate as the district's needs change and spacious enough to transfer to other settings. At present, several districts in the region surrounding Milwaukee are adapting the portal platform, and their efforts soon may reveal some insights about the scalability of the portal model, as well as how successfully the portal's designers have navigated a balance among the four core tensions this chapter delineates.

IMPLICATIONS FOR STAKEHOLDERS

Collectively, prevalent themes in conference discussions—partisanship, degrees of customization and generalizability, modes of evaluation and research—all signal fundamental questions about the relationship of professional development to the transformation of participants' practices, of their roles in the teaching profession, and of schooling. As is evident from the cases presented in this volume, our field is in the process of moving away from professional development programs that focus on individual knowledge and skills. Instead we are moving toward models that include individual knowledge-building as one component in an integrated process. Within this, teachers, schools, and districts can engage in coordinated efforts to reflect on and redefine their professional roles and practices, as well as the policy context in which teachers operate.

Our stance in hosting this conference is that such a paradigmatic shift is arduous but essential. In that spirit, we offer the following implications of our analysis in this chapter. We hope readers from various stakeholder groups find these implications helpful as they consider the teacher professional development issues that relate most directly to their own concerns. More important, we ask that readers recognize the interconnectedness of their partisan interests and goals with those of other stakeholder groups, using a deeper understanding of these complex interactions to enhance our collective thinking about how to accomplish a paradigm shift.

The implications below are organized by primary stakeholder group. For each group, we offer overall framing concepts as well as a few concrete examples. Though we recognize that the effects of these implications often ripple across several groups, we resort to categories as an organizing tool and encourage readers to consider them as a set of interrelated and mutually referential distinctions.

Funders should support both the refinement of sophisticated research methodologies and related empirical research on current and new models. These studies should aim to provide evidence of whether, how, and why online teacher professional development affects student achievement and the institutional evolution of schools. What counts as evidence should be defined from several perspectives, with data generated by both qualitative and quantitative measures. The following ideas represent only a handful of possible scholarly initiatives:

- Fund research on both boutique and general programs, as well as on informal learning structures that support the continued learning of groups of program alumni;
- Embed program evaluation and empirical research in requests for proposals and encourage mixed-methods studies that develop deep understanding of complex program dynamics;
- Fund studies of effective but small programs that are expanding to determine whether their success and quality are attainable at scale;
- Prioritize funding programs that
  - collaborate across different stakeholder groups (such as university–school district partnerships, or partnerships between technological

product developers and educators) that will design and study online teacher professional development models;

- fund design-based research about the evolution of online teacher professional development models in preference to standard comparative studies of a program to a "control" condition;

• Support grantees in considering sustainable business models for programs from inception; and

• As reliable evidence about online teacher professional development's impact is accumulated, support conferences to share knowledge, as well as a Web-based national clearinghouse to assist in client identification and selection of quality programs based on alternative models.

Policymakers and regulators should recognize that school reform cannot succeed without an ongoing investment in transformational teacher professional development. Policies for school funding should be refined to enable sustained investment in human capacity-building. Requirements for recertification should be altered to recognize the affordances provided by online and blended models of professional development. Being guided by these understandings would result in

• Generating requests for proposals that promote a balance between empirical research and program evaluation;

• Creating a recertification system that includes alternative models of teacher learning (for instance, virtual learning, programs that use emerging interactive media); and

• Developing flexible policies for teacher compensatory time, release days, industry externships, and summer work to provide incentives that promote teacher participation in comprehensive professional development.

Administrators and school leaders should view professional development as a vital element of comprehensive, transformational change. They should understand and attend to teachers' reasons for participating in professional development, ranging from outside incentives to the intrinsic motivation of intellectual and professional growth. They should not only challenge teachers to improve practice, but also provide institutional and structural supports that encourage teacher risk-taking, reflection, collaboration, and leadership. As part of teacher supervision, administrators and school leaders should focus on individualized learning plans for teachers, holding teachers accountable for pursuing, applying, and demonstrating their own learning. The following specific ideas reflect some actionable steps that reflect these implications:

- Recognize that the vitality of schools depends on ongoing learning, and move to foster a culture of continuous change;
- Create a culture that supports groups of teachers engaging in professional development (for example, prioritizing reimbursement for whole departments over incentives for individual teachers);
- Facilitate in-house research on the kinds of professional development models that might best serve local needs;
- Offer greater incentives, rewards, and new kinds of career advancement opportunities for teachers willing to commit to multiple programs or more integrated programs that address carefully defined and articulated learning goals;
- Develop incentives for individual participants in professional development to disseminate what they have learned throughout the school, such as
  - Sharing their experiences with colleagues;
  - Forming informal learning structures, such as critical friends groups;
  - Creating portfolios to document teacher and student learning after professional development;
- Offer evaluations and recommendations of programs to help school staff select the best offerings for pursuing their professional and personal learning goals, and to position them to benefit from the incentives and rewards mentioned above;
- Encourage greater connection between school learning and economic needs by forming partnerships with local companies that support summer externships for teachers, student internships, and ongoing school-industry dialogue; and
- Work with teachers unions to allow for different constructs of teachers' work, career path, and incentives, in the service of developing better strategies for teachers' professional learning.

Readers will note that many of these recommendations apply to professional development in general, rather than just to online programs.

CONCLUSION

Sophisticated application of advances in information technology has dramatically altered the nature of work in many sectors of society, resulting in greater effectiveness and productivity. Education is intrinsically a human-centered enterprise, so the primary contribution of computers and telecommunications is not to automate what people do, but instead to empower teachers in their own learning and in helping students learn. We believe that evolving and applying more effective models of online and blended teacher professional development is key to helping our society toward a bright future. We hope that the insights from this book will provide direction for the challenges that lie ahead.

Notes

INTRODUCTION
The Evolution of Online Teacher Professional Development
Chris Dede

1. W. Hawley and L. Valli, "The Essentials for Effective Professional Development: A New Consensus," in *Teaching as the Learning Profession: Handbook of Policy and Practice*, ed. L. Darling-Hammond and G. Sykes (San Francisco: Jossey-Bass, 1999), 127–150.
2. K. M. Killeen et al., "School District Spending on Professional Development: Insights Available from National Data (1992–1998)," *Journal of Education Finance* 28, no. 1 (2002): 25–49.
3. H. Borko, "Professional Development and Teacher Learning: Mapping the Terrain," *Educational Researcher* 33, no. 8 (2004): 3–15.
4. M. Barnett, *Issues and Trends Concerning Electronic Networking Technologies for Teacher Professional Development: A Critical Review of the Literature*, paper presented at the annual meeting of the American Educational Research Association (2002).
5. C. Dede, "Why Design-Based Research Is Both Important and Difficult," *Educational Technology* 45, no. 1 (2005): 5–8.

CHAPTER 1
An Overview of Current Findings from Empirical Research
Pamela L. Whitehouse, Lisa A. Breit, Erin M. McCloskey, Diane Jass Ketelhut, and Chris Dede

1. A substantially longer version of this study is available at http://gseweb.harvard.edu/%7Euk/otpd/final_research_overview.pdf.
2. D. P. Ausubel, "The Use of Advance Organizers in the Learning and Retention of Meaningful Verbal Material," *Journal of Educational Psychology* 51, no. 5 (1960), 267–272.
3. A list of these is available at http://www.gse.harvard.edu/~dedech/oTPD_list.pdf.
4. S. J. Derry et al., "From Ambitious Vision to Partially Satisfying Reality: An Evolving Socio-Technical Design Supporting Community and Collaborative Learning in

Teacher Education," in *Designing for Virtual Communities in the Service of Learning,* ed. S. Barab et al. (Cambridge: Cambridge University Press, 2004), 256–295.

5. M. Hawkes and K. Good, "Evaluating Professional Development Outcomes of a Telecollaborative Technology Curriculum," *Rural Educator* 21, no. 3 (2000), 5–11; and M. Hawkes and A. Romiszowski, "Examining the Reflective Outcomes of Asynchronous Computer-Mediated Communication on Inservice Teacher Development," *Journal of Technology and Teacher Education* 9, no. 2 (2001), 285–308.

6. M. Barnett et al., "Using Emerging Technologies to Help Bridge the Gap between University Theory and Classroom Practice: Challenges and Successes," *School Science and Mathematics* 102, no. 6 (2002), 299.

7. A. Porter et al., *Does Professional Development Change Teaching Practice? Results from a Three-Year Study* (Washington, DC: U.S. Department of Education, 2000), 10.

8. C. M. Clarke and H. Hollingsworth, "Elaborating a Model of Teacher Professional Growth," *Teaching and Teacher Education* 18 (2002), 947–967.

9. B. J. Fishman et al., "Linking Teacher and Student Learning to Improve Professional Development in Systemic Reform," *Teaching and Teacher Education* 19, no. 6 (2003), 643–658.

10. D. C. Neale et al., "Implementing Conceptual Change Teaching in Primary Science," *The Elementary School Journal* 91, no. 2 (1990), 109–131.

11. M. Riel and L. Polin, "Online Learning Communities: Common Ground and Critical Differences in Designing Technical Environments," in *Designing for Virtual Communities* (see note 4), 16–50.

12. S. Barab et al., "Developing an Empirical Account of a Community of Practice: Characterizing the Essential Tensions," *Journal of the Learning Sciences* 11, no. 4 (2002), 489–542.

13. P. D. Sherer et al., "Online Communities of Practice: A Catalyst for Faculty Development," *Innovative Higher Education* 27, no. 3 (2003), 183–194.

14. E. F. Koku and B. Wellman, "Scholarly Networks as Learning Communities," in *Designing for Virtual Communities,* 299–337.

15. S. C. Yang and S. F. Liu, "Case Study of Online Workshop for the Professional Development of Teachers," *Computers in Human Behavior* 20, no. 6 (2004), 733–761.

16. L. Schaverien, "Teacher Education in the Generative Virtual Classroom: Developing Theories through a Web-Delivered, Technology-and-Science Education Context," *International Journal of Science Education* 25, no. 12 (2003), 1.

17. J. Wearmouth et al., "Computer Conferencing with Access to a 'Guest Expert' in the Professional Development of Special Educational Needs Coordinators," *British Journal of Educational Technology* 35, no. 1 (2004), 81–93.

18. R. Nemirovsky and A. Galvis, "Facilitating Grounded Online Interactions in Video-Case-Based Teacher Professional Development," *Journal of Science Education and Technology* 13, no. 1 (2004), 67–79.

19. K. A. Renninger and W. Shumar, "The Centrality of Culture and Community to Participant Learning at and with the Math Forum," in *Designing for Virtual Communities,* 181–209.

20. K. Job-Sluder and S. Barab, "Shared 'We' and Shared 'They' Indicators of Group Identity in Online Teacher Professional Development," in *Designing for Virtual Communities*, 377–403; Barnett et al.; S. Turner et al., "Impact of a Professional Development Program on Teachers' Self-Efficacy" (paper presented at the National Council of Teachers of Mathematics Annual Meeting, Philadelphia, April, 2004); and Fishman et al.

21. E. Dutro et al., "When State Policies Meet Local District Contexts: Standards-Based Professional Development as a Means to Individual Agency and Collective Ownership," *Teachers College Record* 104, no. 4 (2002), 787–811.

22. J. Leach et al., "Deep Impact: A Study of the Use of Hand-Held Computers for Teacher Professional Development in Primary Schools in the Global South," *European Journal of Teacher Education* 27, no. 1 (2004), 5–28.

23. J. Harris and N. Grandgenett, "Teachers' Authentic E-Learning," *Learning and Leading with Technology*, 30 (2002).

24. C. Mouza, "Learning to Teach with New Technology: Implications for Professional Development," *Journal of Research on Technology in Education* 35, no. 2 (2002), 272–289; and D. D. Curtis and M. J. Lawson, "Exploring Collaborative Online Learning," *Journal of Asynchonous Learning Networks*, 5 (2001), 21–34.

25. WestEd, *Teachers Who Learn, Kids Who Achieve: A Look at Schools with Model Professional Development* (2000), available from http://www.wested.org/online_pubs/teachers_who_learn/TeachLearn.pdf.

26. K. E. Rudestam and J. Schoenholtz-Read, "Overview: The Coming of Age of Adult Online Education," in *Handbook of Online Learning*, ed. K. E. Rudestam and J. Schoenholtz-Read (Thousand Oaks, CA: Sage Publications, 2002), 3–28.

27. A. Bruckman, "Co-Evolution of Technological Design and Pedagogy in an Online Learning Community," in *Designing for Virtual Communities*, 239–255.

28. Bruckman.

29. L. Harasim et al., *Learning Networks: A Field Guide to Teaching and Learning Online* (Cambridge, MA: MIT Press, 1996); and R. M. Palloff and K. Pratt, *Building Learning Communities in Cyberspace* (San Francisco: Jossey-Bass, 1999).

30. E. Joy and F. E. Garcia, "Measuring Learning Effectiveness: A New Look at No-Significant-Difference Findings," *Journal of Asynchronous Learning Networks* 4, no. 1 (2000), 22–37.

31. H. Borko, "Professional Development and Teacher Learning: Mapping the Terrain," *Educational Researcher* 33, no. 8 (2004), 3–15.

Additional Sources for Table 1

Barab, S., MaKinster, J., & Scheckler, R. (2004). Designing system dualities: Characterizing online community. In S. Barab, R. Kling, & J. H. Gray (Eds.), *Designing for virtual communities in the service of learning*. Cambridge, England: Cambridge University Press.

Barab, S. A., Barnett, M., & Squire, K. (2002). Developing an empirical account of a community of practice: Characterizing the essential tensions. *Journal of the Learning Sciences, 11,* 489–542.

Barnett, M. (2002, April). *Issues and trends concerning electronic networking technologies for teacher professional development: A critical review of the literature.* Paper presented at the annual meeting of the American Educational Research Association, New Orleans, LA.

Broady-Ortman, C. (2002). Teachers' perceptions of a professional development distance learning course: A qualitative case study. *Journal of Research on Technology in Education, 35,* 107–138.

Brown, A., & Green, T. (2003). Showing up to class in pajamas (or less!): The fantasies and realities of on-line profesional development. *Clearing House, 6,* 148–152.

Clarke, C. M., & Hollingsworth, H. (2002). Elaborating a model of teacher professional growth. *Teaching and Teacher Education, 18,* 947–967.

Curtis, D. D., & Lawson, M. J. (2001). Exploring collaborative online learning. *Journal of Asynchronous Learning Networks, 5*(1), 21–34.

Derry, S. J., Seymour, J., Steinkuehler, C., Lee, J., & Siegel, M. A. (2004). From ambitious vision to partially satisfying reality: An evolving socio-technical design supporting community and collaborative learning in teacher education. In S. A. Barab, R. Kling, & J. H. Gray (Eds.), *Designing for virtual communities in the service of learning* (pp. 256–295). Cambridge, England: Cambridge University Press.

Desimone, L., Porter, A., Birman, B. F., Garet, M. S., & Yoon, K. S. (2004). How do district management and implementation strategies relate to the quality of the professional development that districts provide to teachers? *Teachers College Record, 104,* 1265–1312.

Dutro, E., Fisk, M. C., Koch, R., Roop, L. J., & Wixson, K. K. (2002). When state policies meet local district contexts: Standards-based professional development as a means to individual agency and collective ownership. *Teachers College Record, 104,* 787–811.

Fishman, B. J., Marx, R. W., Best, S., & Tal, R. T. (2003). Linking teacher and student learning to improve professional development in systemic reform. *Teaching and Teacher Education, 19,* 643–658.

Harlen, W., & Doubler, S. (2004). Online professional development: Science inquiry in the online environment. In C. Vrasidas & G. V. Glass (Eds.), *Current perspectives on applied information technologies: Online professional development for teachers* (pp. 87–104). Greenwich, CT: Information Age.

Harris, J., & Grandgenett, N. (2002). Teachers' authentic e-learning. *Learning and Leading with Technology, 30.*

Hawkes, M., & Good, K. (2000). Evaluating professional development outcomes of a telecollaborative technology curriculum. *Rural Educator, 21*(3), 5–11.

Hawkes, M., & Romiszowski, A. (2001). Examining the reflective outcomes of asynchronous computer-mediated communication on inservice teacher development. *Journal of Technology and Teacher Education, 9,* 285–308.

Herring, S. C. (2004). Computer-mediated discourse analysis: An approach to researching online behavior. In S. Barab, R. Kling, & J. H. Gray (Eds.), *Designing for virtual communities in the service of learning* (pp. 338–376). Cambridge, England: University of Cambridge Press.

Job-Sluder, K., & Barab, S. (2004). Shared "we" and shared "they" indicators of group identity in online teacher professional development. In S. Barab, R. Kling, & J. H. Gray (Eds.), *Designing for virtual communities in the service of learning* (pp. 377–403). Cambridge, England: University of Cambridge Press.

Kabilan, M. K. (2004). Online professional development: A literature analysis of teacher competency. *Journal of Computing in Teacher Education, 21*(2), 51–55.

King, K. P. (2002). Identifying success in online teacher education and professional development. *Internet and Higher Education, 5,* 231–246.

King, K. P., & Dunham, M. D. (2005). Finding our way: Better understanding the needs and motivations of teachers in online learning. *International Journal of Instructional Technology and Distance Learning, 2*(1), 11–26.

Koku, E. F., & Wellman, B. (2004). Scholarly networks as learning communities. In S. Barab, R. Kling, & J. H. Gray (Eds.), *Designing for virtual communities in the service of learning* (pp. 299–337). Cambridge, England: Cambridge University Press.

Leach, J., Patel, R., Peters, A., Power, T., Ahmed, A., & Makalima, S. (2004). Deep impact: A study of the use of hand-held computers for teacher professional development in primary schools in the Global South. *European Journal of Teacher Education, 27*(1), 5–28.

McKeown, M. G., & Beck, I. L. (2004). Transforming knowledge into professional development resources: Six teachers implement a model of teaching for understanding text. *Elementary School Journal, 104,* 391–408.

Mouza, C. (2002). Learning to teach with new technology: Implications for professional development. *Journal of Research on Technology in Education, 35,* 272–289.

Neale, D. C., Smith, D., & Johnson, V. (1990). Implementing conceptual change teaching in primary science. *Elementary School Journal, 91,* 109–131.

Nemirovsky, R., & Galvis, A. (2004). Facilitating grounded online interactions in video-case-based teacher professional development. *Journal of Science Education and Technology, 13*(1), 67–79.

O'Connor, D., & Ertmer, P. A. (2003). *Today's coaches prepare tomorrow's mentors: Sustaining results of professional development.* Columbus, OH: Mid-Western Educational Research Association Conference.

Picciano, A. G. (2002). Beyond student perceptions: Issues of interaction, presence, and performance in an online course. *Journal of Asynchronous Learning Networks, 6*(1), 21–39.

Porter, A., Garet, M. S., Disimone, L., Yoon, K. S., & Birman, B. F. (2000). *Does professional development change teaching practice? Results from a three-year study.* Washington, DC: U.S. Department of Education.

Renninger, K. A., & Shumar, W. (2004). The centrality of culture and community to participant learning at and with the math forum. In S. A. Barab, R. Kling, & J. H. Gray

(Eds.), *Designing for virtual communities in the service of learning* (pp. 181–209). Cambridge, England: University of Cambridge Press.

Richardson, J. C., & Swan, K. (2003). Examing social presence in online courses in relations to students' perceived learning and satisfaction. *Journal of Asynchronous Learning Networks, 7*(1), 68–88.

Riel, M., & Polin, L. (2004). Online learning communities: Common ground and critical differences in designing technical environments. In S. Barab, R. Kling, & J. H. Gray (Eds.), *Designing for virtual communities in the service of learning* (pp. 16–50). Cambridge, England: Cambridge University Press.

Schaverien, L. (2003). Teacher education in the generative virtual classroom: Developing theories through a web-delivered, technology-and-science education context. *International Journal of Science Education, 25,* 1451–1469.

Schlager, M., & Fusco, J. (2004). Teacher professional development, technology, and communities of practice: Are we putting the cart before the horse? In S. Barab, R. Kling, & J. Gray (Eds.), *Designing virtual communities in the service of learning.* Cambridge, England: Cambridge University Press.

Sherer, P. D., Shea, T. P., & Kristensen, E. (2003). Online communities of practice: A catalyst for faculty development. *Innovative Higher Education, 27,* 183–194.

Turner, S., Cruz, P., & Papakonstantinou, A. (2004, April). *Impact of a professional development program on teachers' self-efficacy.* Paper presented at the annual meeting of the National Council of Teachers of Mathematics, Philadelphia.

Wang, M., Sierra, C., & Folger, T. (2003). Building a dynamic online learning community among adult learners. *Educational Media International, 40*(1–2), 49–61.

Wearmouth, J., Smith, A. P., & Soler, J. (2004). Computer conferencing with access to a "guest expert" in the professional development of special educational needs coordinators. *British Journal of Educational Technology, 35*(1), 81–93.

WestEd. (2000). Teachers who learn, kids who achieve: A look at schools with model professional development. Retrieved October 20, 2005, from http://www.wested.org/online_pubs/teachers_who_learn/TeachLearn.pdf.

Yang, S. C., & Liu, S. F. (2004). Case study of online workshop for the professional development of teachers. *Computers in Human Behavior, 20,* 733–761.

CHAPTER 2
EdTech Leaders Online

Glenn M. Kleiman and Barbara Treacy

1. Information on the South Carolina Online Professional Development program was provided by Mike Thun, education associate, South Carolina Department of Education Office of Technology, who directs this program.

2. D. Sparks and S. Hirsh, *A New Vision for Staff Development* (Alexandria, VA: Association for Supervision and Curriculum Development, 1997).

3. G. Kleiman, *Meeting the Need for High-Quality Teachers: e-Learning Solutions,* paper presented at the U.S. Department of Education Secretary's No Child Left Behind

Leadership Summit (July 12–13, 2004), available from http://nationaledtechplan.
org/documents/Kleiman-MeetingtheNeed.pdf

4. National Staff Development Council, *E-Learning for Educators: Implementing the Standards for Staff Development* (Oxford, OH: Author, 2001), available from http://www.nsdc.org/library/authors/elearning.pdf; and Kleiman.

CHAPTER 3
Piaget Goes Digital

Martha Stone Wiske, David Perkins, and David Eddy Spicer

1. National Commission on Teaching and America's Future, *What Matters Most: Teaching for America's Future* (1996), available from http://www.nctaf.org/publications/WhatMattersMost.pdf; and National Commission on Teaching and America's Future, *No Dream Denied: A Pledge to America's Children* (2003), available from http://www.nctaf.org/dream/report.pdf.

2. E. Drago-Severson, *Helping Teachers Learn: Principal Leadership for Adult Growth and Development* (Thousand Oaks, CA: Corwin Press, 2004); and J. W. Little, "Teachers' Professional Development in a Climate of Educational Reform," *Educational Evaluation and Policy Analysis* 15, no. 2 (1993): 129–151.

3. D. K. Cohen, "A Revolution in One Classroom: The Case of Mrs. Oublier," *Educational Evaluation and Policy Analysis* 12, no. 3 (1990): 327–345.

4. National Academy of Education, *Recommendations Regarding Research Priorities: An Advisory Report* (Evaluative/Feasibility report no. PPB-1999-6307) (Washington, DC: National Academy of Education, 1999).

5. D. N. Perkins, *King Arthur's Round Table: How Collaborative Conversations Create Smart Organizations* (New York: Wiley, 2003); and J. Pfeffer and R. I. Sutton, *The Knowing-Doing Gap: How Smart Companies Turn Knowledge into Action* (Boston: Harvard Business School Press, 1999).

6. M. Eraut, "Knowledge Creation and Knowledge Use in Professional Contexts," *Studies in Higher Education* 10, no. 2 (1985), 117–133.

7. D. A. Schön, *The Reflective Practitioner: How Professionals Think in Action* (New York: Basic Books, 1983).

8. M. Eraut, *Developing Professional Knowledge and Competence* (London: Falmer Press, 1994), 25.

9. J. Piaget et al., *The Essential Piaget*, 100th anniversary ed. (Northvale, NJ: J. Aronson, 1995).

10. Cohen.

11. B. S. Edwards, "The Challenges of Implementing Innovation," *Mathematics Teacher* 93, no. 9 (2000), 777.

12. J. Brehm, *A Theory of Psychological Reactance* (New York: Academic Press, 1966).

13. P. Cobb et al., "Situating Teachers' Instructional Practices in the Institutional Setting of the School and District," *Educational Researcher* 32, no. 6 (2003), 13–24; F. Levy and R. J. Murnane, *The New Division of Labor: How Computers Are Creating*

the Next Job Market (Princeton: Princeton University Press; New York: Russell Sage Foundation, 2004); National Research Council, *How People Learn: Brain, Mind, Experience, and School* (Washington, DC: National Academy Press, 2000); and Partnership for 21st Century Skills, *Learning for the 21st Century: A Report and Mile Guide for 21st Century Skills* (2003), available from http://www.21stcenturyskills.org/downloads/P21_Report.pdf.

14. R. Kegan, "What 'Form' Transforms? A Constructive-Developmental Approach to Transformative Learning," in *Learning as Transformation: Critical Perspectives on a Theory in Progress,* ed. J. Mezirow (San Francisco: Jossey-Bass, 2000), 35–70.

15. J. A. Moon, *Reflection in Learning and Professional Development: Theory and Practice* (London: Kogan Page, 2000).

16. M. Huberman, "Networks That Alter Teaching: Conceptualisations, Exchanges and Experiments," in *Teacher Development: Exploring Our Own Practice,* ed. A. Craft et al. (London: Paul Chapman in association with the Open University, 2001), 141–159.

17. M. Carnoy et al., *The New Accountability: High Schools and High-Stakes Testing* (New York: Routledge, 2003); and R. F. Elmore, *School Reform from the Inside Out: Policy, Practice, and Performance* (Cambridge, MA: Harvard Education Press, 2004).

18. C. H. Weiss, "How Can Theory-Based Evaluation Make Greater Headway?" *Evaluation Review* 21, no. 4 (1997), 501–525; and C. H. Weiss, *Evaluation: Methods for Studying Programs and Policies,* 2nd ed. (Upper Saddle River, NJ: Prentice Hall,1998), 55–71.

19. M. S. Wiske and D. Perkins, "Dewey Goes Digital: The Wide World of Online Professional Development," in *Scaling Up Success: Lessons Learned from Technology-Based Educational Improvement,* ed. C. Dede et al. (San Francisco: Jossey-Bass, 2005); and Wiske et al., "New Technologies to Support Teaching for Understanding," *International Journal of Educational Research* 35, no. 5 (2001), 483–501.

20. T. Blythe, *The Teaching for Understanding Guide* (San Francisco: Jossey-Bass, 1998); and M. S. Wiske, ed., *Teaching for Understanding* (San Francisco: Jossey-Bass, 1998).

21. Wiske 1998, 21.

22. D. N. Perkins, "Understanding Understanding," in Blythe, 22.

23. M. S. Wiske et al., *Teaching for Understanding with New Technologies* (San Francisco: Jossey-Bass, 2005).

24. J. W. Little et al., *Teacher Learning, Professional Community, and Accountability in the Context of High School Reform* (Descriptive no. RD97124001) (Washington, DC: National Partnership for Excellence and Accountability in Teaching, 1999); National Research Council; R. Putnam and H. Borko, "What Do New Views of Knowledge and Thinking Have to Say About Research on Teacher Learning?" *Educational Researcher* 29, no. 1 (2000), 4–15; and E. Wenger, *Supporting Communities of Practice: A Survey of Community-Oriented Technologies* 1, no. 3 (2001), retrieved May 7, 2002, from http://www.ewenger.com/tech/.

25. Perkins, 46–51.

26. D. Eddy Spicer, "Contacts and Context: How Three Professionals Understand the Collegial Environment of an Online Course as an Aspect of Meaningful Professional Engagement" (paper presented at the annual meeting of the American Educational Research Association, 2002).

27. H. Soule, *Online Teacher Professional Development: Exploring Lessons from Namibia and Uganda* (2004), available from http://www.dot-com-alliance.org/resourceptrdb /uploads/partnerfile/upload/293/Online_Teacher_Professional_Development_ Uganda_Namibia.pdf.

28. L. Hetland et al., "Bridging the Gap between Schools and Universities: Networked Technologies as Support for Better Teaching" (paper presented at the annual meeting of the American Educational Research Association, 2004).

29. D. Eddy Spicer et al., *Project COOL: Year One Evaluation Report* (Massachusetts DOE Fund 170b) (Cambridge, MA: Harvard Graduate School of Education, 2004).

30. Hetland et al.

31. Wiske and Perkins.

32. A. Collins et al., "Design Research: Theoretical and Methodological Issues," *Journal of the Learning Sciences* 13, no. 1 (2004), 15–42; and The Design-Based Research Collective, "Design-Based Research: An Emerging Paradigm for Educational Inquiry," *Educational Researcher* 32, no. 1 (2003), 5–8.

33. D. Eddy Spicer et al., "Quality Assurance 'Middleware' for Gauging Learning Effectiveness in Online Teacher Professional Development" (paper presented at the annual meeting of the American Educational Research Association, 2005).

34. The authors would like to thank WIDE World researcher/statistician Roland Stark for providing the data collection, analysis, and reporting in this section.

35. Improvement in teaching practice and in student learning are each based on five-item scales with internal consistencies of .8 to .9.

36. Based on six- and four-item scales, respectively, with internal consistencies and test–retest r of .8 to .9. For computer attitudes, $D = .13$, $N = 367$, $p < .0005$; for attitudes toward online communication, $D = .30$, $N = 367$, $p < .0005$.

37. On the three portions of the assessment, $\chi^2 (1) = 7.3$, 6.7, and 3.7; $\varphi = .31$, .30, and .22; $p < .01$, $p = .01$, and $p = .06$, respectively.

CHAPTER 4
PBS TeacherLine and Concord Consortium's Seeing Math Secondary
Rob Ramsdell, Raymond Rose, and Mary Kadera

1. The contents of this chapter were developed in part under grants from the Department of Education. However, the contents do not necessarily represent the policy of the Department of Education, and the reader should not assume endorsement by the Federal Government.

2. Stands for Mid-Continent Research for Education and Learning.

3. A distinct course is defined as a unique course title with its own syllabus and course content.

4. Hezel Associates, *Initial Year 5 Findings from the Evaluation of PBS TeacherLine* (2005).

5. Hezel Associates, *Year 3 Evaluation of PBS TeacherLine* (2005).

6. Hezel Associates, 2005.

7. The examples shared here, as well as other interactives and resources, are available at http://seeingmath.concord.org/resources.html and http://teacherline.pbs. org/teacherline/resources/techresources.cfm.

8. R. Carter and F. Harik, "Thursday's Lesson: Warming Up to Quadratics with the Parabola Web," *Concord* (Fall 2004), pp. 12–13, available from http://www.concord. org/publications/newsletter/2004-fall-newsletter.pdf.

9. This price does not include graduate credit, and pricing for graduate credit (if a participant chooses this option) varies between institutions.

10. Adams State College and Indiana University are current providers of graduate credit on nationally offered courses, and additional credit options are organized by PBS member stations.

11. J. Richardson, "Online Professional Development: Concern About the Standards of Distance Education," *School Administrator* (October 2001).

12. M. Stein and E. Bassett, *Uncovering K–12 Professional Development Opportunities* (Boston: Eduventures, 2004).

CHAPTER 5
EMentoring for Student Success

Roberta Jaffe, Ellen Moir, Elisabeth Swanson, and Gerald Wheeler

1. R. Blank and D. Langesen, *State Indicators of Science and Mathematics Education* (Washington, DC: Council of Chief State School Officers, 2001); L. Lewis, *Teacher Quality: A Report on Teacher Preparation and Qualifications of Public School Teachers* (NCES 1999080) (Washington, DC: National Center for Education Statistics, 1999); and I. R. Weiss, *Report of the 2000 National Survey of Science and Mathematics Education* (Chapel Hill, NC: Horizon Research, 2001).

2. M. B. Allen, *Eight Questions on Teacher Preparation: What Does the Research Say?* (Denver, CO: Education Commission of the States, 2003).

3. S. Veenman, "Perceived Problems of Beginning Teachers," *Review of Educational Research* 54 (1984), 143–178; and S. P. Gordon and S. Maxey, *How to Help Beginning Teachers Succeed* (Alexandria, VA: Association for Supervision and Curriculum Development, 2000).

4. E. Britton et al., eds., *Comprehensive Teacher Induction* (Dordrecht, the Netherlands: Kluwer Academic Publishers, 2003); S. J. Odell and L. Huling, *Quality Mentoring for Novice Teachers* (Indianapolis: Kappa Delta Pi, 2000); S. Feiman-Nemser et al., "Beyond Support: Taking New Teachers Seriously as Learners," in *A Better Beginning: Supporting and Mentoring New Teachers*, ed. M. Scherer (Alexandria, VA: Association for Supervision and Curriculum Development, 1999), 3–12; L. Huling-Austin, "Research on Learning to Teach: Implications for Teacher Induction and Mentor-

ing Programs," *Journal of Teacher Education* 43, no. 3 (1992), 173–80; K. Stansbury and J. Zimmerman, *Lifelines to the Classroom: Designing Support for Beginning Teachers* (San Francisco: WestEd, 2002); and S. Villani, *Mentoring Programs for New Teachers: Models of Induction and Support* (Thousand Oaks, CA: Corwin Press, 2002).

5. J. A. Luft et al., "Contrasting Landscapes: A Comparison of the Impact of Different Induction Programs on Beginning Secondary Science Teachers, Practices, Beliefs, and Experiences," *Journal of Research in Science Teaching* 40, no. 1 (2003), 77–97; J. A. Luft and N. C. Patterson, "Supporting Beginning Science Teachers," *Journal of Science Teacher Education* 13, no. 4 (2002), 267–282; J. A. Luft, "Changing Inquiry Practice and Beliefs? The Impact of a One-Year Inquiry-Based Professional Development Program on the Beliefs and Practices of Secondary Science Teachers," *International Journal of Science Education* 23, no. 5 (2001), 517–534; and M. Garet, A. Porter, L. Desimone, B. Birman, and K. Joon, "What Makes Professional Development Effective? Results from a National Sample of Teachers," *American Educational Research Journal* 38, no. 4 (2001), 915–945.

6. American Federation of Teachers, "Mentor Teacher Programs in the States," *American Federation of Teachers Educational Issues Policy Brief* 5 (1998), 1–13.

7. Garet et al.; and L. Lambert, *Building Leadership Capacity in Schools* (Alexandria, VA: Association for Supervision and Curriculum Development, 1998).

8. Z. Berge, "Computer Conferencing and the Online Classroom," *International Journal of Educational Telecommunications* 3, no. 1 (1997); and M. P. Collins and Z. L. Berge, "Moderating Online Electronic Discussion Groups" (paper presented at the annual meeting of the American Educational Research Association, Chicago, IL, March 24–28, 1997).

9. L. Darling-Hammond and D. L. Ball, *Teaching for High Standards: What Policymakers Need to Know and Be Able to Do* (CPRE Joint Report Series, JRE-04) (Philadelphia: CPRE Publications, 1997); and S. L. Sanders and J. C. Rivers, *Cumulative and Residual Effects of Teachers on Future Student Academic Achievement* (Knoxville: University of Tennessee Value-Added Research and Assessment Center, 1996).

10. L. Darling-Hammond, "Teacher Quality and Student Achievement: A Review of State Policy Evidence," *Education Policy Analysis Archive* 8 (2000), available at http://epaa.asu.edu/epaa/v8ni/; B. Chaney, "Student Outcomes and the Professional Preparation of 8th Grade Teachers in Science and Mathematics" (manuscript prepared for NSF grant RED 9255255) (Rockville, MD: Westat, 1995); and C. A. Druva and R. D. Anderson, "Science Teachers' Characteristics by Teacher Behavior by Student Outcomes: A Meta-Analysis of Research," *Journal of Research in Science Teaching* 20, no. 5 (1983), 467–479.

11. R. M. Ingersoll, *Teacher Turnover, Teacher Shortages, and the Organization of Schools* (Seattle: Center for the Study of Teaching and Policy, 2001).

12. Garet et al.

13. P. Keeley, *Maine LabNet Moderators Guide* (Augusta, ME: Maine Mathematics and Science Alliance, 2004); J. Ravitz, "An ISD Model for Building Online Communities: Furthering the Dialogue," *Proceedings of the Annual Conference of the Asso-*

ciation for Educational Communications and Technology (Albuquerque, NM: 1997), available from http://www.bie.org/Ravitz/isd_model.html; L. E. Slocum et al., "Online Chemistry Modules: Interaction and Effective Faculty Facilitation," *Journal of Chemical Education* 81, no. 7 (2004); and P. Taylor, "An Examination of the Effect of Facilitation Training on the Development and Practice of Participants in an Online Induction Program for Teachers of Science and Mathematics" (dissertation proposal, Montana State University, Bozeman, 2005).

14. G. Collison et al., *Facilitating Online Learning: Effective Strategies for Moderators* (Madison, WI: Atwood Publishing, 2000).

15. Taylor.

16. B. Ford, *eMSS Year 3 Formative Evaluation Report* (Chapel Hill, NC: Horizon Research, Inc., March 2005).

17. L. Bice, "Construction of Knowledge about Teaching Practice and Educating Students from Diverse Cultures in an Online Induction Program" (doctoral dissertation, Montana State University, Bozeman, 2005).

18. S. Kocyba and P. Taylor, "The Evolution of Distance Mentoring Relationships: From Survival to Reflective Practice" (paper presented at the annual conference of the National Association for Research in Science Teaching, Vancouver, BC, 2004).

19. Z. Berge and S. Mrozowski, "Review of the Research in Distance Education, 1990 to 1999," *American Journal of Distance Education* 15, no. 3 (2001), 5–19; R. Paloff and K. Pratt, *Building Learning Communities in Cyberspace: Effective Strategies for the Online Classroom* (San Francisco: Jossey-Bass, 1999).

20. Bice, "Construction of Knowledge."

21. Bice, "Construction of Knowledge."

22. E. Stacey, "Collaborative Learning in an Online Environment," *Journal of Distance Education* 14, no. 2 (1999), 14–33.

23. Kocyba and Taylor; L. Bice, "Is Teacher Knowledge Affected by a Distance Mentoring Model?" (paper presented at the annual conference of the American Educational Research Association, Montreal, 2005); and Bice, "Construction of Knowledge."

CHAPTER 6
Science Learning and Teaching

Susan J. Doubler and Katherine Frome Paget

1. K. Hammerness et al., "How Teachers Learn and Develop," in *Preparing Teachers for a Changing World: What Teachers Should Learn and Be Able to Do,* ed. L. Darling-Hammond and J. Bransford (San Francisco: Jossey-Bass, 2005), 358–389.

2. Hammerness et al.

3. D. C. Lortie, *Schoolteacher: A Sociological Study* (Chicago: University of Chicago Press, 1975).

4. M. Kennedy, "The Role of Preservice Teacher Education," in *Teaching as the Learning Profession: Handbook of Policy and Practice,* ed. L. Darling-Hammond and G.

Sykes (San Francisco: Jossey-Bass, 1999), 54–85; and H. A. Simon, "Problem Solving in Education," in *Problem Solving in Education: Issues in Teaching and Research,* ed. D. T. Tuna and R. Reif (Hillsdale, NJ: Erlbaum, 1980), 81–96.

5. P. L. Grossman et al., "Appropriating Tools for Teaching English: A Theoretical Framework for Research on Learning to Teach," *American Journal of Education* 108, no. 1 (1999), 1–29.

6. M. T. Tatoo, "Examining Values and Beliefs about Teaching Diverse Students: Understanding the Challenges for Teacher Education," *Educational Evaluation and Policy Analysis* 18, no. 2 (1996), 155–180; and M. Wideen et al., "A Critical Analysis of the Research on Learning to Teach: Making the Case for an Ecological Perspective on Inquiry," *Review of Educational Research* 68, no. 2 (1998), 130–178.

7. L. Shulman, "Knowledge and Teaching: Foundations of the New Reform," *Harvard Educational Review* 7, no. 1 (1987), 1–22.

8. Hammerness et al., 382; D. Ball et al., "Interweaving Content and Pedagogy in Teaching and Learning to Teach: Knowing and Using Mathematics," in *Multiple Perspectives on the Teaching and Learning of Mathematics,* ed. J. Boaler (Westport, CT: Ablex, 2000), 83–104; and L. Ma, *Knowing and Teaching Elementary Mathematics: Teachers' Understanding of Fundamental Mathematics in China and in the United States* (Mahwah, NJ: Erlbaum, 1999).

9. M. S. Wiske, ed., *Teaching for Understanding* (San Francisco: Jossey-Bass, 1998).

10. T. Duffy and J. Kirkley, "Introduction: Theory and Practice in Distance Education," in *Learner-Centered Theory and Practice in Distance Education: Cases from Higher Education,* ed. T. Duffy and J. Kirkley (Mahwah, NJ: Erlbaum, 2004), 4.

11. Duffy and Kirkley; J. Bransford et al., "Vanderbilt's AMIGO Project: Knowledge of How People Learn Enters Cyberspace," in *Learner-Centered Theory* (see note 10), 209–234; S. Grabinger, "Design Lessons for Social Education," in *Learner-Centered Theory,* 49–60; and C. Twigg, *Innovations in Online Learning: Moving Beyond No Significant Difference* (Troy, NY: Center for Academic Transformation at Rensselaer Polytechnic Institute, 2001).

12. C. Fosnot, *Enquiring Teachers, Enquiring Learners: A Constructivist Approach to Teaching* (New York: Teachers College Press, 1989).

13. Hammerness et al.

14. National Research Council, *National Science Education Standards* (Washington, DC: National Academy Press, 1996), 59.

15. O. Lee, "Subject Matter Knowledge, Classroom Management and Instructional Practice in Middle School Science Classrooms," *Journal of Research in Science Teaching* 32, no. 4 (1995), 423–440; and W. Harlen and C. Holroyd, "Primary Teachers' Understanding of Concepts of Science: Impact on Confidence and Teaching," *International Journal of Science Education* 19, no. 1 (1997), 93–105.

16. H. Asoko, "Learning to Teach Science in the Primary School," in *Improving Science Education: The Contribution of Research,* ed. R. Millar et al. (Buckingham, UK: Open University Press, 2000), 79–93.

17. D. H. Monk, "Subject Area Preparation of Secondary Math and Science Teachers and Student Achievement," *Economics of Education Review* 13, no. 2 (1994), 125–145.

18. D. Perkins, "What Is Understanding?" in *Teaching for Understanding,* ed. M. S. Wiske (San Francisco: Jossey-Bass, 1998), 39–57.

19. D. Ball and G. McDiarmid, "The Subject Matter Preparation of Teachers," in *Handbook for Research on Teacher Education,* ed. W. R. Houston (New York: Macmillan, 1990); and R. Duschl, "Making the Nature of Science Explicit," in *Improving Science Education* (see note 16), 79–93.

20. R. Driver et al., "Establishing the Norms of Scientific Argumentation in Classrooms," *Science Education* 84, no. 3 (1996), 287–312; and J. Ziman, *Public Knowledge: An Essay Concerning the Social Dimension of Science* (Cambridge: Cambridge University Press, 1986).

21. National Research Council; and Bransford et al.

22. T. Kuhn, *The Structure of Scientific Revolutions* (Chicago: Chicago University Press, 1962); D. Kuhn et al., *The Development of Scientific Thinking Skills* (San Diego: Academic Press, 1988); and R. Tweney et al., eds., *On Scientific Thinking* (New York: Columbia University Press, 1981).

23. American Association for the Advancement of Science, *Benchmarks for Science Literacy* (New York: Oxford University Press, 1993), 2–3.

24. W. Harlen and S. Doubler, "Can Teachers Learn through Inquiry On-Line?," *International Journal of Science Education* 26, no. 1 (2004), 1–21.

25. Goodman Research Group, *Lesley/TERC Online Masters Program Summative Evaluation* (Cambridge, MA: Author, 2005); and W. Harlen and C. Altobello, *An Investigation of "Try Science" Studies Online and Face-to-Face* (Cambridge, MA: TERC, 2003).

26. M. Monk and J. Dillon, "The Nature of Scientific Knowledge," in *Good Practice in Science Teaching: What Research Has to Say,* ed. J. Osborne and M. Monk (Buckingham, England: Open University Press, 2000), 72–87.

27. A. Arons, "What Science Should We Teach?" in *Curriculum Development for the Year 2000* (Colorado Springs, CO: Biological Science Curriculum Study, 1989); B. Bell and J. Gilbert, *Teacher Development: A Model from Science Education* (Washington, DC: Falmer Press, 1996); and A. Rosebery and G. Puttick, "Teacher Professional Development as Situated Sensemaking: A Case Study in Science Education," *Science Education* 82 (1998), 649–677.

28. J. Supovitz and H. Turner, *Journal of Research in Science Teaching* 37 (2000), 963–980.

29. Goodman Research Group.

30. D. Schwartz et al., "Designs for Knowledge Evolution: Methods and Measures of a Prescriptive Learning Theory," in *Cognition, Education, and Communication Technology,* ed. P. Gardenfors and P. Johansson (Mahwah, NJ: Erlbaum, in press).

31. M. S. Wiske, ed., *Teaching for Understanding* (San Francisco: Jossey-Bass, 1998).

32. A. Collins et al., "Cognitive Apprenticeship: Making Thinking Visible," *American Educator: The Professional Journal of the American Federation of Teachers* 15, no. 3 (1991), 9.

33. J. Bransford et al., "Rethinking Transfer: A Simple Proposal with Multiple Implications," in *Review of Research in Education* 24A, ed. A. Iran-Nejad and P. Pearson (Washington, DC: American Educational Research Association, 2001), 61–100.

34. K. Sheingold, *Conversations in Learning: Facilitating Online Science Courses* (Cambridge, MA: TERC, 2005), 45.

35. L. Shulman and J. Shulman, "How and What Teachers Learn: A Shifting Perspective," *Journal of Curriculum Studies* 36, no. 2 (2004), 257–271.

36. B. White and J. Frederiksen, "Inquiry, Modeling, and Metacognition: Making Science Accessible to All Students," *Cognition and Instruction* 16, no. 1 (1998), 3–118.

37. Sheingold.

38. J. Bransford and D. Schwarz, "Rethinking Transfer: A Simple Proposal with Multiple Implications," in *Review of Research in Education, Vol. 24* (Washington, DC: American Educational Research Association, 2001), 61–100.

CHAPTER 7
Seminars on Science

Robert V. Steiner, Maritza Macdonald, Rosamond Kinzler, and Myles Gordon

1. We would like to thank Mark St. John, Laura Stokes, Judy Hirabayashi, Anita Smith, and their colleagues at Inverness Research Associates for providing much of the evaluation data that appear in this report. Seminars on Science, the courses, and this chapter have all benefited enormously from the knowledge, experience, skills, and insights of the Inverness staff. We would also like to acknowledge the efforts of Adriana Aquino, Armistead Booker, Michael Broom, David Randle, Kristi Ransick, Francine Stern, and John Yoo for both past and current contributions to Seminars on Science.

2. L. Darling-Hammond, *What Matters Most: Teaching for America's Future* (New York: Teachers College, 1996); The National Commission on Mathematics and Science Teaching for the 21st Century, *Before It's Too Late: A Report to the Nation* (Washington, DC: U.S. Department of Education, 2000); National Research Council, *How People Learn: Brain, Mind, Experience, and School* (Washington, DC: National Academy Press, 2000).

3. National Board for Professional Teaching Standards, "Early Adolescence/Science Standards for National Board Certification" (Washington, DC: U.S. Department of Education, 1997), available from http://www.nbpts.org/candidates/guide/whichcert/18EarlyAdolScience2004.html; and National Research Council, *National Science Education Standards* (Washington, DC: National Academy Press, 1996).

4. J. H. Falk and L. D. Dierking, *The Museum Experience* (Walnut Creek, CA: Alta Mira Press, 2000); G. E. Hein, *Learning in the Museum* (London: Routledge, 1998); G. Wiggins and J. McTighe, *Understanding by Design* (Alexandria, VA: Association for Supervision and Curriculum Development, 1998).

5. M. St. John et al., *The AMNH Seminars on Science Project: Lessons Learned from Phase I* (Inverness, CA: Inverness Research Associates, 2002), available from http://www.inverness-research.org.

6. L. S. Shulman, "Teacher Development: Roles of Domain Expertise and Pedagogical Knowledge," *Journal of Applied Developmental Psychology* 21 (2000), 129–135.

7. Seminars on Science, "Summer (2005) Post-Course Learner Survey Summary" (internal document, July 2005).

8. Seminars on Science.

9. St. John et al.

10. St. John et al.

CHAPTER 8
Embedded Professional Development

Sasha A. Barab, Craig Jackson, and Elizabeth Piekarsky

1. We would like to acknowledge the work of Tyler Dodge in developing figure 1, Scott Warren and Richard Stein in developing the Anytown curriculum, and George Newman for his valuable feedback on this manuscript.

2. M. A. Smylie and J. G. Conyers, "Changing Conceptions of Teaching Influence: The Future of Staff Development," *Journal of Staff Development* 12, no. 1 (1991), 12–16.

3. S. A. Barab et al., "Building a Community of Teachers: Navigating the Essential Tensions in Practice," *Journal of the Learning Sciences* 11, no. 4 (2002), 489–542.

4. J. P. Gee, *What Video Games Have to Teach Us about Learning* (New York: Palgrave, 2003).

5. K. D. Squire, "Games as Ideological Worlds," *Educational Researcher,* in press.

6. Gee; C. A. Steinkuehler, "Videogaming as Participation in a Discourse" (paper presented at the annual conference of the American Association for Applied Linguistics, Arlington, VA, March 25, 2003); S. A. Barab, M. Thomas, T. Dodge, R. Carteaux, and H. Tuzun, "Making Learning Fun: Quest Atlantis, A Game without Guns," *Educational Technology Research and Development* 53, no. 1 (2005), 86–108.

7. S. A. Barab, M. Thomas, T. Dodge, K. Squire, and M. Newell, "Critical Design Ethnography: Designing for Change," *Anthropology & Education Quarterly* 35, no. 2 (2004), 254–268.

8. S. A. Barab, A. Arici, and C. Jackson, "Eat Your Vegetables and Do Your Homework: A Design-Based Investigation of Enjoyment and Meaning in Learning," *Educational Technology* 65, no. 1 (2005), 15–21.

9. D. L. Ball and D. K. Cohen, "Reform by the Book: What Is—or Might Be—the Role of Curriculum Materials in Teacher Learning and Instructional Reform?" *Educational Researcher* 25, no. 14 (1996), 6–8.

10. J. R. Savery and T. M. Duffy, "Problem-Based Learning: An Instructional Model and Its Constructivist Framework," in *Constructivist Learning Environments: Case Studies*

in Instructional Design, ed. B. G. Wilson (Englewood Cliffs, NJ: Educational Technology Publications, 1996), 135–148.

11. L. Vygotsky, *Mind in Society: The Development of Higher Psychological Processes* (Cambridge, MA: Harvard University Press, 1978).

12. Ball and Cohen.

13. J. D. Bransford, A. O. Brown, and R. R. Cocking, eds., *How People Learn: Brain, Mind, Experience, and School* (Washington, DC: National Academy Press, 2002).

14. M. B. Miles, introduction to *Professional Development in Education: New Paradigms and Practices,* ed. T. Guskey and M. Huberman (New York: Teachers College, 1995), vii.

15. D. Ball, "Teacher Learning and the Mathematics Reforms: What We Think We Know and What We Need to Know," *Phi Delta Kappan* 77 (1996), 500–508; and E. M. Willis, "Technology: Integrated into, Not Added onto, the Curriculum Experiences in Pre-Service Teacher Education," *Computers in the Schools,* 13, no. 1/2 (1997), 141–153.

16. Smylie and Conyers; and L. Darling-Hammond, "Quality Teaching: The Critical Key to Learning," *Principal* 77, no. 1 (1997), 5–11.

17. These protocols and the idea of Critical Friends Groups forming around these protocols were developed by the National School Reform Faculty (see http://www.nsrfharmony.org/).

18. D. A. Schön, *The Reflective Turn: Case Studies in and on Educational Practice* (New York: Teachers College, 1991), 68.

19. C. Lewis and I. Tsuchida, "Planned Educational Change in Japan: The Shift to Student-Centered Elementary Science," *Journal of Educational Policy* 12, no. 5 (1997), 313–331.

20. D. A. Schön, *Educating the Reflective Practitioner: Toward a New Design for Teaching and Learning in Professions* (San Francisco: Jossey-Bass, 1987).

21. Schön 1991.

22. J. Dewey, *Experience and Education* (New York: Collier Macmillan, 1938).

23. J. Dewey, *How We Think* (New York: D. C. Heath, 1933).

24. S. Barab, J. G. MaKinster, J. Moore, D. Cunningham, and the ILF Design Team, "Designing and Building an Online Community: The Struggle to Support Sociability in the Inquiry Learning Forum," *Educational Technology Research and Development* 49, no. 4 (2001), 71–96.

25. A. Collins et al., "Cognitive Apprenticeship: Teaching the Crafts of Reading, Writing, and Mathematics," in *Knowing, Learning, and Instruction: Essays in Honor of Robert Glaser,* ed. L. B. Resnick (Hillsdale, NJ: Erlbaum, 1989), 453–494.

26. Barab, MaKinster, et al.

27. S. A. Barab and T. Duffy, "From Practice Fields to Communities of Practice," in *Theoretical Foundations of Learning Environments,* ed. D. Jonassen and S. M. Land (Mahwah, NJ: Erlbaum, 2000), 25–56; J. Lave and E. Wenger, *Situated Learning: Legitimate Peripheral Participation* (New York: Cambridge University Press, 1991); A. Sfard, "On

Two Metaphors for Learning and the Dangers of Choosing Just One," *Educational Researcher* 27, no. 2 (1998), 4–12.

CHAPTER 9
Online Teacher Professional Development

Thomas M. Duffy, Jamie R. Kirkley, Rodrigo del Valle, Larissa V. Malopinsky, Carolyn M. Scholten, Gary R. Neely, Alyssa Wise, and Ju-Yu Chang

1. The development of LTTS was funded, in part, by the Fund for the Improvement of Postsecondary Education (FIPSE), U.S. Department of Education Learning Anytime Anywhere Program, USDE Grant # P339B990108-01.

2. B. Dodge, "WebQuests: A Technique for Internet-Based Learning," *Distance Educator* 1, no. 2 (1995), 10–13.

3. J. Bransford et al., *How People Learn: Brain, Mind, Experience, and School,* expanded ed. (Washington, DC: National Academy Press, 2000); J. S. Brown et al., "Situated Cognition and the Culture of Learning," *Educational Researcher,* Jan–Feb (1989), 32–42; and T. M. Duffy and D. H. Jonassen, *Constructivism and the Technology of Instruction : A Conversation* (Hillsdale, NJ: Erlbaum, 1992).

4. J. R. Savery and T. M. Duffy, "Problem-Based Learning: An Instructional Model and Its Constructivist Framework," in *Constructivist Learning Environments: Case Studies in Instructional Design,* ed. B. G. Wilson (Englewood Cliffs, NJ: Educational Tech Pubs, 1996), 135–148.

5. C. T. Fosnot, *Constructivism: Theory, Perspectives, and Practice* (New York: Teachers College Press, 1996), ix.

6. E. Wenger, *Communities of Practice: Learning, Meaning, and Identity,* 1st paperback ed. (Cambridge: Cambridge University Press, 1999).

7. Brown et al.

8. G. A. Griffin, "Crossing the Bridge: The First Years of Teaching" (paper presented at a hearing of the National Commission on Excellence in Teacher Education, Austin, TX, 1984).

9. L. Desimone et al., "Effects of Professional Development on Teachers' Instruction: Results from a Three-Year Longitudinal Study," *Educational Evaluation and Policy Analysis* 24, no. 2 (2002), 81–112.

10. D. Linn and S. Spicer, *NCLB: Teacher Quality Promising Practices,* 2003, available from http://www.nga.org/center/divisions/1,1188,C_ISSUE_BRIEF^D_5268,00.html.

11. M. Kennedy, *Form and Substance in Inservice Teacher Education* (Research Monograph no. 13) (Madison, WI: National Institute for Science Education, 1998); V. Richardson and P. Placier, "Teacher Change," in *Handbook of Research on Teaching,* ed. V. Richardson (Washington DC: American Educational Research Association, 2001), 905–947; and G. Sykes and T. Bird, "Teacher Education and the Case Idea," *Review of Research in Education* 18 (1992), 457–521.

12. L. Darling-Hammond, "Research and Rhetoric on Teacher Certification: A Response to 'Teacher Certification Reconsidered,'" *Education Policy Analysis Archives* 10, no. 36 (2002), available from http://epaa.asu.edu/epaa/v10n36.html.

13. L. S. Shulman, "Those Who Understand: Knowledge Growth in Teaching," *Educational Researcher* 15, no. 2 (1986), 4–14.

14. P. C. Blumenfeld et al., "Motivating Project-Based Learning: Sustaining the Doing, Supporting the Learning," *Educational Psychologist* 26, nos. 3 and 4 (1991), 369–398.

15. B. Parsad et al., *Teacher Preparation and Professional Development* (Washington, DC: National Center for Education Statistics, 2001); T. B. Corcoran, *Helping Teachers Teach Well: Transforming Professional Development* (New Brunswick, NJ: Consortium for Policy Research in Education, 1995); and Kennedy.

16. Parsad et al.

17. Richardson and Placier; and B. Showers and B. Joyce, "The Evolution of Peer Coaching," *Educational Leadership* 53, no. 6 (1996).

18. Parsad et al.

19. J. P. Scribner, "Teacher Learning in Context: The Special Case of Rural High School Teachers," *Education Policy Analysis Archives* 11, no. 12 (2003), available from http://epaa.asu.edu/epaa/v11n12/.

20. T. Duffy and J. Kirkley, "Introduction: Theory and Practice in Distance Education," in *Learner-Centered Theory and Practice in Distance Education: Cases from Higher Education* (Mahwah, NJ: Erlbaum, 2004), 3–16.

21. T. M. Duffy et al., *Online Teacher Professional Development: Design Principles, Their Instantiation, and Learning Outcomes* (unpublished manuscript).

22. J. Hedberg, "Ensuring High Quality Thinking and Scaffolding Learning in an Online World," in *Proceedings of the Australian Society for Computers in Tertiary Education* (2002), 261–270, available from http://www.ascilite.org.au/conferences/auckland02/proceedings/papers/166.pdf.

23. R. S. Prawat and R. E. Floden, "Philosophical Perspectives on Constructivist Views of Learning," *Educational Psychology* 29, no. 1 (1994), 37–48.

24. S. A. Barab et al., "Designing System Dualities: Characterizing a Web-Supported Teacher Professional Development Community," in *Designing for Virtual Communities in the Service of Learning*, ed. S. A. Barab et al. (Cambridge, England: Cambridge University Press, 2004), 53–90; and K. A. Renninger and W. Shumar, "Community Building with and for Teachers: The Math Forum as a Resource for Teacher Professional Development," in *Building Virtual Communities: Learning and Change in Cyberspace*, ed. K. A. Renninger and W. Shumar (New York: Cambridge University Press, 2002), 60–95.

25. G. Ball et al., "Lifelike Computer Characters: The Persona Project at Microsoft Research," in *Software Agents*, ed. J. M. Bradshaw (Menlo Park, CA: AAAI/MIT Press, 1997), 191–222.

26. Hezel & Associates, *Year 3 Evaluation of PBS TeacherLine* (September 2003); and G. Osman and T. Duffy, "Online Teacher Professional Development and Implementa-

tion Success: The Learning to Teach with Technology Studio (LTTS) Experience" (in preparation).

27. T. Duffy et al., "Engaging in Issues of Theory, Pedagogy, and Practicality to Develop an Online, Mentored, Professional Learning Environment for PreK–12 Teachers: The Learning to Teach with Technology Studio" (in review).

28. Duffy et al. (in review).

29. A. Wise et al., "The Effects of Teacher Social Presence on Student Satisfaction, Engagement, and Learning," *Journal of Educational Computing Research* 31, no. 2 (2004), 247–271.

30. Osman and Duffy (in preparation).

31. Duffy et al. (in review).

32. R. del Valle and T. Duffy, "Online Learning: Learner Characteristics and Their Approaches to Managing Learning," *Computers in Human Behavior* (in review).

33. C. J. Bonk, "Navigating the Myths and Monsoons of Online Learning Strategies and Technologies" (paper presented at the E-education Without Borders Conference, Abu Dhabi, United Arab Emirates, February, 2003); and R. Carnwell, "Approaches to Study and Their Impact on the Need for Support and Guidance in Distance Learning," *Open Learning* 15, no. 2 (2000), 123–140.

34. S. A. Barab and T. Duffy, "From Practice Fields to Communities of Practice," in *Theoretical Foundations of Learning Environments,* ed. S. M. L. D. Jonassen (Mahwah, NJ: Erlbaum, 2000), 25–56.

35. M. Schlager et al., "Evolution of an On-line Education Community of Practice," in *Building Virtual Communities: Learning and Change in Cyberspace,* ed. K. A. R. A. W. Shumar (New York: Cambridge University Press, 2002), 129–158.

36. M. Schlager and J. Fusco, "Teacher Professional Development, Technology, and Communities of Practice: Are We Putting the Cart before the Horse?" in *Designing Virtual Communities in the Service of Learning,* ed. S. Barab et al. (New York: Cambridge University Press, 2004), 120–153.

37. G. Osman et al., "Learning through Collaboration: Student Perspectives" (in review).

38. Barab and Duffy.

39. M. Riel, "Cross-Classroom Collaboration in Global Learning Circles," in *The Cultures of Computing,* ed. S. L. Star (Oxford: Blackwell, 1995), 219–242.

CHAPTER 10
Teachers' Domain Professional Development

Ted Sicker

1. Teachers' Domain is a registered trademark of the WGBH Educational Foundation. All rights reserved. The author thanks Denise Blumenthal, director of WGBH Educational Productions, and Shelley Pasnik of EDC/CCT for their review of this chapter.

CHAPTER 11
Processes Supporting the Regional Evolution of Effective Professional Development
Ilona E. Holland, Chris Dede, and Kathy Onarheim

1. D. W. Redovich, "197 Bogus Graduation Rate Studies and Reality from Wisconsin" (2004), available from http://www.jobseducationwis.org/197%20Bogus%20 Education%20Studies%20from%20Harvard%20and%20the%20Truth%20from %20Wisconsin.doc; J. P. Greene, "Graduation Rates for Choice and Public School Students in Milwaukee" (Milwaukee: School Choice Wisconsin, 2004), available from http://www.schoolchoiceinfo.org/data/research/grad_rate.pdf.

2. C. Dede and R. Nelson, "Technology as Proteus: Digital Infrastructures That Empower Scaling Up," in *School Success: Lessons Learned from Technology-Based Educational Innovation*, ed. C. Dede, J. Honan, and L. Peters (New York: Jossey-Bass, 2005), 110–132.

3. Partnership for 21st Century Skills, "Learning for the 21st Century" (2003), available from http://www.21stcenturyskills.org.

4. Dede and Nelson, 121.

5. K. Bielaczyc and A. Collins, "Learning Communities in Classrooms: A Reconceptualization of Educational Practice," in *Instructional Design Theories and Models*, vol. 2, ed. C. M. Reigeluth (Mahwah, NJ: Erlbaum, 1999).

6. Bielaczyc and Collins.

7. Bielaczyc and Collins.

8. J. Bransford et al., eds., *How People Learn: Brian, Mind, Experience, and School* (Washington, DC: National Academy Press, 1999).

9. J. Lave and E. Wenger, *Situated Learning: Legitimate Peripheral Participation* (New York: Cambridge University Press, 1991).

10. M. Sheehan and A. Jafari, *Designing Portals: Opportunity and Challenges* (Hershey, PA: IRM Press, 2003).

11. C. Dede, "Enabling Distributed-Learning Communities via Emerging Technologies," in *Proceedings of the 2004 Conference of the Society for Information Technology in Teacher Education (SITE)* (Charlottesville, VA: American Association for Computers in Education, 2004).

12. M. S. Wiske et al., "Piaget Goes Digital: Negotiating Accommodation of Practice to Principles," in this volume.

13. Dede, 11.

14. D. Sullivan, *Proven Portals: Best Practices for Planning, Designing and Developing Enterprise Portals* (Boston: Addison-Wesley, 2004), 73.

15. Sullivan, 69.

16. C. Dede, L. Breit, D. Ketelhut, E. McCloskey, and P. Whitehouse, *An Overview of Current Findings from Empirical Research on Online Teacher Professional Development* (Cambridge, MA: Evolving a Research Agenda for Online Teacher Professional Development Conference, 2005).

17. Dede et al.

18. G. A. Moore, *Crossing the Chasm,* rev. ed. (New York: Harper Perennial, 1999).

19. C. Coburn, "Rethinking Scale: Moving Beyond Numbers to Deep and Lasting Change," *Educational Researcher* 32, no. 6 (2003): 3–12.

20. C. Dede, "Scaling Up: Evolving Innovations beyond Ideal Settings to Challenging Contexts of Practice," in *Cambridge Handbook of the Learning Sciences,* ed. R. K. Sawyer (Cambridge: Cambridge University Press, in press).

21. M. Stein and E. Bassett, *Uncovering K–12 Professional Development Opportunities* (Boston: Eduventures, 2004).

22. L. Moody, *Lessons from Milwaukee: Issues of Sustainability and Scale* (in preparation); CESA #1 Annual Report (Brookfield, WI: Cooperative Education Service Agency, May 17, 2005).

23. Dede et al.

CHAPTER 12
Core Tensions in the Evolution of Online Teacher Professional Development

Diane Jass Ketelhut, Erin M. McCloskey, Chris Dede, Lisa A. Breit, and Pamela L. Whitehouse

1. C. Dede, "Planning for 'Neomillennial' Learning Styles: Implications for Investments in Technology and Faculty," in *Educating the Net Generation,* ed. J. Oblinger and D. Oblinger (Boulder: EDUCAUSE Publishers, 2005), 226–247.

2. C. Dede et al., *Transforming Education for the 21st Century: An Economic Imperative* (Chicago: Learning Point Associates, 2005).

3. J. E. Stiglitz, *Globalization and Its Discontents* (New York: W. W. Norton, 2002).

4. Business Roundtable, *Tapping America's Potential: The Education for Innovation Initiative* (Washington, DC: Author, 2005), 1.

5. P. Stevens and M. Weale, *Education and Economic Growth* (London: National Institute of Economic and Social Research, 2003).

6. J. Temple, *Growth Effects of Education and Social Capital in the OECD Countries* (CEPR Discussion Paper No. 2875) (Bristol, England: University of Bristol, 2001).

7. R. Barro, *Education and Economic Growth* (Paris: Organization for Economic Cooperation and Development, 2000).

8. Organization for Economic Co-operation and Development, *The Well-Being of Nations: The Role of Human and Social Capital* (Paris: Author, 2001).

9. Organization for Economic Co-operation and Development, *Innovation in the Knowledge Economy: Implications for Education and Learning* (Paris: Author, 2004).

10. Task Force on the Future of American Innovation, *The Knowledge Economy: Is the United States Losing Its Competitive Edge?* (Washington, DC: Author, 2005), available from http://www.futureofinnovation.org/PDF/Benchmarks.pdf.

11. Business–Higher Education Forum, *A Commitment to America's Future: Responding to the Crisis in Mathematics and Science Education* (Washington, DC: Author, 2005).

12. Federal Reserve Bank of Dallas, *What D'Ya Know? Lifetime Learning in Pursuit of the American Dream* (annual report) (Dallas: Author, 2004).

13. R. M. Jones, "Local and National ICT Policies," in *Technology, Innovation, and Educational Change: A Global Perspective,* ed. R. B. Kozma (Eugene, OR: International Society for Technology in Education, 2003), 163–194.

14. F. Levy and R. J. Murnane, *The New Division of Labor: How Computers Are Creating the Next Job Market* (Princeton: Princeton University Press, 2004).

15. Levy and Murnane, 75.

16. Levy and Murnane, 94.

17. Dede et al.

18. T. L. Friedman, *The World Is Flat: A Brief History of the Twenty-First Century* (New York: Farrar, Straus, and Giroux, 2005).

19. C. Dede, J. P. Honan, and L. Peters, eds., *Scaling Up Success: Lessons Learned from Technology-Based Educational Improvement* (San Francisco: Jossey-Bass, 2005), 53.

20. A. Collins et al., "Design Research: Theoretical and Methodological Issues," *Journal of the Learning Sciences* 13, no. 1 (2004): 15–42.

21. C. Dede, "Why Design-Based Research Is Both Important and Difficult," *Educational Technology* 45, no. 1 (2005), 5–8.

About the Contributors

Sasha A. Barab is an associate professor in Learning Sciences, Instructional Systems Technology, and Cognitive Science at the Indiana University School of Education.

Lisa A. Breit is a professional development consultant and a doctoral student in Learning and Teaching at the Harvard Graduate School of Education.

Ju-Yu Chang is a research assistant at the Indiana University School of Education.

Chris Dede is the Timothy E. Wirth Professor in Learning Technologies at the Harvard Graduate School of Education.

Rodrigo del Valle is director of Continuing Education and Graduate Studies at the Universidad Católica de Temuco, Chile.

Susan J. Doubler is a project director at TERC and an associate professor at Lesley University.

Thomas M. Duffy is the Barbara Jacobs Professor of Education and Technology at the Indiana University School of Education.

Myles Gordon is vice president for education at the American Museum of Natural History.

Ilona E. Holland is a lecturer on education at the Harvard Graduate School of Education.

Craig Jackson is project manager and design manager for the Quest Atlantis Project at The Center for Research on Learning and Technology, Indiana University Bloomington.

Roberta Jaffe is science education coordinator of the New Teacher Center at the University of California Santa Cruz.

Mary Kadera is managing director of K–12 Education at PBS.

Diane Jass Ketelhut is a lecturer at the Harvard Graduate School of Education.

Rosamond Kinzler is director of the National Center for Science Literacy, Education, and Technology at the American Museum of Natural History.

Jamie R. Kirkley is a doctoral candidate at Indiana University.

Glenn M. Kleiman is vice president of Education Development Center, Inc., and a lecturer at the Harvard Graduate School of Education.

Maritza Macdonald is senior director of professional development at the American Museum of Natural History.

Larissa V. Malopinsky is a project manager at the Indiana University School of Education.

Erin M. McCloskey is a doctoral candidate at the Harvard Graduate School of Education.

Ellen Moir is executive director of the New Teacher Center at the University of California Santa Cruz.

Gary R. Neely is a programmer at the Indiana University School of Education.

Kathy Onarheim is director of technology services at CESA #1.

Katherine Frome Paget is a senior research scientist at TERC and Education Development Center, Inc.

David Perkins is a senior professor of education at the Harvard Graduate School of Education.

Elizabeth Piekarsky is a teacher of highly gifted fourth-grade students at University Elementary School in Bloomington, Indiana.

Rob Ramsdell is senior director of PBS TeacherLine.

Raymond Rose is vice president of the Concord Consortium.

Carolyn M. Scholten is a research associate at the Indiana University School of Education.

Ted Sicker is executive producer of Teachers' Domain at the WGBH Educational Foundation.

David Eddy Spicer is research manager of WIDE World at the Harvard Graduate School of Education.

Robert V. Steiner is the project director of Seminars on Science at the American Museum of Natural History's National Center for Science Literacy, Education, and Technology.

Elisabeth Swanson is director of the Science/Math Resource Center at Montana State University.

Barbara Treacy is managing project director of the EdTech Leaders Online Program at Education Development Center, Inc.

Gerald Wheeler is executive director of the National Science Teachers Association.

Pamela L. Whitehouse is a lecturer at the Harvard University Extension School.

Alyssa Wise is a research associate at the Indiana University School of Education.

Martha Stone Wiske is a lecturer on education at the Harvard Graduate School of Education.

Index

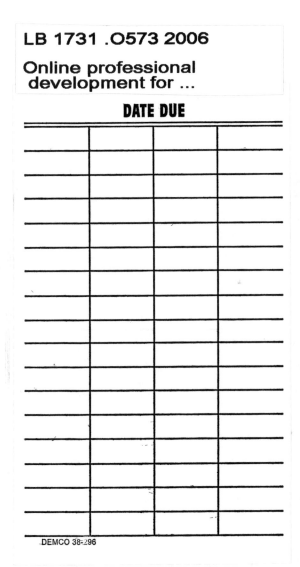